# DecideBetter!
## For College

Michael E. McGrath

DecideBetter!
Improve Your Life Through Better Decisions

## The Decide Better! Series

*Decide Better! for a Better Life*
*Decide Better! for College*
*Decide Better! Decision-a-Day Calendar*

Available in Fall 2009

*Decide Better! for Business Success*

# DecideBetter! for College

## Michael E. McGrath
## Christopher K. McGrath

**motivation** PUBLISHING

Addison, Texas

Published by

Motivation Publishing
16633 Dallas Pkwy, Suite 280
Addison, TX 75001

For more information, visit http://www.DecideBetter.com.

Printed in the United States of America

Cover and text design by Bookwrights

All author photos © Michelle Lindsay Photography

Library of Congress Control Number: 2008942205

ISBN-13: 978-1-935112-03-7

10 9 8 7 6 5 4 3 2 1

First Edition

*This book is dedicated to all high school seniors, college students, and their parents who have to navigate college life individually and together. We wish you luck in making the best possible decisions for your academic life.*

# Contents

# Acknowledgments

Many people were involved with the production of this book in the Decide Better! series—too many to mention—but a number of people were absolutely crucial to its completion. First, we would like to thank our families, including Diane and Becca, as well as Molly, for their support and patience during this process.

Second, we would like to recognize the hard work, fortitude, and determination of Trudi Pevehouse, who is a truly enduring example of someone who can handle all of life's challenges with strength and always with a smile. We would also like to thank Jennifer Cary for her inspiration and for keeping us on track and working tirelessly in pursuit of the Decide Better! vision.

As for the writing and style of this book, we are truly indebted to Barbara Darling for her revisions to the manuscript that made the final book more readable. Carrie Klein has also provided many invaluable edits and comments that have greatly improved the book. We also appreciate the skills of Sharon Goldinger and Mayapriya Long for their hard work on editing and designing this book. In addition, we would like to thank Lindy Kirk for her humor and ability to interject a light touch into what is commonly seen as very sober and difficult subject matter. In addition, Allison Retan made many general contributions toward the completion of the book.

Moreover, we owe an enormous debt of gratitude to Jerry Flanagan, a lifelong friend and someone who has dedicated his life to working with college students and helping them to succeed. We are truly lucky to have you as a friend and a resource for this book.

We also greatly appreciate the work of David, Laura, and Lauren at the Strategic Vision team for their assistance with promoting Decide Better! and providing invaluable help in getting the message about the importance of making better decisions out to the public through the media.

Finally, we would like to thank the rest of our families, including Mike and Sarah, Jill and Carmen, Matty, Callie, and Drew, and Carolyn and Carrie, for providing us with the support and inspiration for this book.

# Introduction

College is a journey—a journey that starts you on the path to the rest of your adult life. Throughout this college journey you will make many decisions, some that may not seem important and some that will shape your future. In a way, it's unfair that you need to make life-changing decisions now, before you've had the time to hone your decision-making skills. That's why we wrote this book. The purpose of this book is to help you make better decisions at this critical period of your life.

Making choices need not be a migraine-inducing process. The decisions you have ahead of you as you prepare for college are manageable once you apply a bit of structure. You can treat this book as your personal counselor. Manipulate the contents to your advantage. Skip around if you want to, but do the work, and you will indeed land squarely at the gateway to your future.

The first stage of your college journey starts when you are still in high school because that's when you decide where to attend college. By the end of your junior year, or at the latest by the beginning of your senior year, you plunge into the college application process by deciding which colleges you will apply to. At this time your decisions (and follow through!) start kicking into high gear. You won't be able to attend the best college for you if you don't apply. Chapter 2 helps get you off to a good start by explaining how to make the decision about where to apply. We help you leapfrog over the traps that often bog down the application process.

After you get your applications out, it's up to the colleges to make their decisions. Chapter 3 will give you some insights into the "black box" of college acceptance decisions. Understanding the admission process allows you to craft your applications in ways that will increase your chance that the black box will accept your application. Once your acceptance letters arrive, you need to make *your* selection decision—and this is typically a very important decision. Chapter 4 provides a thorough decision-making process and an example that you can easily follow to learn how to make the best decision for you. The remaining chapters in section I address specific decisions you may face during your application and acceptance period, such as being wait-listed, applying early, and taking a year off before attending college.

The second stage of your journey is your transition into college from high school. For most students, the transition means leaving home, family, and friends to start an entirely new life. During this stage you will be making some decisions that will impact your next four years. You will find advice and decision techniques to balance your life (chapter 8), pick extracurricular activities (chapter 16), select a roommate (chapter 19), establish your new relationship with your parents (chapter 21), and decide how to pay for college (chapter 22). You may want to read these chapters over the summer before you leave for college.

Making good decisions doesn't stop when you enter college. In fact you will continually make even more important decisions as a student. You will find useful guidance, advice, and techniques that broaden your opportunities for genuine success in section II, which helps you with academic decisions. Deciding on your college major is, in fact, a "major" decision. Comparing your decision techniques to the game of chess helps make the process easier. While you expect to graduate in four years, you may be surprised to know that most students do not. You can control this outcome by determining your priorities and following through with your actions. During your college years you may also have to make decisions on what to do in the summer and whether to study abroad for a semester. Proven approaches for making these decisions are offered as well. Many students face a decision about whether to transfer to another school, and if you must make this decision, the information in chapter 13 will help you through it.

Your college experience will not be limited to studying. You also want to have fun, which involves decisions too—decisions about partying, drinking, and how to spend your time. Some of you may face decisions about whether to live on-campus or off, or maybe in a fraternity or sorority house. Section III provides valuable insights into making these important social decisions and helps you avoid the pitfalls of poor choices. Anticipating the unintended consequences of your decisions is a critical concept that could even save your life. The challenges you will face as you make your own boundary decisions—now that you are free from the boundaries your parents set for you—are also addressed in section III.

You will also need to make relationship decisions, and this is the focus of section IV. You'll have to make important decisions about roommates, dating, and your relationship with your parents. College is a good time to learn how to make relationship decisions as you will encounter them throughout your life.

In section V you'll find advice on how to make important financial decisions. For perhaps the first time, you will be on your own financially, and it is up to you to make sound financial choices. Too many college students end up with unmanageable credit card debt by the time they graduate. This section offers information that will help you make good decisions on using credit cards, spending, and paying for college.

The final stage of your college journey is the milestone of graduation. You need to prepare for life beyond college. What do you want to do after you graduate? The final section of the book helps you with this decision. You'd be wise to address it well before you have your diploma in hand. You'll also learn how the decision skills you developed in college can apply to the rest of your life.

Our mission at Decide Better! is to help people make better decisions and improve their lives. We seek to achieve this through a series of books, media interviews, presentations and speeches, and resources on our Web site. *Decide Better! for College* is one of a series of books, each focused on decisions in all aspects of life. Some of the lessons in this book build on those in our first book, *Decide Better! for a Better Life*, which is a general guide to better decisions.

*Decide Better! for College* provides you with a road map for this journey so that you can see the decisions you need to make and how you can best make them. We've found that, for most students, these decisions aren't obvious, so we identify the decisions you need to make throughout the stages of your college journey. We use decision worksheets and decision tables throughout the book to help you through the process. You can easily download copies of these from our Web site: http://www.DecideBetter.com/college.html.

Many stories and examples are used throughout the book to illustrate decisions. These are fictionalized, disguised, modified, and composite stories of typical experiences. Any resemblance to real people or real situations is coincidental.

It is also important to note that we wrote this book for parents, as well. Each chapter contains notes to parents to help them determine when they should participate in each decision-making process—and when they shouldn't. For parents, letting go of children and sending them off to college can be difficult. Parents want what's best for their children. They want you to be successful, to stay out of trouble, and to make your own decisions. But sometimes these desires are in conflict.

You can use this book in several ways. First, understand that if your parents have given you this book, it's probably because they want to provide you with useful, expert advice on decisions that they know you will be making. Second, you should share this book with your parents and ask for their advice where it might be appropriate or helpful. This book is a road map to refer to along the college journey, so you and your parents need your own copies. And you should take your copy along to college with you. Ask your parents questions, encourage good communication, and maybe point out something in the book they might read and use that as a conversation opener. They may have a helpful point of view.

When college-bound teens take flight and parents become empty nesters, no one's lives will be the same. This transition is a unique time for all involved. Why not decide to make the most of the experience?

Your college journey should be exciting and get you off to the best start on your adult life. We hope this book inspires you and helps you make better decisions so that your journey is even better.

# Section I.

## Application and Selection Decisions

**D**eciding which college to attend, and deciding even before that which colleges you will apply to, may be one of the most important series of decisions in your entire life. The college you attend will have a big impact on your future, including what career you will have, where you live, who many of your friends will be, what many of your interests will be, and possibly even who you will marry. You will be at college for four years, and you want to get the most out of that time. The goal of this section is to help you get your life on the right track from the beginning by helping you make the right decision on where to go to college.

This first section of the book is focused on application and selection decisions, and it contains seven chapters. The first is a basic overview of the decision on whether to go to college. We are biased here—we think you should. But it's still a decision that you have to make. After you've made that decision, and you've (hopefully) decided to go to college, the next three chapters provide the core information you need to help you through the application and acceptance decisions that you will have to make. Chapter 2 provides you with a practical process for deciding where to apply. This is where many students start off wrong by not applying to the right schools. If you don't apply to a particular college, you won't be able to go there. It's as simple as that. While it may take a little work to determine which schools to apply to, there is no doubt that it is worth the effort to do it right. We understand that deciding which colleges to apply to can seem daunting and a bit unwieldy at first. And you cannot take the process lightly. Moreover, if you don't adequately determine what you're looking for in a college and which colleges meet those needs, you're likely to end up at a school that's not a good fit for you. Using a structured process for filtering, sorting, and ranking schools gives you the best shot at realizing your dreams for the most fulfilling college life.

While the decision on where to apply is under your control, the decision on where you get accepted isn't. Whether a college accepts your application is more of a "black box" decision. Chapter 3 describes how colleges make their decisions on who to accept, who to reject, or who to put on the waiting list. By understanding as much as possible about how this black box works, you can position yourself to get it to work more in your favor.

Eventually, the acceptance or rejection letters appear in your mailbox. The big, fat ones typically indicate that you've been accepted. The skinny ones generally bear disappointing news. So then what? It's decision time again, and chapter 4 will help you to decide which college you will go to. This critical decision is a difficult one for many students. This chapter provides you with an easy-to-use decision worksheet to compare your college alternatives. By weighing the importance of the criteria that you think are critical to your college experience, you can make your final decision with the confidence that you have selected the best match from among your viable options. An electronic version of the worksheet is also available on our Web site if you prefer to use that. A shortened version can also be found there if you are unable to spend the time to use the comprehensive version.

The next three chapters focus on special issues by addressing specific decisions that may or may not be applicable to you, depending upon your specific circumstances. Chapter 5 focuses on how to make the best decision about whether to take a year off between high school and college to accomplish some specific goal or to get some experience that you believe would be valuable. The information will help you to make this decision in a very deliberate and structured way to ensure you have thoroughly evaluated your options. This lesson can also apply if you're considering taking a year off after you've enrolled in college but before you graduate.

Chapter 6 focuses on making the decision about whether to apply for early college admission. You may have many good reasons to apply early, as well as many bad reasons. If you're considering whether to apply for early admission, this chapter will help you to make the decision that is best for you. Finally, chapter 7 focuses on the decisions that you will need to make if you're waitlisted at a school that you want to go to. You can take a number of actions if you find yourself in this situation, and this chapter will help you to figure out the best decisions you can make under these circumstances.

# Chapter 1

# To Go or Not to Go
## That Is the Question

One of our good friends has a daughter, let's call her Daisy, who is very smart, motivated, and somewhat of an overachiever. However, in the middle of her senior year of high school, Daisy acquired a nasty case of burnout. She was having trouble getting to class and attending her after-school activities, and she couldn't even imagine signing up for another four years of academic stress and chaos. She decided she could rely on her several solid skills, skip college, and head straight into the working world. After all, how would college algebra help her in the real world? After months of struggling in minimum-wage jobs where she got zero respect and people treated her like she wasn't smart, she began to think maybe college wasn't such a bad idea. In today's world, people often have to see to believe, so perhaps she needed a college degree for others to believe she was smart and to actually land a decent job that challenged her mind and fulfilled her dreams! Less than a year after she proclaimed college unnecessary, Daisy found herself front row and center in a lecture hall, scribbling notes like her future depended on it—because it did.

If you're still trying to decide whether to go to college, we will give you some advice: yes, go to college. This book does not give advice on *what* decisions you should make; it gives you advice on *how* to approach the decisions that you're going to face and how to make them using tools that will ensure the best outcomes. But when it comes to deciding whether to go to college,

> ### Note to Parents
> *It's your job as a parent to make sure that your children make good decisions when it comes to going to college or not. Encourage them to go to college!*

**Most Common Reasons for Not Going to College:**

- I can't afford it.
- I want to make money right now and not waste it on college.
- A college degree doesn't guarantee I will get a job.
- A college degree isn't worth anything these days.
- I can learn more and faster by teaching myself.
- College will take up too much of my precious time.
- I can take any classes I want online for free.

we will always suggest that you go. That being said, the decision remains yours to make.

When we speak with high school students who aren't convinced that college is right for them, time and time again money is the top factor for not going to college. We agree that it takes a lot of money to pay for college. On the other hand, many ways exist to combat the high costs of college. Student loans are the most common of these. While you will have to pay these off after graduation, you can take a long time to do so and can typically take a break from your payments if you incur some type of hardship. In addition, you can take the interest on your college loan payments as a tax deduction, which reduces the overall amount actually paid. (See chapter 22 for more information about paying for college.)

Borrowing may be a humbling decision, but you could find that the outcome after four years of college may be well worth it. While student loans are generally designed to help you cover tuition costs, many of them also pay for your living expenses. Some students also worry about supporting their families or paying for other outside expenses that the loans won't cover. This still doesn't mean college isn't an option. These students need to be creative and come up with a plan for how to do it—one that will likely involve working while in school, something millions of students in college are doing at this very moment. So before you say "It's just too expensive for me" and decide not to pursue a college education, remember that you have financial options. When you're comparing the positives and negatives, if money were not a factor, how would that affect your decision?

# The Million-Dollar Decision

Speaking of money, members of the American workforce with a college education are far more likely to have a higher income than those who have only a high school diploma. Data from the United States Census Bureau indicates that workers with a bachelor's degree or higher do much better in terms of their income than those without a college degree. As Figure 1-1 shows in terms of real wages for full-time, year-round employees, high school graduates average $30,400 in salary per year, while those with a bachelor's degree average $52,200 per year, a significant difference of $21,800, or 72 percent.

**FIGURE 1-1   Annual Income by Education Level**

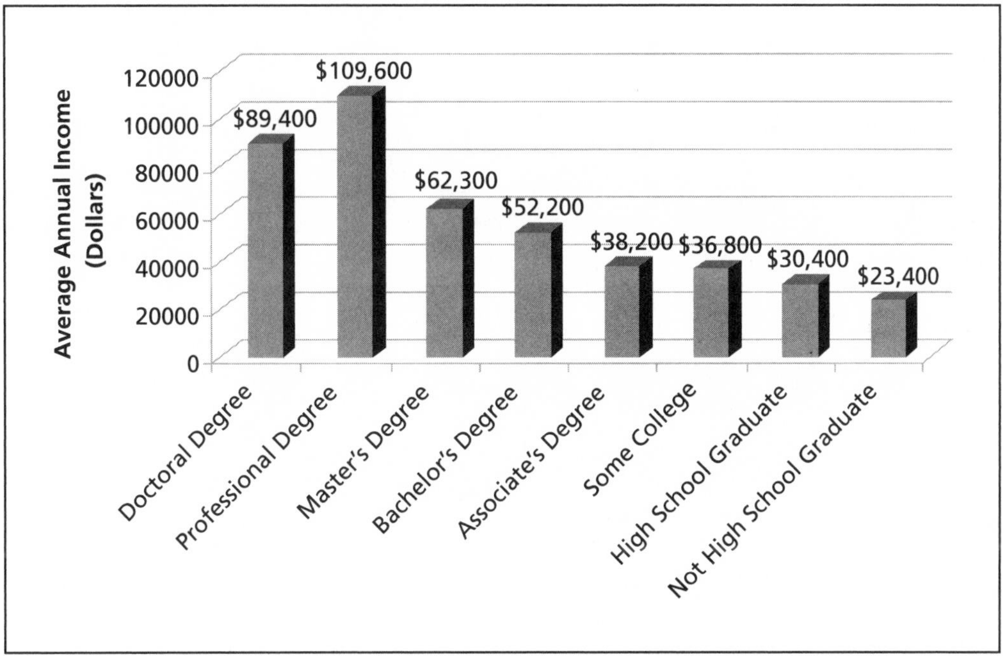

If you look at the lifetime averages, the numbers are even starker. According to the Census Bureau, full-time, year-round employees with a high school diploma earn $1.2 million in the lifetime of their careers, while those with a bachelor's degree earn $2.1 million during their careers. That's a whopping $900,000 more, or 75 percent! (See Figure 1-2.) Does that sway your thinking about whether college is worth it? It's sometimes hard to justify spending the money on college up front instead of saving it. But you should actually think of education expenses as savings, not spending, because they are an investment in future income, as these figures prove. You may pay $100,000 for college, but according to these estimates, you're going to recoup $900,000 on this investment.

Permit us to give you one more example. At 18, Matt had zero interest in school. Come to think of it, he never enjoyed school, but to appease his parents, he enrolled in a few classes at the local community college after high school. Within a

**FIGURE 1-2  Lifetime Income by Education**

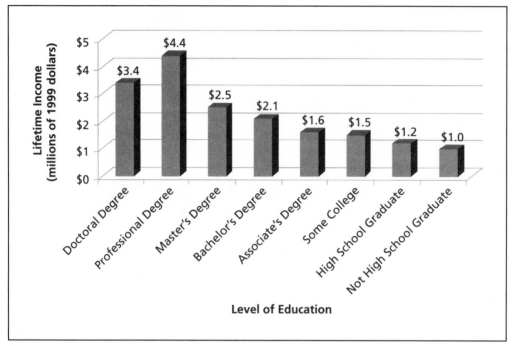

Source: U.S. Census Bureau

few months, he withdrew completely from these classes to focus on work. He had a job that provided a pretty decent income—especially given his age. It was unfulfilling, but as long as he could pay his rent and bills and have extra "fun money," he didn't really care. Let's fast-forward a few years. Matt is now 26 and is still working at the same job. The only difference is that all of his friends—the same ones who were starving and broke throughout college while Matt had money—have graduated, have gotten nice jobs, and are now the ones treating him to dinner. His salary has barely increased in eight years due to a lack of growth in the company. Matt has hit the top of his earnings ladder, while his friends are just stepping onto the first rung. Besides, what seemed like a nice paycheck when he was 18 is inadequate now that he's older and his interests and tastes have evolved. What is he to do? Well, to make a long story short, Matt decided to go to school, but it was not easy. While his friends were making money, enjoying their weekends, and occasionally taking trips, Matt was restricted to a student schedule—taking classes around his work schedule and spending his weekends studying. As they say, hindsight is always 20/20 and, in this case, Matt clearly understood he should have made the tough choice and gone to college long ago.

## How to Decide

If you're in the midst of deciding whether to go to college, the best approach is to determine the benefits and drawbacks of going or not going. To do this, you should take out a sheet of paper and write down what you see as the positives and negatives of going to college. (You can also do this on your computer instead.) Put a line down the middle of the sheet of paper and write "Positives" and "Negatives" at the top of each column. Give yourself at least a few days to compile your list—a few weeks would be even better—because you won't be able to think of all of the factors that you should consider for this important life decision at one time. Then you need to give yourself time to think them through. Only once you believe you've considered every factor should you make the decision.

The key to this decision is the time frame you look at. You will have more money in the next four years if you don't go to college. But statistics show that you will earn much more over the remainder of your lifetime if you do graduate from college. So make two sections of your worksheet. Label the top section *Short Term*, covering the next four to five years, and label the bottom section *Long Term*, covering the rest of your life. Then write out the positives and negatives for each. Step back, weigh them, and decide.

## To Sum Up

Should you go to college? Yes.

# Chapter 2

## Oh, the Places You Can Go

### There Are So Many Schools. How Do You Decide Where to Apply?

After six months of struggling through being unhappy while living in a coed dorm that had a community bathroom and enduring classes of 400 students that were taught by inaccessible professors, Natalie realized she had made a huge mistake when deciding which college to attend. The cute boys she'd seen on campus when she visited last year seemed to have vanished. She suspected the cafeteria hadn't received a fresh batch of produce since her visit either. One weekend, hoping to have two days with a boy-free bathroom, Natalie decided to visit a friend at another college. After visiting that campus and talking with her friend, Natalie knew she should have applied there. She could have gotten in, and she would have had a great experience. But she hadn't thought about that school during the

> **Note to Parents**
>
> *The best way to help your children when they're choosing which schools to apply to is by encouraging them to use a sound decision process. You may have some good advice, but you don't have to spend four years at the school—they do.*

application decision process—it simply hadn't appeared on her collegiate radar. Natalie, like thousands of other college students every year, had made a bad decision and landed at a school that was completely wrong for her. Had she more adequately researched her college possibilities using a better and more structured decision method, she could have avoided that athlete's foot breeding ground of a bathroom and ended up at the perfect school for her.

Another student we know, Jenna, simply ignored the college application process during her senior year of high school because she was too busy. She was a good student, but she was a focused athlete—she was a star basketball player at her high school. Throughout the basketball season, she trained and played basketball for a minimum of five hours per day and completely forgot about applying for college. It's not that she didn't want to go to college—she did want to go—but she was so involved in the basketball season that she forgot, applications were due during that time. By the time she realized it, all of the deadlines had passed. Fortunately for Jenna, she knew someone who worked in the admissions department at a college and who was able to bend the rules for her and allow her to apply late. She was subsequently accepted to that college. Unfortunately for her, however, she wasn't able to choose wisely which colleges to apply to—she was required to go to the only one she could because she neglected the application deadlines.

> The college you attend will define the rest of your life, so it makes sense to invest the time to make the best decision, beginning with the decision about where to apply.

With more than 4,200 colleges and universities in the United States, it's initially overwhelming to decide which ones are "application worthy." Should you just pick some off of a list because their names are familiar? Are you and your best friends simply choosing all the same ones in hopes of attending college together? What about the colleges your parents attended—you know, the names that pop up in stories involving the phrase "those were the best four years of my life"? Or will you make your decision by throwing a dart at a map and applying to the schools in that target area?

Many factors are involved in selecting colleges you would consider attending. In many ways, the college you attend will define the rest of your life. Many people make lifelong friends at college, form connections that are useful in careers, find life partners, learn in-depth information about their majors, and increase their mental acuity and reasoning abilities. A poor choice has ramifications you definitely should avoid. It makes sense to invest adequate time to conduct your search using reliable decision-making techniques. What amount of time is it worth to you to achieve your best outcome?

# Prepare to Spend Some Time

Selecting colleges is serious business. You must work at it! We estimate that you might spend roughly 190 to 275 hours completing the full cycle of college review and application procedures. We know it sounds like a lot of time, but you'll see that it's absolutely worth it. Expect to plan time for these activities:

| | |
|---|---|
| Reviewing catalogs and online information, discussing colleges with parents, teachers, and counselors | 25 hours |
| Visiting campuses (including travel, tours, meetings, and class attendance) | 75–100 hours |
| Completing applications and essays | 50 hours |
| Studying for and taking SATs and ACTs | 25–75 hours |
| Finalizing decisions | 15–25 hours |

Rather than approaching these activities haphazardly, take advantage of the Decide Better! decision process to avoid wasting time. The time you invest in these strategies substantially increases your ability to make sound and realistic decisions so that your four years at college are your dream come true, not your worst—and most expensive—nightmare.

The U.S. Department of Education has found that as many as 60 percent of college students attend more than one college before they receive their bachelor's degrees. While people change schools for various reasons, the vast majority of those students simply chose poorly in the beginning. By putting in the necessary time and effort to make the best decision, you can avoid being one of those transfer students.

# There Is a College for You

While having so many schools to choose from may seem overwhelming, the good news is, with more than 4,200 potential choices, you should be able to find the perfect fit for you. Begin by taking the decision seriously. As you work through the process defined in this book, you will identify your best possible options. No matter what your grade point average (GPA) and test scores are, you can find the "right choice." At the conclusion of this elimination process, you should be prepared to apply to a range of schools, each of which can be categorized on a spectrum based on how likely you are to get in.

# Five Steps, Five Categories Get You Started

Where do you begin? Glad you asked. This chapter lays out a simple five-step process that leads you to your final selection: the colleges that meet your selection criteria and to which you will apply. Think about your selection process as having a file card for each of the 4,200 potential colleges. You begin to sort or eliminate the cards, eventually narrowing them to five piles, which are your five college categories that match your likelihood of being accepted to each one and your desire to attend each one.

Since it wouldn't be beneficial to simply deal the cards randomly into the five categories, you need a system for deciding which schools fit in which category. That's where the Decide Better! decision-making process comes in. Instead of using a hypothetical deck of cards, we devised a system that uses five steps—basically five rounds of sifting to help you narrow your choices. You will systematically eliminate the schools that do not fit your criteria and ultimately identify the ones that are perfect for you—your final top college picks. These are the schools to which you will apply. You don't need to spend any time defining the process. You just need to implement these five steps:

1. *Filtering*—Based on the criteria you deem to be crucial to any school you apply to, filter out and eliminate all schools that don't meet those needs.

2. *Sorting*—Based on your academic profile, sort each of the remaining schools into one of five categories: Target, Reach, Fallback, Out of My Reach, and Too Far Back.

3. *Ranking*—Relying on a rough evaluation, tentatively rank each school in each category in the order that you believe fits your needs.

4. *Evaluating*—Based upon your rough rankings, perform a more detailed evaluation of each school and then rerank them according to the information you uncover.

5. *Deciding*—Using the rankings you created in the previous step, decide how many schools you are going to apply to in each category, and then do it.

As you venture down the college application path, it's important to utilize all accessible resources. In terms of tangible material, independent college guides, college Web sites, independent Web sites, and information you've gathered from specific schools can serve as great resources. In terms of intangible resources, our theory is that the more opinions you have, the better off you will be. Parents, teachers, college counselors, friends, and siblings can all be valuable sources of information and offer fresh perspectives. (Of course, you don't have to do everything they advise.) We particularly recommend keeping your parents involved in this process and incorporating their advice when considering which schools to apply to. Their life experiences provide a significant resource that's yours, free for the asking! Plus, keeping them in the loop will help them appreciate your final decision about where to send applications. Their support makes life much easier for everyone.

To help demonstrate this process of deciding where to apply, we're going to use Will, a high school student, as an example. He began this process late in his junior year and reached the finish line in the winter of his senior year. Our intention is not to set Will up as the poster boy for applying to college and to imply that you should mimic him exactly. His example serves as a reference point to help you understand the process and all of the factors involved in this decision. After all, this is the first step in one of the most important decisions you'll make in your life!

## Step 1: Filtering

Begin step one in this process by identifying the criteria that are crucial to your decision—the "deal breakers." Deal breakers are any desired criteria that a particular college lacks or a characteristic that somehow conflicts with what you want. A deal breaker eliminates that college from consideration—period. Maybe the deal breaker is the college's geographic location; maybe it's the types of academic programs offered; maybe it's the social atmosphere; and maybe it's all of the above and more. What exactly are your needs or desires in a school? What do you want to get out of your time in college? During this first step, you should consider only the deal breakers—the factors that a school must possess or it's off the list. After consulting many students as they attempt to make this decision, we've found that the following list defines the most common categories college students considered when deciding where to apply:

- *Location*—Region of the country, location in relation to home, amenities of location, climate, etc.
- *Academics*—Academic specialties, specific professors, overall quality of education, academic facilities, faculty-student ratio, etc.
- *Social Factors*—Student demographics, living arrangements, availability of fraternities and sororities, extracurricular activities, sports teams, etc.
- *Cost*—Overall tuition, housing costs, transportation costs, etc.

- *Other Characteristics*—Prestige of school, size of school, public versus private university, liberal arts colleges versus broad-based national universities, size of classes, beauty of campus, religious affiliation, etc.

Please don't simply write this list down verbatim and decide these are your criteria. This is merely a jumping-off point. Ultimately, your list of deal breakers has to be completely individualized—straight from your heart and your head. For example, you may decide that you want a school in New England that has a particular religious affiliation. You can then filter out all of the schools that don't meet those two criteria, and you will be left with a much smaller number of schools to examine. Take out a sheet of paper (or create a document on your computer) and list your own requirements for selecting a college. Be sure that your deal breakers are not too limiting. For example, you'll be hard-pressed to find a school that meets your needs for intramural mud wrestling, class sizes of five to eight students, and a stellar Astrology department. You should have only two or three absolute deal breakers—for example, that you definitely want to go to a medium-sized liberal arts school. Considering too many criteria as deal breakers is unwise and may limit your choices unnecessarily.

Determine which criteria you consider deal breakers and remove from consideration any schools that don't meet these requirements.

Our friend Will decided that his filter criteria, or deal breakers, were these:

- The school should be a liberal arts school with approximately 2,000 to 8,000 students.
- The school must provide the opportunity for him to write for the student newspaper.
- The school must have the option for him to play on an intramural sports team, since he doesn't want to spend the time required to play on the school's intercollegiate teams.

Will narrowed his choices to these criteria after refining his requirements over the course of a week and a half. He worked with his parents and college counselor to revise each filter factor and create a set of characteristics that truly defined what he wanted in any school he considered attending. He initially thought that he would limit the schools to those that were within a half-hour drive of the ocean, since he liked to sail, but then he realized that he probably wouldn't be spending much time sailing during the school year. So he eliminated this requirement completely. Additionally, in terms of the location, Will initially wanted to limit his choices to schools in New England, where he grew up. After more thought, he realized this was not a deal breaker. He knew that he may prefer to stay there, but at this point in his search, he should still consider schools outside that area, so he removed that from his list. He also decided that he wouldn't limit the school based upon the academic programs available, since he was still on the fence regarding a major, though he was leaning toward either journalism or political science. Will also was uncertain whether he would be interested in joining a fraternity, so he decided not to limit his choices based on that at this point in the process. At first, he hadn't included a limit on the size of the school. However, while speaking with his college counselor about the traits his dream school would possess, the counselor told him to consider school size in his decision. After thinking about it for a few days and talking it over with his parents, Will agreed with that assessment and added school size as a filtering factor, which is now reflected on his list.

> **Note to Parents**
>
> *Here's a helpful hint: let your children sort the schools on their own first and then sit down with them to go over how they did it, helping them to confirm whether they've placed each school on the correct list.*

Here's an example of what not to do when filtering out schools. Lisa was an above-average student in high school, although she was not at the top of her class. She came from a modest background and was definitely concerned about how to pay for college. When she was determining which schools to apply to and filtering out schools using this first step, she mistakenly overemphasized cost as a deal breaker. She included a number of cost factors in her filtering, with schools' overall tuitions as most important. Lisa considered any schools that estimated tuition, room, and board at more than $25,000 per year to be out of her price range, and she automatically filtered them out. She also considered travel costs as an important deal breaker, especially for high-priced schools that were farther away from home than a four-hour drive or a relatively inexpensive direct flight. A number of very good schools still remained on her list, so she wasn't too concerned. Because of cost factors, however, Lisa did filter out the school she'd initially considered her top choice.

Lisa's best friend, Amy, on the other hand, came from a very similar financial background, but Amy decided not to filter out her top-choice schools based on high tuition. Due to her process, Amy ended up applying to the same school that had once been Lisa's top choice. Amy was accepted to that school, and the school offered her a substantial financial assistance package that included loans and scholarships. In the end, Lisa was accepted to an adequate school, but she never forgave herself for filtering out schools that may have been a better fit simply because they seemed financially unreachable. She always wondered whether she could have received enough financial aid to attend her dream school if she had not been scared off by the price tag.

We like to remind students who are going through this process and have concerns about the cost of going to college that they won't know what type of financial assistance they can get until they apply and are accepted. You shouldn't include expense as the most important factor in your decision at this point. What you can do is keep one or two schools on your list as "financial backups." These backups cover you in case you find that financial packages fall short and you cannot afford any of the other schools that accepted you. In other words, you shouldn't filter out a particular school because it's too expensive, but you can actively consider a school that's more budget-friendly.

## Step 2: Sorting

Step two in the process is to begin sorting the schools that remain on your list into five categories based upon your academic profile. Your academic profile should consist of your GPA, your standardized test scores, the level of coursework you have taken (such as advanced placement, or AP, courses), the type of high school you attend (such as a college-prep school), the activities you are involved in both in school and outside of school, and any other factors that you believe define your academic profile. There are even online resources available to help you determine your academic profile. It is fairly easy to categorize these schools, and don't worry if you're not 100 percent sure which category to place them in. You can always move them in the next step of the process.

You should sort the schools you are considering applying to into these five categories:

- *Target*—Those schools that you think you will get into based on your academic profile
- *Reach*—Those schools that are a little above your academic profile
- *Fallback*—Those schools that you are very confident you will get into
- *Out of My Reach*—Those schools that are impossible for you to get into based on your academic profile
- *Too Far Back*—Those schools that are well below your academic ability

In order to complete this step in a coordinated manner, you can simply take a sheet of paper and draw two lines down it (or do this on a computer) to create three columns. Label the column on the left *Fallback*, the one in the center *Target*, and the one on the right *Reach*. Using a second sheet of paper, you can create two columns for the schools you are removing from consideration—at least for the time being. Label these two categories as *Out of My Reach* and *Too Far Back*. As you do this, you should be categorizing all of the schools that weren't filtered out in step 1. At this point, you shouldn't worry about ranking each school, just be sure to put them into the correct column.

**Factors to Use to Measure Your Academic Profile:**

- Your GPA
- Your class rank
- Your SAT or ACT scores
- The number of AP courses you have taken
- Your extracurricular activities

To place your schools in the correct category, begin with a preliminary evaluation of the school. You can do this process in a number of ways. We recommend dividing and conquering using three levels of information about each school under consideration.

The first sorting includes the schools you have made a predetermination about and have already decided which column to place them into, at least preliminarily. Your college counselor, for example, may have given you a list of schools to consider in a particular category. These recommendations may have also come from your parents, teachers, or others who know you and have knowledge about particular schools. Regardless of whether your advisors are correct or incorrect about ranking these schools in the Reach or Target categories, for example, place them in the category they have told you for this step. You can move them later. Will, our example student, did this with a number of schools. Based on the recommendations of his college counselor, his teachers, and his parents, he placed three schools in his Fallback category, five in his Target category, and two in his Reach category.

The second sorting includes schools that, for one reason or another, you want to place in your Target category, your Out of My Reach category, or any of the other categories. This may be because you are already hoping to go to particular schools or because you think that they are appropriate for you. Sorting at this level may also include placing schools because of their reputations. For example, schools that have a very high level of academic prestige that you are certain you are not going to be accepted to should be placed in the Out of My Reach category. Likewise, schools that you believe do not fulfill your educational goals should go in the Too Far Back or Fallback categories. Again, you can move any of these schools later.

Here is how Will filtered his schools. He had pretty strong grades, but not nearly strong enough to be a serious candidate for any of the Ivy League schools. He also had relatively strong SAT scores, with a combined total of 1260 for the verbal and math sections. He started by placing all of the Ivy League schools in the Out of My Reach category. In addition, he had a list of schools that he believed lacked the educational advantages he sought, so he placed those in his Too Far Back category. Some other schools were placed in his Fallback category, his Target category, and his Reach category.

The third and final sorting includes schools for which you have no pre-existing personal context. No one has recommended them to you so you are relying more on facts. Undertaking some preliminary research will help you decide into which category to place them. For example, you can look at the average GPA and SAT scores for the school and determine how your scores rank in comparison. These numbers are widely available and can be easily found online, in the materials you receive from the schools, or in any college guide. You may also want to consider outside sources that aren't affiliated with colleges, such as the annual rankings of colleges provided by *U.S. News & World Report*, which can be very helpful. Not only does the magazine rank the schools, it also provides a breakdown of the average SAT scores, class rank, GPA, and acceptance rate for incoming freshmen. In fact, Will used this resource, and it provided him with fresh input for the schools about which he had gathered only limited information.

> ### Note to Parents
> *It's crucial that you work with your children during this process because they may not know exactly where their academic profile fits in with the schools they're sorting.*

If the average GPA and SAT scores of a school are far above yours, the school may either be a Reach or an Out of My Reach; if the numbers are similar to yours (within a close range), the school may be a Target; and if the numbers fall below yours, they may be a Fallback or a Too Far Back. Will completed the requirements for this step by placing additional schools into his Target category, his Fallback category, and his Reach category. He also placed dozens of other schools in either his Too Far Back or his Out of My Reach categories.

After completing step 2's sorting process, you should have a number of schools in the Reach, Target, and Fallback categories on your list. This number will vary by individual, but a dozen or so in each of these categories is a good minimum. Overall, a good range to shoot for is 30 to 40 schools in the three categories, combined; 50 is probably too many. (If you've got too many, you should repeat this sorting step to eliminate some more schools that you think are not right for you, based upon your research up to this time.) At this point in your process, you should not be considering schools listed in your Out of My Reach and Too Far Back categories. Keep these lists, though, because you can always come back to them and move the schools to another category as you see fit.

Figure 2-1 shows the schools on the lists of our example student, Will. As you can see from the way that he organized his list, he sorted liberal arts schools based upon the low and high ends of the SAT scores of students they accepted. Since his SAT score was 1260, he decided that schools that accept students with a 1270 or higher were Reach schools, while those that accept a 1260 as an average were Target schools, and those that accept a 1260 in the higher end of their students were Fallback schools. He had a total of 38 schools on his list, including 13 on his Target list, 12 on his Reach list, and 13 on his Fallback list.

**FIGURE 2-1   Sorting Schools**

| Fallback (1060–1380) | Target (1130–1460) | Reach (1270–1530) |
|---|---|---|
| • St. Lawrence Univ. (56) | • Davidson College (9) | • Williams College (1) |
| • Wheaton College (56) | • Hamilton College (17) | • Amherst College (2) |
| • Drew University (63) | • Colgate University (17) | • Swarthmore College (3) |
| • Hobart & Willm. Smith (63) | • Bates College (24) | • Middlebury College (5) |
| • Muhlenberg College (71) | • Colorado College (26) | • Bowdoin College (7) |
| • Lewis & Clark College (80) | • Kenyon College (32) | • Haverford College (10) |
| • Allegheny College (85) | • Occidental College (36) | • Claremont McKenna (11) |
| • St. Mary's College (87) | • Union College (40) | • Wesleyan University (11) |
| • Goucher College (91) | • Franklin & Marshall (40) | • Vassar College (11) |
| • Ohio Wesleyan Univ. (97) | • Dickinson College (44) | • Oberlin College (20) |
| • Westmont College (106) | • Skidmore College (47) | • Colby College (22) |
| • Stonehill College (106) | • Gettysburg College (48) | • Barnard College (30) |
| • Bennington College (106) | • Pitzer College (49) | |

*Rankings in parentheses provided by *U.S. News & World Report*.

Once he placed the schools into those categories, he simply listed the schools in the order of their overall rank based on the 2006 *U.S. News & World Report* college ranking issue. Some schools placed in the Target category had a higher rank than other schools placed in the Reach category because of the difference in SAT scores. For example, you can see that Davidson College, ranked ninth overall, was on his Target list, while Barnard, which was ranked 30th, is in his Reach column. He categorized them this way because Barnard's spread of SAT scores for current students was higher than his score and higher than some other schools with a higher rank. He still has the opportunity to change his prioritization of the schools based on his interest in them during the next step.

# Step 3: Ranking

Step 3 involves ranking your Fallback, Target, and Reach schools. This includes making an initial evaluation of each school, and much of this will be based on your instincts and initial impressions. Do you believe the school is one you want to consider? Usually the best way to start is by ranking the schools listed on your Target list. Then rank the schools on your Reach list and finally rank the schools on your Fallback list.

When ranking the schools in step 3, begin with those for which you already have information from previous experiences, impressions, or information you've garnered in any other way. Do you have a good impression of a school and believe it would be a good fit? Rank it high on your list. Do the same for schools that teachers, parents, and college counselors have recommended, as long as you believe they are providing you with good information and not just guessing.

Once you have gone through the schools for which you already have gathered a lot of information, move on to those for which your information is more limited. Use the resources available to you to make a rough estimate of how close you think that school is to what you envision as your perfect school and how closely it matches your academic profile. Useful tools for determining this include college guides, materials sent by the schools to you, the official college Web site, and other information that you can find on the Internet about the school. There are actually Web sites that can predict your chances of getting into a specific college based upon your GPA, your class rank, and your test scores. Don't spend too much time on this, however, since the goal is to make a rough decision about where each school should fall on your three lists.

This additional research should also help you to double-check whether you've placed the schools on the correct list in the previous step. If you determine that a particular school may actually be a Reach or a Fallback, instead of a Target school, for example, then revise the list accordingly.

**Methods for Researching Schools:**

- Read college materials
- Read materials provided on college Web sites
- Look at the course offerings for the current and upcoming years
- Read information about the schools on other Web sites and blogs
- Read the student newspapers
- Speak with current students or alumni
- Visit and tour the schools
- Interview admissions officers
- Contact one or more professors
- Spend a night in a dorm with a current student

After this additional basic evaluation, Will found that he liked several schools more than others, and he reordered his lists. His new prioritization is shown in Figure 2-2. As you can see, his preferences are significantly different than the *U.S. News & World Report* college rankings since he reordered the schools according to which ones were most suited to his tastes. Simply relying on the magazine's rankings of the schools would not uncover how closely each of the schools reflected Will's particular college needs and wishes.

**FIGURE 2-2   Initial Ranking of Schools**

| Fallback (1060–1380) | Target (1130–1460) | Reach (1270–1530) |
|---|---|---|
| 1. Goucher College (91) | 1. Bates College (24) | 1. Vassar College (11) |
| 2. Hobart & William Smith (63) | 2. Colgate University (17) | 2. Middlebury College (5) |
| 3. Drew University (63) | 3. Hamilton College (17) | 3. Bowdoin College (7) |
| 4. Wheaton College (56) | 4. Skidmore College (47) | 4. Amherst College (2) |
| 5. St. Lawrence University (56) | 5. Union College (40) | 5. Haverford College (10) |
| 6. Lewis & Clark College (80) | 6. Davidson College (9) | 6. Wesleyan University (11) |
| 7. St. Mary's of Maryland (87) | 7. Colorado College (26) | 7. Claremont McKenna (11) |
| 8. Ohio Wesleyan (97) | 8. Kenyon College (32) | 8. Williams College (1) |
| 9. Bennington College (106) | 9. Dickinson College (44) | 9. Swarthmore College (3) |
| 10. Muhlenberg College (71) | 10. Pitzer College (49) | 10. Colby College (22) |
| 11. Allegheny College (85) | 11. Franklin & Marshall (40) | 11. Oberlin College (20) |
| 12. Westmont College (106) | 12. Gettysburg College (48) | 12. Barnard College (30) |
| 13. Stonehill College (106) | 13. Occidental College (36) | |

*Rankings in parentheses provided by *U.S. News & World Report*.

## Step 4: Evaluating

Step 4 involves a much more in-depth evaluation of your schools to create a final list, ranked in the order in which you believe you will apply. Based upon the rough rankings created in the previous step, you should perform this detailed evaluation in the order listed in each category, working across the categories. This evaluation should begin with a final look at the resources you glanced through in the step 3 ranking, including the materials sent by the colleges, the official college Web sites, and other information available about each school on additional Web sites.

One method we have found useful in this step is to "try on" each school to see if it fits. Just as you would try on clothes or shoes before you buy them, you should try on each of the schools in your mind to check for a good fit. How would your life be different if you attended school A as opposed to school B? How would you enjoy the academics at the school? How would you enjoy the social life? How would you enjoy the campus? The weather? The professors? The travel from home to school? The types of courses available? Does the community in which the school is located provide the amenities you seek, such as cultural events, restaurants, movie theaters, shopping, and recreational activities? You want to make decisions that lead you to the highest degree of positives for each school. College should not be four years of torture!

Step 4 requires a lot of work, but it will pay off in the end. To accomplish this step correctly, you need to have a plan that focuses your time and attention in the most effective way. Researching schools includes a wide range of activities, from the least time intensive (reading the materials produced by the college) to the most time intensive (visiting the school and spending the night in a dorm with a student). The least time-intensive methods are also the ones that produce the least helpful results and, as you may have guessed, the most time-intensive methods provide the most helpful results. Establish a plan that enables you to maximize your time, implementing different research methods for schools higher on your list than those lower down your list. The Methods to Research Schools sidebar highlights some of the research methods to use in your evaluation. Because of the time involved, you will need to decide which research methods to use for which schools. Some methods you will likely elect to undertake for only a few schools on the list. Others you may want to perform for all of the schools. While we recommend engaging in the more detailed research for the schools at the top of your lists, this isn't a hard-and-fast rule. If you have determined a clear first choice and you already know you're going to apply to that school, you probably don't need to spend a night in one of its dorms to support your decision.

*Just as you would try on clothes or shoes before you buy them, you should try on each of the schools in your mind to see if they fit.*

As you perform this detailed research, you will begin to truly learn what it would be like to be a student at each school. You may find that a school you had previously ranked first on your Target list, for example, doesn't actually fit your needs after all, so you decide that you should either rank it lower or remove it from the list. That's okay. This step is designed to help you weed out the schools that aren't right for you. You may also find that a school you previously considered as a Reach school is actually within your Target list, so you should move it to the appropriate list and alter your rankings appropriately. Throughout this process, you should continually reassess the schools that are on the list, the categories they're in, and the order in which you've ranked them.

*You should definitely consider bouncing ideas off other people before you come to your final decision, including your parents, friends, teachers, college counselor, and anyone else you think would be helpful.*

Step 4's evaluation process helps you complete your priorities and finalize the list of schools to which you are going to consider applying. If you inadvertently eliminate a school that may have been the perfect fit for you because you didn't do the necessary research, you will end up like Natalie in our example, kicking yourself for a long time. You will only apply to some of the schools on your list, so the priority you assign to them at this step is crucial. Trying on the schools was something that we recommended for Will, and he agreed. He figuratively tried on the schools in all of these ways and really learned a lot about how he would fit into the various schools on his list. He removed some of them from consideration completely. Some others he reranked either higher up or lower down on his lists. His new configuration is shown in Figure 2-3.

**FIGURE 2-3   Final Ranking of Schools**

| Fallback (1060–1380) | Target (1130–1460) | Reach (1270–1530) |
|---|---|---|
| 1. Goucher College (91) | 1. Hamilton College (17) | 1. Amherst College (2) |
| 2. Hobart & William Smith (63) | 2. Skidmore College (47) | 2. Middlebury College (5) |
| 3. Ohio Wesleyan University (97) | 3. Colgate University (17) | 3. Wesleyan University (11) |
| 4. St. Mary's College of Maryland (87) | 4. Bates College (24) | 4. Colby College (22) |
| 5. Lewis & Clark College (80) | 5. Union College (40) | 5. Williams College (1) |
| 6. Drew University (63) | 6. Davidson College (9) | 6. Swarthmore College (3) |
| 7. Wheaton College (56) | 7. Dickinson College (44) | 7. Haverford College (10) |
| 8. St. Lawrence University (56) | 8. Kenyon College (32) | |
| | 9. Colorado College (26) | |

*Rankings in parentheses provided by *U.S. News & World Report.*

# Step 5: Deciding

Once you have completed the thorough evaluation for step 4, the obvious last step in the process is to make your final decision about which schools to apply to. While the previous steps were very time consuming, they were all preparation for this significant decision. Now you can approach this decision with the knowledge that you are completely prepared to make good choices. Having followed the Decide Better! process, you can press forward with confidence, rather than panic.

How are you going to make the final decision? It's important to select a range from each of your three categories, depending upon how many schools overall that you want to apply to. If you determine that you want to apply to eight schools, for example, which is a pretty good starting place for your consideration, you may want to apply to two schools on your Reach list, two on your Fallback list, and four on your Target list. If you want to apply to nine schools, you could apply to two or three on your Reach list, two or three on your Fallback list, and the remaining number on your Target list. The average student applies to approximately six different schools.

Will decided he would do the extra work on the applications and apply to a whopping 11 schools. One of Will's friends, Jeff, took a different approach. He decided that he was going to apply to seven schools—six from his Reach list and only one school from his Target list. In the end, Will's approach worked better than Jeff's, as Jeff was rejected from all of the schools he applied to and had to wait until the next school year to begin his college career.

You will most likely have more schools on your three lists than you can possibly apply to, but if you've done your work correctly, your schools are ranked in the sequential order of your level of interest in applying to them. However, your application decision does not necessarily mean you automatically pick only your very top choices. You very well may elect not to apply to the top two schools on your Reach list, the top four schools on your Target list, and the top two schools on your Fallback list. For a variety of reasons you may want to include a certain amount of variation in the schools you select. If the top four schools on your Target list are all in the Northeast, for example, you might decide that you want to adjust your selections to include some geographic variety. In this case, you may want to consider applying to one or two schools that are further down in your priorities (and that are not located in the Northeast) in addition to several from the top of your priorities. This decision may more completely satisfy your needs. You also may want to consider whether the schools you're applying to accept the common application. If they do, you may be inclined to increase the number of schools you apply to. In fact, as you can see from Figure 2-4, Will applied to 11 schools, including numbers 1, 3, and 4 from his Reach list; numbers 1, 2, 3, 5, and 8 from his Target list; and numbers 1, 3, and 6 from his Fallback list.

**FIGURE 2-4   Selected Schools**

| Fallback (1060 – 1380) | Target (1130 – 1460) | Reach (1270 – 1530) |
|---|---|---|
| 1. Goucher College (91) | 1. Hamilton College (17) | 1. Amherst College (2) |
| 2. Hobart & William Smith (63) | 2. Skidmore College (47) | 2. Middlebury College (5) |
| 3. Ohio Wesleyan University (97) | 3. Colgate University (17) | 3. Wesleyan University (11) |
| 4. St. Mary's College of Maryland (87) | 4. Bates College (24) | 4. Colby College (22) |
| 5. Lewis & Clark College (80) | 5. Union College (40) | 5. Williams College (1) |
| 6. Drew University (63) | 6. Davidson College (9) | 6. Swarthmore College (3) |
| 7. Wheaton College (56) | 7. Dickinson College (44) | 7. Haverford College (10) |
| 8. St. Lawrence University (56) | 8. Kenyon College (32) | |
| | 9. Colorado College (26) | |

*Rankings in parentheses provided by *U.S. News & World Report*.

# To Sum Up

Deciding which schools could possibly be your home for the next four years can be a daunting and stress-inducing task. These institutions affect your future education, your future friends, your future earning potential, and possibly even your future spouse! And this future begins with deciding where to apply. Far too many students end up at the wrong college because they didn't apply to the right ones. Won't it be reassuring to know that you invested the appropriate time and brain-power to make this major decision wisely?

In this chapter we introduced a five-step process to guide your decision. By following this straightforward process, you can be assured that your decision is sound.

# Chapter 3

# The Black Box

## How Colleges Make Their Admission Decisions

**J**acqueline received good grades in high school and decent SAT scores, so she was confident that she would get into one of the two schools she applied to. After all, her GPA and SAT scores were above the lower end of the range for each school. So she was terribly surprised when she received thin envelopes—rejections from both colleges. Jacqueline was a victim of the black box decision process used by colleges. She erroneously assumed that she qualified for acceptance by the two schools because she met the lower end of the published range for them. You don't have control over the way colleges make their acceptance decisions, and their decision-making process is not as straight-forward as meeting their minimum GPA and SAT requirements.

For those of you who enjoy roller coasters, you know that there's nothing like the rush of adrenaline that comes from complete and utter lack of control as you swoosh up and down. For those few minutes, your fate is in the hands of the Amusement Park Gods, and there is nothing between you and the sky but an uncomfortable metal seatbelt. For those of you who hate roller coasters, chances are you hate relinquishing control.

A much more important instance in which you lack control while other people stand between you and your

*Note to Parents*
*Do you know how colleges make their admissions decisions? Understanding the process will help you and your children "work" the system and get admitted to the best schools.*

fate is the college admission process. But rather than causing you to throw your hands up in the air and to scream like a lunatic, this situation tends to induce indigestion, insomnia, and possibly hair loss. The question is, how do colleges decide who gets admitted and who gets a painfully thin envelope containing the standard, "Oh, so close! But still far away! Thanks anyway for your interest and that $50 application fee, of course"? It's often considered to be a black box—a hidden process that seems random and that is kept secret from everyone else, as Figure 3-1 illustrates.

**FIGURE 3-1 The Black Box**

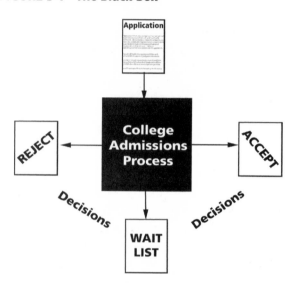

After extensive research, interviews with several officials charged with making these decisions, and a review of previous admission decisions, we've come up with information that can help you fine-tune your college admission attempts and increase your chances of being accepted to the schools that suit you best. Many of the tips and the basics for this chapter have come from research conducted by the National Association for College Admission Counseling. (For more about the resources provided by NACAC, please visit http://www.nacacnet.org.)

While the criteria that schools use to determine who gets accepted may change from year to year and vary from school to school, some important baselines can help you understand the decision process better. Understanding how each admissions staff makes its decisions helps you know which areas to emphasize in your applications. What are the main components that college admission personnel use to make their decisions?

# Key Considerations for Admission

First, and usually most important, admissions personnel review your academic standing, which comprise the following information:

- Your high school GPA, or how you've done overall in your high school coursework
- Your standardized test scores, which would be either your SATs or your ACTs
- The grades you've received in any college preparatory courses, including AP courses

Admissions personnel consider these factors to be most important because they indicate how well suited students are to succeed in the coursework the colleges offer. These criteria form a baseline of student achievement and may immediately qualify or disqualify candidates. For instance, some schools will decide not to consider students for acceptance (except under special circumstances) if their GPA is below 2.8 and/or their SAT scores are below 1500. Each school sets its own minimum acceptance baseline for these criteria and usually publishes that baseline front and center in the admission information.

Even so, students who rank well on each of these factors have no guarantee that they will get into a top school. In addition, some students who do not have stellar ratings in these factors will get accepted to a top school. At the elite schools, it's difficult to determine what you need to do to qualify. Harvard regularly rejects hundreds of student applicants who received perfect scores of 800 on the SAT math exam. Yale rejects applicants who scored a perfect 2400 on the three-part SAT, and Princeton turns away hundreds of high school applicants with 4.0 grade point averages.

The next most important category that admissions personnel consider includes these four additional academic factors that may tip your academic scale over that of competing students:

- Your class rank
- Your application essay or writing sample
- Your college counselor or advisor recommendations
- Your teacher recommendations

These combined factors help colleges narrow the field to applicants who fit the schools' academic parameters. While admissions staff may weed out certain candidates who don't meet their threshold of initial baseline criteria, they will apply the secondary set of criteria to decide which of the applicants who met their first round of criteria rise above the rest. Those who don't stand out are usually tossed into the reject or defer piles or, at a minimum, are not advanced into the pile of first-choice students.

Nonacademic and personal factors comprise the third selection category. Essentially, these encompass extracurricular activities and the face-to-face presentations to the schools (if applicable). Involvement in various activities shows colleges that students are able to both focus on their studies and maintain a wide variety of interests. This indicates effective time management, which is a desirable attribute for college students given the choices and diversions they face. These are the nonacademic and personal factors:

- Your interview with admissions personnel, if one is available
- Your extracurricular activities, including your previous employment experience
- Your demonstrated commitment to studying at their school, which they can judge by how you impress them during your interview, how well you might integrate into their campus environment, and how they believe you can add to their overall academic atmosphere

> By gaining insight into how admissions officers make their decisions, you can better understand how to get into their school.

These third-level considerations are typically the factors that set one applicant apart from another, in essence serving as the next level "tip" factors. The nonacademic and personal factors allow admissions personnel to understand *who* you are, not just how well you do in your coursework and how well you can handle standardized tests. Personality and personal interests are important to admissions staff—albeit less important than academics—so they really do want to get to know you before they make an admission decision.

The fourth important category of factors used in deciding incoming freshman classes is relatively new. A small subset of schools now also consider these evolving academic factors:

- Your performance on state-based graduation exam scores, which are usually used to determine the ability of a student to actually graduate from high school
- Your performance on standardized subject tests, including the subject tests within the SAT system and advanced placement tests

As these factors become more widely used by high school systems throughout the country, they are very likely to continue to infiltrate admission decisions. They are still not considered as important to your overall academic performance as GPA and SAT scores are, but schools do add these results, if available, to their assessment mix.

The fifth and final category of factors used by a vast majority of schools for acceptance decisions encompasses these factors over which students have little to no control:

- Your ability to pay the tuition, which is important because, while colleges may provide a high level of financial aid to some of the top students, the only way most schools can provide this support is by having other students enrolled who are able to pay the full tuition

- Your race or ethnicity, which is important when schools are looking for a particular level of diversity in their classes

- Your state or county of residence, which is very important not only for state schools, but also for schools that want to recruit candidates from diverse regional areas

- Your relationship with college alumni, which is important both because alumni indicate a pattern of academic success that, by association, intimates your potential success and because alumni donations are a critical element of colleges' financial stability

Colleges may use these factors in their admission processes for a variety of reasons, even though they may seem unfair to you or other students. Colleges like to maintain certain levels of diversity, including academic diversity and diversity of interests, as well as ethnic and geographic diversity. You really have limited—or no—influence over these factors and whether the schools will choose to rely on these factors in their admission decisions. Still, it is important for you to understand the multifaceted approaches used for admission to colleges.

Armed with this knowledge, how can you use your understanding of their decision process for your own benefit? Let's go through these factors step by step so that you can see how to improve your chances of admission to the schools of your choice. While performing the following evaluations, you will determine how to keep upgrading your application, thus improving your chances for success. Your goal is to keep moving your application forward through the process toward acceptance and to avoid the "application denied" piles.

# Primary Academic Factors

First, let's focus on the academic factors, including your GPA, your standardized test scores, and your grades in college-prep courses. You can work to improve your SAT scores by taking a preparation program. Studies have shown that these programs do improve standardized test scores. SAT and other standardized tests are used by many colleges as the primary screening criteria. The scores help them compare students across many schools in a standardized way, and we can't overstate their importance. Even if you have great participation in high school activities, you are unlikely to pass this first screen if your SAT scores are well below the range for that college. Exceptions could be made, however, if your activities included an Olympic gold medal or you are one of the top athletes in the country.

SAT scores are also important for the prestige of a college. Colleges are regularly ranked, and SAT scores are an important criterion in the ranking. Colleges are therefore constantly trying to improve the SAT scores in their incoming classes. Most colleges want to show charts to trustees that reflect an improving trend in SAT scores with each class.

In 2008, Baylor University in Texas tried to improve its SAT scores by offering its admitted freshmen a $300 campus bookstore credit to retake the SAT and $1,000 a year in merit scholarship aid for those who raised their scores by at least 50 points. Of that year's freshman class of more than 3,000, 861 students received the bookstore credit and 150 students qualified for the $1,000-a-year merit aid. The program raised Baylor's average SAT score for incoming freshmen to 1210 from about 1200, according to John Barry, vice president for communications and marketing. That score is one of the factors taken into consideration for the rankings compiled by *U.S. News & World Report* and other sources.

**Primary Academic Criteria:**

- GPA
- Standardized test scores
- Achievement in AP level courses

If you're in the application phase of your senior year, you may think you can do little to improve these factors, but that's not necessarily true. Can you find ways to improve your GPA, your test scores, and how well you do in advanced placement courses? You can—and should—focus on excelling at your coursework, particularly your advanced courses. While you may have to send your current grades with your application before you have your fall semester grades, by making a determined effort to improve your grades in that semester, you can show the colleges your commitment to scholarship. Make the decision now to do that, and then send in your new-and-improved grades as an update to your application. Overall, for these primary academic factors, you do have the ability to make improvements. How determined are you? Will you make a conscious decision to improve this critical category of factors?

# Secondary Academic Factors

Now let's review the second set of factors. To begin with, while many high schools have stopped ranking their students for a number of reasons, class rank is still considered a significant determiner of how well a student can handle the stresses of college classes. One director of admissions from a liberal arts school told us that class rank is a much more accurate indicator of how well a student will do in classes than SAT scores. The reason is that SAT scores simply reflect achievement on a single test, while the class rank reflects the overall ability of students to thrive in their environment. If your school does assign a rank to its students, then you can be sure that your rank will be a fairly important factor in your likelihood of being offered admission.

The other factors involved in this second set are much easier for you to address, but you need to make conscious decisions to maximize these factors. Since nearly all schools require an essay or high school course writing sample, let us begin there. The vast majority of schools require a specific admission essay, usually one that is on a topic of their choosing. You must decide what you're trying to convey to the people who will be reading it and how you plan to differentiate yourself from the other applicants. You need to prove that you are a good student, that you are a good match for their school, and that you will bring some type of unique quality that adds to their academic and social environments. While they can get a sense of your previous accomplishments from your application details (where you've worked, what courses you've taken, and your extracurricular activities), your essay is your chance for them to get to know you on a personal level. It brings your personality into the application process.

> **Criteria That Tip the Scale:**
> - Class rank
> - Essay/writing sample
> - Recommendations

This opportunity—and you really should consider this an opportunity, particularly if you don't believe your academic record will be enough for you to gain admission—allows you to showcase your written communications skills. Work with your parents, teachers, college counselors, and a writing tutor (if necessary) to determine what topic you want to write about. Don't, however, let anyone write the essay for you. The colleges will be able to tell—remember that the colleges also have another writing sample from you that was included with your SAT or ACT score reports. Use a dictionary and a thesaurus to verify your word usage and spelling. Dig out your grammar book and check sentence structure. Have someone reliable proofread your essay before you

*Note to Parents*

*You can be of particular assistance in helping your children decide what to write about in the essay because you may be able to remind them of something impressive they did several years ago but had forgotten about.*

submit it. You can really benefit from availing yourself of these safeguards to ensure that you have written a truly top-caliber essay.

Your letters of recommendation are another important variable in this second category of college admission factors. These are typically from your college counselor, advisor, current teachers, or a college alumnus. If deciding whom to ask for recommendations is difficult for you, please seek your parents' input.

One student we advised on the admission process, Jeremy, told us that he was going to ask his theater teacher to write his recommendation to college, where he intended to major in physics. While it was clear that compared to his other teachers this teacher knew the most about him, we told him to be careful about blindly asking the theater teacher when other teachers also knew him very well. If he were planning to major in theater, we would have told him to consider asking his theater teacher. He told us he was also close to his physics teacher, and in the end, he decided it would be better to ask that teacher to write his recommendation.

# Nonacademic Factors

The nonacademic factors that make up the third category involve making a number of important decisions that will significantly affect your admission chances. The first of these factors is how well you do in your interview. If the top-pick schools you're applying to offer an interview, you may decide that this venture is worthwhile.

Demonstrating your high level of interest in the school is often the factor that can put your application ahead of others.

Make the decision now about whether you're going to do an interview and what you're going to try to accomplish during it. How are you going to portray yourself to the interviewer? If the interviewer comes away knowing one more fact about you than he or she had known before the interview, what do you want that to be? You may even want to role play an interview with a friend or one of your parents.

Your extracurricular activities are also a significant discriminator in the acceptance process. Do you play an instrument or a sport? Are you an artist, poet, or writer? Do you act in plays or design the set or the lighting for these plays? Are you involved in any student organizations such as student government, the student newspaper, or some other group? What are your interests outside of class? Do you volunteer in the community? These activities are very important to admissions personnel because they add additional layers to your profile. They set you apart from other applicants and round out your personality above and beyond your grades. In addition, being involved in extracurricular activities shows the admissions officers that you are able to manage your time wisely, even when you are involved in a wide variety of activities. Finally, they are important because the social atmosphere on a campus is crucial to any healthy college. Having qualified students who want to be involved in activities outside of class is important to maintain a well-rounded and active campus.

Being a multifaceted student involved in a variety of activities increases your likelihood of being admitted into your top-pick schools, but you need to decide what selling points you're going to present to the schools. Look at your current involvement in high school activities and determine which of these you plan to continue in college. If you're not planning on playing sports in college, you may want to notch up your involvement in activities other than—or in addition to—sports. Art, music, and other similar activities are also commonly offered in college, for example. In general, you should be involved in a variety of activities that can show the breadth of your interests, but you should also make a conscious decision about which of these you believe will enhance your chances of college admission. While the duration of your involvement is a factor, it's never too late to decide to participate in an outside activity. If you believe that you're not active enough, decide today to become more involved.

The final component of the nonacademic category of factors is your demonstrated interest in the school. Let's use Derek to exemplify the importance of this component. Derek applied to a school that was definitely a Reach school at the higher end of his qualification range. He really had his sights set on the school, though, and considered it his first choice. He decided that he would pursue this school over all else and tailored his entire application approach to exactly those items that would help his admission chances. The school offered an early decision option, and while he knew his chances of admission during the early period were limited, he decided to apply anyway.

> **Nonacademic Criteria:**
> - Admissions interview
> - Extracurricular activities
> - Your demonstrated level of interest in the school

He interviewed with an admissions officer during the early decision period and explained why he believed this was the one school that mattered to him and why he would be a good addition to the school. Much to his chagrin, he was not accepted during the early decision period, but his application was held over for consideration during the regular admission period. During this time, he continued to update the school with academic information to add to his original application. He maintained contact by e-mail with the admissions officer with whom he had interviewed, explaining his continued interest in being considered for admission. When the admission letter finally arrived in April, he was thrilled to learn that he was accepted. In an e-mail communication, the admissions officer told Derek that one of the factors that tipped his application over the top was the level of interest he had demonstrated in the school. His efforts had paid off.

Demonstrating your high level of interest in the school is often the factor that can put your application ahead of others. You can do this for yourself by making a decision about how you are going to show your interest to admissions personnel. Derek showed his interest through applying early, explaining his interest during his interview, updating his application for the regular admission period, and maintaining contact with the admissions department. You should form your own strategy to demonstrate your level of interest in the schools that you are applying to, whether you have a clear first choice or not.

# New Academic Factors

The next category of factors considered by admissions personnel is much like the first academic category in terms of how well you can control them. The first of these criteria is how well you perform on the state-based graduation exams that are becoming increasingly prevalent. Prepare for these tests as seriously as you would for your SAT or ACT exams. Where required, these scores are sent to the schools you apply to, and while schools give more weight to your SAT or ACT scores, they will not ignore your state graduation exams.

You should also decide whether you are going to take any of the standardized subject tests, which are tests focused on one or more subjects and are offered by the organizers of the SAT or the ACT. If you already know you are going to pursue physics in college, for example, and you have focused your applications to show your ability and desire to study physics, you should seriously consider taking the physics subject test offered by SAT. If you are tailoring your application around your desire to study physics and you decide not to take the subject test, the admissions personnel might question why you decided not to take it. If more specific tests are offered for your focus area of study, you should make a decision about whether to take these tests, and if you do, you should be prepared to score high on them.

**New Academic Criteria:**

- State-based graduation exams
- Standardized subject tests

# Uncontrollable Factors

You may have almost no control over the final group of criteria that admissions personnel rely on. For instance, your ability to pay the tuition may depend on many factors over which you have little control, including your parents' level of financial contribution and any financial assistance from outside sources. Colleges use this ability-to-pay factor because they obviously need money to run the school. They admit a lot of students who are highly qualified but unable to pay the full tuition and then offer them financial aid and grants. This is balanced, though, by also admitting students who do not require financial assistance. How this balancing act affects your acceptance chances may depend upon the schools' current financial needs.

> Some factors that admissions personnel consider are completely out of your hands.

The second factor—your race or ethnicity—is wholly uncontrollable by you. Colleges like to admit a diverse set of students because diversity attracts more diversity and keeps enrollments strong. You also do not have much control over the location where you reside. Many schools—particularly state schools—are required to admit a certain number of in-state students and may also prefer student representation from many different cities and counties in their state. Other schools may choose to admit students from diverse locations but may not be seeking students from your location at the time you want to enroll. If the school is located in the Northeast, for example, and the vast majority of the applicants are from that area but the school wants more geographical diversity, being from the Southwest may be an asset that can boost your admission chances.

Julian, a student we worked with, was ranked fifth in his class at a medium-sized Texas high school and was hoping to go to a top school. He had very good grades, a high GPA, relatively high scores on the SATs, and was involved in a fair number of extracurricular activities. He also had strong recommendations. All of those qualifications should mean a fair chance of being admitted to a highly ranked school. He was concerned, however, about the other four classmates whose class rankings were higher than his. Fortunately for Julian, however, all four of them applied—and were accepted to—major universities in their home state of Texas. Julian decided that he really wanted to attend Princeton, and while he wasn't the highest ranked student at his high school, he still got in. How much his Texas residency and the decisions of those students who were ranked above him played in his admission is unknown, but those factors certainly didn't hurt.

The final fairly uncontrollable factor is the relationship between the applicants and college alumni. Fortunately for you as an applicant, this may be something you can change. If you have a relationship with an alumnus, don't ignore it. You need to foster that relationship and use it to increase your chances of admission. Have the alumnus write a recommendation for you even if the school doesn't specifically ask for one. If the alumnus has a relationship with an admissions officer or other administrative personnel, that can certainly be an enormous advantage for you. But you need to be proactive and ask for help from the alumnus. If you don't already have a relationship with someone who attended a school you are interested in, try to find one. You may not be successful, but it shouldn't be for lack of trying. Ask around. Check with your parents, your friends and their parents, and your teachers. Check online for college alumni offices and contact them for local alumni contacts. You may find that you're closely associated with an alumnus and didn't know it. Most people enjoy helping others and would welcome the opportunity to assist an aspiring college-bound student. All you need to do is find the person and ask for the support.

**Uncontrollable Criteria:**
- Ability to pay tuition
- Race or ethnicity
- Residence location
- Relationship with alumni

# New Admission Models

Recently, many colleges throughout the country have been testing out new admission software that can help them pinpoint which students to accept and which ones to offer various levels of financial aid to. These models enable the schools to better reach their enrollment targets in terms of academic profiles, as well as geographic, ethnic, and financial diversity. The software indicates a particular student's likelihood of enrolling in the school if admitted and the amount of financial aid and scholarships to offer to increase this likelihood. Included in the software's process, to the dismay of many applicants, are factors such as whether a student's parents attended the school. If they did, the school may offer less financial aid or scholarships since the student is more likely to pay full tuition to attend because of these existing school ties. The software is designed to calculate many variables, such as a student's relationship with the school, financial resources, class rank, grades, SAT scores, residence, and ethnic background. It will then suggest decisions the admissions personnel should make to bring the best mix of students into the college.

## To Sum Up

The more you know about the admission process the more you can leverage this knowledge to make the right decisions during every step of the application process. By understanding how admissions personnel make their decisions, you can tailor your approach to your applications accordingly and maximize your chances of being accepted.

Colleges make decisions on whether to accept you or not. From your perspective this decision process is like a mysterious black box. In this chapter, you gained some insights into that black box. Use these insights to improve your chances of it working in your favor.

# Chapter 4

## The Big Decision

### Making the Final Decision on Where to Go

**M**ichelle was considering what college to attend and had several great opportunities. She talked about the differences between her choices with her classmates and her parents. In the end, she decided to turn down opportunities at some very good private schools even though she had been offered generous scholarships. Instead, she elected to attend the state college because her boyfriend was going there. Her parents were upset, and, ironically, she broke up with her boyfriend a month after they started college, and she switched schools after her first year. Michelle obviously made a bad decision on where to go to college. Will you?

**Note to Parents**
*Your children can't—and shouldn't—make this decision on their own. You need to help them understand their priorities and help them make an informed decision, not one based on emotion.*

You've waded through the college application process and finally reached the finish line. You are a rare physical specimen, a model of tenacity, perseverance, and incredible stamina. You've endured writing essays and filling out applications. You've survived studying and taking and perhaps retaking the SATs or ACTs. You've made it through grueling interviews with admissions officers and being seen with your parents while visiting schools. Then you waited for months and months to find out what your future will hold for you and where you'll spend the next four years. And, let's face it, all that hard work and time you spent—when you could have been out with your friends instead—was worth it. Finally, the day came when the envelopes started arriving. Some were thick and some were pathetically thin, but you now know which schools want you and which schools don't. The waiting game is over! But now what? Perhaps your initial excitement and relief is being replaced by anxiety and panic. What should you do? First, breathe. Next, you need to make a decision!

How on Earth do you make this monumental decision—the one that dictates the next four years of your life? How do you make that final choice of which college will someday be your alma mater? By how each school "feels" to you? By how close it is to home? By how close the school is to the schools your friends attend? By how good the cafeteria food is? Maybe you should have your friends put the envelopes behind their backs, and you can start picking hands until you've narrowed it down to two envelopes. Then, you can play "eeny, meeny, miny, moe" to determine the lucky school that will be taking your tuition money. This may sound silly, but unless you take a fair and deep look at each of your options, giving them equal consideration, then you may as well just pick one at random.

> This is probably the most important decision you've ever made in your life so you should approach it as such.

## Look Long Term, Not Just Short Term

Which college to attend is probably the most important decision you will make in your life thus far, and the decision will have a tremendous impact on the rest of your life, so take the time to make the best decision you can. Your decision should be a calculated process that leads you to the best choice based upon the criteria that are the most important to *you*. So how do you do this? We've created a decision worksheet that you can download from our Web site at http://www.DecideBetter.com/college.html. Filling this out helps you to identify which criteria are the most important to you and to rate how each of the schools matches these criteria. The worksheet will automatically calculate which school meets your criteria best, enabling you to make the most informed decision possible. Download the worksheet and follow along with it in front of you or just review the portions of the worksheet that are outlined in this chapter.

We've had opportunities to provide just such decision-making assistance to a number of high school seniors and their parents. The student we followed in the second chapter, Will, provides a good example of how to apply this decision-making process. We will use his example throughout this chapter to demonstrate how to best implement this important decision.

If you remember, Will applied to 11 schools, including five from his Target list (Hamilton College, Skidmore College, Colgate University, Union College, and Kenyon College), three from his Reach list (Amherst College, Wesleyan University, and Colby College), and three from his Fallback list (Goucher College, Ohio Wesleyan University, and Drew University). He was accepted into six very good liberal arts schools, including one from his Reach list (Colby College), three from his Target list (Skidmore College, Union College, and Kenyon College), and two from his Fallback list (Goucher College and Drew University). To help Will make his decision, we provided him with our Decide Better! college decision work sheet. To simplify his decision process, he narrowed his choices to four before beginning step 1 of the process: Colby College, Skidmore College, Union College, and Goucher College. Four steps are covered in the worksheet: 1) determine your decision categories and criteria, 2) assign each decision criterion a weight, 3) assess your selected colleges, and 4) make that big decision about which school to attend. Read on to master these four steps that will lead to your college acceptance decision.

### Top Factors Not to Use as the Only Factor for Choosing a College:

- Because it's ranked high in magazines
- Because your girlfriend, boyfriend, or best friend goes there
- Because the cost is low
- Because a specific person recommended it to you (parents, college counselor, friends, etc.)
- Because the guide book looks good
- Because it's a party school
- Because your mother or father went there
- Because it has a good football team
- Because the college interviewer was nice

## Step 1: Determine Your Decision Categories and Criteria

The decision worksheet includes five general categories that should be included in your decision-making process. Each of these categories is further broken down into four to seven different individual criterion. The first step in the process is to decide how important each general category is to you. These categories and their criteria include:

- ❗ *Location*—close to home, close to friends, climate, and urban or rural location
- ❗ *Academics*—availability of major, availability of back-up major, quality of faculty, general academic environment, flexible or structured curriculum, level of academic pressures, faculty to student ratio, use of technology, and quality of academic facilities

❶ *General Characteristics*—school prestige, school size, public versus private university, disability friendly, campus demographics, religious affiliation, housing quality, campus appearance, and the feel or your intuition

❶ *Costs*—net tuition costs, student loan availability, work-study availability, room and board costs, and travel costs

❶ *Social Life*—Greek life availability, extracurricular activities, overall social environment, housing options, sports teams to watch, and opportunity to play on sports team

Each category on the worksheet also includes a number of blank lines so you can enter topics that are important to you that have not been included on the worksheet. Take advantage of these by determining the characteristics and entering them into the worksheet before you proceed to the next step. Assign a weight to these new entries, as well. You can also change your mind about any or all of these weightings, and the numbers in the worksheet will reflect any changes you make.

How do you determine the importance of each of these five categories? Much of it depends on the relative importance each holds for you and your parents. How important is the cost and availability of financial aid? How about the academics or the social life or the location? Would you prefer to attend a school near your home or one that is farther away? How about the other characteristics of the school, such as the size or prestige or religious affiliation? You need to make that determination, and after doing so, you should assign each of these decision categories a percentage value so that the total of all the five categories will add up to 100 percent.

Here is the breakdown that Will chose: Location (10 percent), Academics (40 percent), General Characteristics (15 percent), Costs (25 percent), and Social Life (10 percent). When you define these percentages according to your own priorities, go through them one time first and then go back and analyze each of the categories again. You may find that you tweak the numbers here and there, and while it may be easier for you to choose round numbers, don't feel like you can't choose 22.5 percent, for instance, for one of the categories, as long as the totals add up to 100 percent. Remember, you need to get the relative importance of each category in comparison to the others. (You can always go back and change your percentage breakdown at any point later in the process.) Once you have decided the

*Note to Parents*
This is the most important step for you! Participate in the process of weighing the criteria and make sure the relative importance fits for you, too. Then let your children do the rest. You can be confident that they will make a good decision.

level of importance for each category, enter that information into the correct space on the decision work sheet.

When deciding the level of importance he wanted to assign to each of the categories, Will started with Academics, since he knew that they held the most importance to him. He thought this category should constitute a little less than half of his decision, and he assigned it 40 percent. He next looked at Location, which he believed was not very important. He realized that it would be nice to be able to get to school and back home relatively easily, and he knew he wanted to be close to a city, but he didn't want location to be the determining criterion. He still thought it should have some impact so he assigned it 10 percent. As for Social Life, because he had some specific interests for extracurricular activities, he assigned Social Life 10 percent. He had yet to assign the remaining 40 percent and began to consider how much the Cost of the school mattered in his decision. He knew that all of the schools he had applied to had similar costs and that, while he wanted to get a good value for his education, he knew he could take out loans for the amount that his parents could not contribute. He decided costs were worth 25 percent of his decision and believed that the remaining 15 percent should be assigned to the last category, General Characteristics.

## Step 2: Assign Each Decision Criterion a Weight

The next step is to look at each category and decide the importance of each individual criterion within the broader categories. While you should try to be as accurate as possible about this, you can go back and change these values at any time during the process. When assigning a weight to each criterion, you should select 0 if the individual criterion is not important in the slightest, and up to 5 if the criterion is extremely important to your decision. The vast majority should be assigned a 2 or a 3, with only the least or most important criterion receiving a 0 or a 5. If a particular criterion is completely irrelevant to you, you should assign it a 0 so that it does not skew your results. Don't hesitate to customize the decision worksheet to your own interests by adding or substituting criteria.

**FIGURE 4-1  Weighting of Location Criteria**

| Location | 10 | % | Weight |
|---|---|---|---|
| Close to home | | | 3 |
| Close to friends | | | 2 |
| In climate you want | | | 2 |
| In urban or rural area | | | 2 |
| | | Total points | 9 |

Location Criteria: Figure 4-1 provides a breakdown of the weight of each of the criteria in the Location category on Will's decision work sheet. He wanted to attend a school with easy access to home, which generally meant either a drive of up to four hours or a direct flight from his house in Chicago. While this wasn't the most important criterion for him, he figured that he should include it with the moderate weighting of 3. As for the proximity to his friends, he decided that was less important, but if it were possible to attend a school near his friends, then he would. He decided that the climate wasn't overly important to him, but that he would prefer a Northern climate, since that was where he grew up. As for the environment, it was very important for him to be in an area that was not too rural. While being in the inner city wasn't necessarily what he was looking for, he certainly didn't want to be somewhere he considered to be in the middle of nowhere. So he decided to set this as a 2.

**Academic Criteria:** Figure 4-2 provides a breakdown of the weight of each of the criteria in the Academics category on Will's decision worksheet, for which he had assigned the greatest percentage of importance out of all of the categories (40 percent). Will knew how important it was for each school to have his first-choice major, which was political science. Since he still wanted the option to change his mind about his major, he gave this criterion a weighting of 4. As for his second potential major, which was likely to be business, he decided that it was less important that each school have it and gave it a weighting of 2. The reputation and competence of the professors at each school was of high importance so he decided to assign this criterion a relatively high weighting of 4. The same held true for the general academic environment because he believed it was important for the school to have students and faculty who considered academics as the most important component of a college education.

**FIGURE 4-2 Weighting of Academic Criteria**

| Academics | 40 | % | Weight |
|---|---|---|---|
| Has your first choice major | | | 4 |
| Has your second choice major options | | | 2 |
| Has professors you admire | | | 4 |
| General academic environment | | | 4 |
| Curriculum (flexible or structured) | | | 3 |
| Level of academic pressures | | | 2 |
| Average class size | | | 4 |
| Use of technology in education | | | 2 |
| Quality of academic facilities | | | 3 |
| **Total points** | | | **28** |

While many schools have a very structured curriculum with a lot of general requirements, Will decided he preferred a school with a more flexible curriculum and assigned a 3 for the weight of this criterion. Less important to him was the level of academic pressure. He knew he could handle a high level of pressure but wasn't particularly interested in looking for the school with the highest amount of academic pressure so he assigned the criterion a 2. As for the average class size, he was looking for a school offering more classes that would be taught with fewer students, as opposed to offering more large, lecture-style classes with hundreds of students. This criterion was pretty important to him, and he assigned it a 4. He decided it was moderately important to him how prevalent the use of technology was in the teaching process at each of the schools so he assigned this criterion a weighting of 2. He also thought it was important to have academic facilities that were in good shape and relatively modern so he rated the quality of academic facilities a 3.

**General Characteristics Criteria:** Figure 4-3 provides a breakdown of the assigned weights in the General Characteristics category of Will's decision work sheet, for which he assigned an overall importance level of 15 percent. While he didn't think the prestige of the school was the most important aspect, he also didn't think it was inconsequential, and he assigned it a weight of 4. As for the size of the school, he didn't want an enormous university with tens of thousands of students, but he likewise didn't want a school with fewer than a couple thousand people. He felt pretty strongly about it so he assigned a 4 to the size criterion. (He had previously made the decision to only apply to schools that fit this criterion, so all of the schools on this list would be similar.) He didn't want to go to a public university, and again, since he had not applied to any major universities, he simply assigned a weight of 2 to this criterion. He has no disabilities so he assigned a 0 there.

He believed that the demographics were fairly important, as he didn't want to go to a school at which everyone had a background similar to his own, so he entered a 2 for this criterion. As for religious affiliation, he would prefer to go to a school without a religious affiliation, so he entered a weighting of 3. He wanted to ensure that the housing options did not consist of old, rundown buildings. He wanted them to be on the newer side, and this was fairly important to him, so he gave this a weight of 4. He also preferred a campus that had some natural beauty to it, rather than just brick and mortar, so he also gave this criterion a 4. Based upon his campus visits, he felt that his intuition about the schools was crucial, so he gave this criterion a weight of 5, the highest.

**FIGURE 4-3  Weighting of General Criteria**

| General Characteristics | 15 | % | Weight |
| --- | --- | --- | --- |
| Prestige of school | | | 4 |
| Size of school | | | 4 |
| Public versus private school | | | 2 |
| Disability friendly | | | 0 |
| Campus demographics | | | 2 |
| Religious affiliation of school | | | 3 |
| Quality of housing | | | 4 |
| Beauty of campus | | | 4 |
| Your "feel" of the school—intuition | | | 5 |
| **Total points** | | | 28 |

Cost Criteria: Next, Will tackled weights for school costs, which can be seen in Figure 4-4. He believed that the overall net tuition cost was clearly the most important factor since it was the most expensive part of the costs he would incur. He assigned it a weight of 5. Since the net cost for tuition included not only the list price for tuition but also the dollar amount of the scholarships offered by each school, this amount would be likely to vary widely from one school to another. In terms of the availability of work-study programs for each school, Will felt this factor was much less important than the net tuition costs, but not irrelevant, so he assigned this criterion a 1. While room and board costs impact the overall cost of attending school, he would have to pay them at all of the schools. The amount of these costs compared to the overall tuition costs are significantly less so he also assigned this criterion a 1. He also wanted travel costs to be considered, and he assigned that criterion a 2.

**FIGURE 4-4  Weighting of Cost Criteria**

| Costs | 25 | % | Weight |
|---|---|---|---|
| Net tuition costs | | | 5 |
| Work-study availability | | | 1 |
| Room and board costs | | | 1 |
| Travel costs | | | 2 |
| | | Total points | 9 |

Social Life Criteria: Figure 4-5 details the breakdown of the final category of criteria in Will's decision worksheet, the school's Social Life, for which he assigned an importance level of 10 percent. While he believed that academia should outweigh social life (as is indicated by the high importance he placed on academics), he had some specific interests when it came to his social life. For example, he already knew he wasn't interested in joining a fraternity, but wasn't concerned about whether a school he might attend had them, so he listed that criterion as irrelevant with a weighting of 0. Because he wanted some activities that interested him to be available, he decided to assign extracurricular activities a 4. When it came to the overall social environment, he realized he was pretty good at fitting in with most people and didn't feel that one particular type of social environment would be vastly important. He assigned a 1 to this criterion. In terms of housing, he

**FIGURE 4-5  Weighting of Social Life Criteria**

| Social Life | 10 | % | Weight |
|---|---|---|---|
| Greek life available | | | 0 |
| Extracurricular activities | | | 4 |
| Overall social environment | | | 1 |
| Housing options | | | 3 |
| Great sports teams to watch | | | 1 |
| Opportunity to play on sports team | | | 1 |
| | | Total points | 10 |

would really need a quiet place to study and knew that many college students do a lot of partying so he wanted to have the flexibility to live on campus or off campus, as well as to have a single room without a roommate. He assigned this criterion a 3. Finally, in terms of college sports teams, he estimated that he would probably watch a few football or basketball games, but this was not overly important to him, so he entered a 1 for this criterion. He also played baseball, but wasn't sure he would pursue this in college. He liked to think that this could be a possibility, though, so he also rated this criterion a 1.

## Step 3: Assess Your Selected Colleges

Once you have completed the second step, the nuts and bolts of your research begins. Now you need to assess how well each of your schools meets your needs in terms of the criteria. When rating each school on the worksheet, base your responses on the following scale.

5—If it meets your needs completely

4—If it meets the vast majority of your needs

3—If it meets some of your needs but not others

2—If it meets only a few of your needs

1—If it doesn't meet any of your needs

**Location Criteria:** Figure 4-6 provides a breakdown of Will's assessment of all the criteria in the Location category, as he determined according to what's important to him. Taking a quick look at how Will filled out this section, you can see that not one of the schools he was accepted to was near his house, but Goucher, in Baltimore, could be reached by a direct flight from Chicago. He therefore rated it the highest, with a 4, followed by a 3 for both Skidmore and Union. Both of those schools would require a direct flight plus a 30-minute drive on either end. Colby, the school in the most remote location of the four schools, would require either a direct flight followed by a significant drive or else an indirect flight and a shorter drive. Thus, he assigned a rating of 1 to Colby. As for proximity to his friends, he rated Skidmore and Union each a 4 since he had a number of friends in Albany, which was near both schools. He rated Colby a 3 since he had other friends in Boston, and he rated Goucher a 2 since he did not have many friends near Baltimore.

He knew he wanted a climate similar to what he was accustomed to in Chicago, and since all the locations were comparable, he assigned them each a 5 with the exception of Goucher, which he rated a 3. In terms of the rural or urban nature of the schools, Will preferred being in a city or close to a city, so he rated Goucher a 5 for

**FIGURE 4-6  Assessment of Location Criteria**

| Location | 10 | % | Weight | Colby College | Skidmore College | Union College | Goucher College |
|---|---|---|---|---|---|---|---|
| | | | | Assessment | | | |
| Close to home | | | 3 | 1 | 3 | 3 | 4 |
| Close to friends | | | 2 | 3 | 4 | 4 | 2 |
| In climate you want | | | 2 | 5 | 5 | 5 | 3 |
| In urban or rural area | | | 2 | 1 | 3 | 3 | 5 |
| Total points | | | 9 | 4.67 | 7.33 | 7.33 | 7.11 |

being in Baltimore, Skidmore and Union each a 3 for being in fairly large towns near bigger cities, and Colby a 1 for being in a small town that was not near a major city.

The worksheet provides a total number of points for this section according to the weight for each criterion and the value for each school in each criterion. For Will's worksheet, since he rated the Location category as being 10 percent of his decision, each school could receive a maximum of 10 points if they each met the criteria fully and received a 5. Skidmore and Union received the highest scores, 7.33 points each, followed by Goucher, which received 7.11 points, and Colby, which received 4.67 points.

**Academic Criteria:** Will rated each school for the next category, Academics, which he considered the most important in making his decision. Figure 4-7 provides a breakdown of his assessment of each criterion included in this category. All four of the schools offered the major that he expected to take, which is political science, so he rated all of them a 5. In terms of having many options that he liked for his second-choice major, he thought Skidmore had the most options, followed by Colby and Union, with Goucher still having many, but fewer. He therefore rated Skidmore a 5, Colby and Union a 4, and Goucher a 3. All of the schools also had very good professors, and after looking at the information about them one more time, he gave Colby a 5 and the remaining schools each earned a 4. In terms of the general academic environment, all four schools had both students and faculty who were extremely serious about their studies, but he decided to rate Colby a 5, Skidmore a 4, and Union and Goucher both a 3.

Will studied very carefully the ways in which the curricula were put together at each school since this was important to him. After reviewing them, he assigned Colby a 5, Skidmore a 4, and Union and Goucher each a 3. Will expected that the level of academic pressure at each school would be roughly equivalent to the general

**FIGURE 4-7  Assessment of Academic Criteria**

| Academics | 40 | % | Weight | Colby College | Skidmore College | Union College | Goucher College |
|---|---|---|---|---|---|---|---|
| | | | | Assessment | | | |
| Has your first choice major | | | 4 | 5 | 5 | 5 | 5 |
| Has your second choice major options | | | 2 | 4 | 5 | 4 | 3 |
| Has professors you admire | | | 4 | 5 | 4 | 4 | 4 |
| General academic environment | | | 4 | 5 | 4 | 3 | 3 |
| Curriculum (flexible or structured) | | | 3 | 5 | 4 | 3 | 3 |
| Level of academic pressures | | | 2 | 4 | 4 | 3 | 3 |
| Average class size | | | 4 | 5 | 5 | 5 | 5 |
| Use of technology in education | | | 2 | 5 | 5 | 5 | 5 |
| Quality of academic facilities | | | 3 | 4 | 5 | 5 | 4 |
| Total points | | | 28 | 38.00 | 36.29 | 33.14 | 31.71 |

academic environment and assigned Colby and Skidmore each a 4 and Union and Goucher each a 3.

In terms of the average class size, the vast majority of classes at all four of these schools had fewer than 20 students, so he rated them all with a 5. (The actual numbers, as of 2006, were that 61 percent of classes at Colby, 67 percent of classes at Union, 69 percent of classes at Skidmore, and 81 percent of classes at Goucher had fewer than 20 students.) Will then considered how each school used technology in its teaching process, and finding that they all did a wonderful job, he rated them all a 5. As for the quality of the academic facilities at each institution, he learned that they were all in very good condition, with a few classrooms in need of upgrades at Colby and Goucher. He decided to rate Skidmore and Union each a 5, while rating Colby and Goucher each a 4. The totals for the Academic category for each school are listed in Figure 4-7. Out of a total of 40 possible points, Colby has 38.00, Skidmore has 36.29, Union has 33.14, and Goucher has 31.71.

**General Characteristics Criteria:** Figure 4-8 provides a breakdown of Will's assessment of each of the criteria in the General Characteristics category. He reviewed the 2006 *U.S. News & World Report* college rankings to help him determine the level of prestige of each school. Among liberal arts schools, Colby was ranked 22nd, Skidmore was ranked 47th, Union was ranked 40th, and Goucher was ranked 91st.

Accordingly, he assigned Colby a 4, and the other three schools each a 3. He also looked at the size of each of the schools, preferring a school with a moderate number of students. As mentioned before, all of the schools he applied to had the number of students he was looking for, so he rated all of them a 5. All four of the schools were private, which was what he was looking for, so they all received a 5 for that category. Because the ability to meet the needs of disabled students did not affect his education, he assigned all four of the schools a 5.

**FIGURE 4-8  Assessment of General Criteria**

| General Characteristics | 15 | % | Weight | Colby College | Skidmore College | Union College | Goucher College |
|---|---|---|---|---|---|---|---|
| | | | | Assessment | | | |
| Prestige of school | | | 4 | 4 | 3 | 3 | 3 |
| Size of school | | | 4 | 5 | 5 | 5 | 5 |
| Public versus private school | | | 2 | 5 | 5 | 5 | 5 |
| Disability friendly | | | 0 | 5 | 5 | 5 | 5 |
| Campus demographics | | | 2 | 5 | 5 | 3 | 4 |
| Religious affiliation of school | | | 3 | 5 | 5 | 5 | 5 |
| Quality of housing | | | 4 | 4 | 4 | 4 | 3 |
| Beauty of campus | | | 4 | 5 | 5 | 4 | 3 |
| Your "feel" of the school—intuition | | | 5 | 3 | 5 | 4 | 4 |
| **Total points** | | | 28 | **13.07** | **13.71** | **12.32** | **11.68** |

Colby and Skidmore had the type of campus demographics he was looking for so he rated each of them a 5, followed by Goucher which he rated a 4, and then Union which he rated a 3. He also preferred a school with no religious affiliation. He therefore rated all four schools with a 5 since none of them had one. Looking at the overall quality of the housing, he rated Colby, Skidmore, and Union all as 4 since he felt they had the nicest on-campus housing, followed by Goucher with a 3. He thought about the level of beauty of each campus he had visited and remembered that they were all pretty nice. He rated Colby and Skidmore each a 5 for having the nicest campuses, with Union receiving a 4, and Goucher a 3.

Finally, he turned to the overall "feel" of the school—something that is very subjective, but also something that was very important to him. (Intuition has proven to be a very strong reason to consider when picking a college.) He thought back to his campus visits and how he felt while there and whether he could envision himself attending them. He remembered that he had the best feeling about Skidmore, followed by both Union and Goucher. He rated Skidmore a 5 and both Union and Goucher a 4. He rated Colby a 3. The totals for each of the schools are listed in Figure 4-8. Out of a total of 15 possible points for this category, Colby received 13.07 points, Skidmore 13.71 points, Union 12.32 points, and Goucher 11.68 points.

**Cost Criteria:** Figure 4-9 provides a breakdown of Will's assessment of the criteria in the Costs category. The tuitions listed for each of the schools were very similar, although Skidmore was the highest at $36,860 per year. When Will considered the scholarships offered by each school, he discovered a significant difference in cost. Goucher offered the highest scholarship which was nearly a third of the tuition, bringing the total cost to only $22,000 per year. Accordingly, he rated Goucher a 5 for tuition costs. Skidmore and Union both offered him smaller scholarships, each bringing the total cost per year to roughly $28,000. He rated each of these two schools a 4. Finally, Colby offered only a minor amount of support, bringing the total tuition for that school to $33,000 per year, so he rated Colby a 3.

**FIGURE 4-9 Assessment of Cost Criteria**

| Costs | 25 | % | Weight | Colby College | Skidmore College | Union College | Goucher College |
|---|---|---|---|---|---|---|---|
| | | | | Assessment | | | |
| Net tuition costs | | | 5 | 3 | 4 | 4 | 5 |
| Work-study availability | | | 1 | 5 | 5 | 5 | 5 |
| Room and board costs | | | 1 | 5 | 4 | 4 | 4 |
| Travel costs | | | 2 | 2 | 3 | 3 | 5 |
| Total points | | | 9 | 16.11 | 19.44 | 19.44 | 24.44 |

All four of the schools offered similar work-study programs for assistance with Will's tuition and living expenses, so he simply rated them all a 5 for this criterion. All four schools' room and board costs hovered close to $10,000, although Colby was slightly less expensive. He therefore rated Colby a 5 for room and board costs and the other three each a 4. He then considered the travel costs to and from school. As mentioned before, Goucher was the easiest to get to since it only required a direct flight, so he rated it a 5. Skidmore and Union each required a direct flight and then a 30-minute drive so he rated each of them a 3. And last, Colby earned a 2 because it required either an indirect flight with a short drive or a direct flight with a long drive.

Out of a possible 25 points, the totals for each school's Costs category were: Colby 16.11, Skidmore and Union both 19.44, and Goucher 24.44.

**Social Life Criteria:** Figure 4-10 provides a breakdown of Will's assessment of each of the criteria in the Social Life category. Since the existence of fraternities was irrelevant to him, he rated all four of them with a 5, though he could have rated them all with any number and it wouldn't have impacted the outcome. In terms of extracurricular activities, the schools were all very similar so he rated them with a 5, with the exception of Skidmore which Will rated at a 4 because he thought Skidmore lacked some of the activities he was interested in. He then looked at the general social environment and was pleased with all four of them. Based on his understanding of the social life on each campus, he rated Skidmore the highest with a 5, and the remaining three schools each a 4.

**FIGURE 4-10   Assessment of Social Life Criteria**

| Social Life | 10 | % | Weight | Colby College | Skidmore College | Union College | Goucher College |
|---|---|---|---|---|---|---|---|
| | | | | Assessment | | | |
| Greek life available | | | 0 | 5 | 5 | 5 | 5 |
| Extracurricular activities | | | 4 | 5 | 4 | 5 | 5 |
| Overall social environment | | | 1 | 4 | 5 | 4 | 4 |
| Housing options | | | 3 | 5 | 4 | 3 | 4 |
| Great sports teams to watch | | | 1 | 4 | 3 | 3 | 3 |
| Opportunity to play on sports team | | | 1 | 3 | 5 | 5 | 5 |
| Total points | | | 10 | 9.20 | 8.20 | 8.20 | 8.80 |

In terms of the way housing would affect his social life, Will found that Colby seemed to have the most options, so he rated it a 5, followed by Skidmore and Goucher, each garnering a 4, with Union trailing at 3. With respect to watching sports teams, Will decided that he was most interested in the sports at Colby, so he rated it with a 4. He was interested in the other schools' teams equally, so he rated them each with a 3. As for playing on a baseball team, Will decided it would not be easy, but that he would have the best chance at Skidmore, Union, or Goucher, so he assigned each of them a rating of 5. Colby would be a little more difficult for him, he believed, so he rated it a 3. The totals out of 10 possible points for the Social Life category were: 9.20 for Colby, 8.20 each for Skidmore and Union, and 8.80 for Goucher.

## Step 4: Make the Decision

Once you have completed the research for each school and filled in a value for each criterion, the worksheet will automatically provide a total, based upon 100 percent total points possible. Those schools that come closest to 100 percent are the ones that most meet your needs according to your worksheet. Figure 4-11 shows the end result for Will's decision worksheet.

As you can see from the figure, Skidmore came in first, meeting 84.98 percent of the needs Will assigned, followed closely behind by Goucher, which met 83.75 percent. Colby, which Will had thought was likely to come in first, actually was in third place with 81.05 percent, followed by Union in last place, with 80.44 percent. In the end, he was comfortable with these results and decided on Skidmore, a decision he is happy with to this day.

You may think that going to a school that meets only 84.98 percent of your criteria means that you haven't applied to or been accepted to the school that is the perfect fit for you. In general, we believe that any school that receives a score above 80 percent is a very good fit for a student; if the school receives a score anywhere from 60 percent to 80 percent, it may or may not be a good fit; and if the school scores below a 60 percent, it's probably time to look at another school. Why would a school that may be the best fit for you only meet 85 percent of your needs? Consider it this way: if you've been accepted to Harvard, it likely won't meet all of your needs perfectly unless it's free and somehow gets moved to your hometown in Kansas or North Carolina or wherever you're from. That's unlikely. When going through this decision-making process, you're going to need to compromise. Are you willing to pay more money for a school with better academics? Are you willing to sacrifice brand new dorms to pay a little less or go to a school with more up-to-date academic facilities? No school will meet 100 percent of your needs, but using the process laid out in this chapter will help you understand which of your needs are most important to you so that you arrive at the outcome that is best for you.

> You know that you need to spend time visiting schools, completing applications, writing essays, and taking standardized tests. But you also need to spend some quality time analyzing information to make the best decision.

Once you have evaluated each school, you shouldn't feel as though you need to accept the exact result of the decision worksheet. That's why we call it a decision worksheet and not a crystal ball. The purpose of this exercise is to help you determine which is the best school for you, not to force the worksheet's decision on you.

While the worksheet is designed for numerical accuracy, if your results are as close as Will's, it may reassure you to go back through all of the criteria to see if you need to change the percentages in any category, redo any weighting, or reexamine the criteria versus your needs. Then reassess the results and consider your decision.

# The Shortcut

Your time is valuable to you, and the process laid out above is a little time-consuming. While we're convinced that you would be best served by following the approach as we've laid it out, we also would rather that you use a structured approach that is not as comprehensive as the one above instead of not using any particular approach at all. For this reason, we have created a shortcut approach for you, based upon the more thorough one just discussed.

To use this shortcut approach, you can condense all of the individual criteria of the five overall categories we've identified—Location, Academics, General Characteristics, Costs, and Social Life. (It is important when using this condensed approach, however, to be sure that you're still considering all of the individual criteria originally listed in each of these broad categories that we identified above.) Instead of following the four-step approach, you will follow a similar three-step approach. Let's use Figure 4-12 to show you how to do this.

As you can see in Figure 4-12, the first step is similar to the first step in the comprehensive process, which entails providing a weight, based upon 100 percent of possible weighting, to each of the five categories. This percentage expresses how important each category is to you. For ease of understanding, we have used the same weighting provided by our sample student for this example as well, which is 10 percent for Location, 40 percent for Academics, 15 percent for General Characteristics, 25 percent for Costs, and 10 percent for Social Life.

During the second step, it helps to use a different point scheme for the shortcut approach than the comprehensive approach uses. You would go through your list of schools, in this case College A, College B, College C, and College D, and you would apply a score from 0 to 100 to each of the colleges based upon how well each meets your needs for each category of criteria. For example, College D gets only a 50 for Location but gets an 80 for Academics.

Once you assign a value to each of the colleges for each of the categories, you then apply the weighting that you've assigned for each category to this score. For example,

**FIGURE 4-11  Summary Assessment**

| | | | | Colby College | Skidmore College | Union College | Goucher College |
|---|---|---|---|---|---|---|---|
| **Location** | **10** | **%** | **Weight** | **Assessment** | | | |
| Close to home | | | 3 | 1 | 3 | 3 | 4 |
| Close to friends | | | 2 | 3 | 4 | 4 | 2 |
| In climate you want | | | 2 | 5 | 5 | 5 | 3 |
| In urban or rural area | | | 2 | 1 | 3 | 3 | 5 |
| **Total points** | | | 9 | 4.67 | 7.33 | 7.33 | 7.11 |
| **Academics** | **40** | **%** | **Weight** | **Assessment** | | | |
| Has your first choice major | | | 4 | 5 | 5 | 5 | 5 |
| Has your second choice major options | | | 2 | 4 | 5 | 4 | 3 |
| Has professors you admire | | | 4 | 5 | 4 | 4 | 4 |
| General academic environment | | | 4 | 5 | 4 | 3 | 3 |
| Curriculum (flexible or structured) | | | 3 | 5 | 4 | 3 | 3 |
| Level of academic pressures | | | 2 | 4 | 4 | 3 | 3 |
| Average class size | | | 4 | 5 | 5 | 5 | 5 |
| Use of technology in education | | | 2 | 5 | 5 | 5 | 5 |
| Quality of academic facilities | | | 3 | 4 | 5 | 5 | 4 |
| **Total points** | | | 28 | 38.00 | 36.29 | 33.14 | 31.71 |
| **General Characteristics** | **15** | **%** | **Weight** | **Assessment** | | | |
| Prestige of school | | | 4 | 4 | 3 | 3 | 3 |
| Size of school | | | 4 | 5 | 5 | 5 | 5 |
| Public versus private school | | | 2 | 5 | 5 | 5 | 5 |
| Disability friendly | | | 0 | 5 | 5 | 5 | 5 |
| Campus demographics | | | 2 | 5 | 5 | 3 | 4 |
| Religious affiliation of school | | | 3 | 5 | 5 | 5 | 5 |
| Quality of housing | | | 4 | 4 | 4 | 4 | 3 |
| Beauty of campus | | | 4 | 5 | 5 | 4 | 3 |
| Your "feel" of the school—intuition | | | 5 | 3 | 5 | 4 | 4 |
| **Total points** | | | 28 | 13.07 | 13.71 | 12.32 | 11.68 |

*Continued on next page*

**FIGURE 4-11 (*Continued*)**

| Costs | 25 | % | Weight | Assessment | | | |
|---|---|---|---|---|---|---|---|
| Net tuition costs | | | 5 | 3 | 4 | 4 | 5 |
| Work-study availability | | | 1 | 5 | 5 | 5 | 5 |
| Room and board costs | | | 1 | 5 | 4 | 4 | 4 |
| Travel costs | | | 2 | 2 | 3 | 3 | 5 |
| Total points | | | 9 | 16.11 | 19.44 | 19.44 | 24.44 |
| Social Life | 10 | % | Weight | Assessment | | | |
| Greek life available | | | 0 | 5 | 5 | 5 | 5 |
| Extracurricular activities | | | 4 | 5 | 4 | 5 | 5 |
| Overall social environment | | | 1 | 4 | 5 | 4 | 4 |
| Housing options | | | 3 | 5 | 4 | 3 | 4 |
| Great sports teams to watch | | | 1 | 4 | 3 | 3 | 3 |
| Opportunity to play on sports team | | | 1 | 3 | 5 | 5 | 5 |
| Total points | | | 10 | 9.20 | 8.20 | 8.20 | 8.80 |
| Overall weighted assessment | | | Total | 81.05 | 84.98 | 80.44 | 83.75 |

College A was given an 80 for Location, but since Location is only weighted at 10 percent, you would take 10 percent of 80 to give you the weighted score or 8 for College A in the Location category. As you can see from this example, the total number of points doesn't always equal the total weighted score, which emphasizes the importance of weighting certain criteria higher or lower than others. Since Academics are more important in this example than Location, the points assigned in the Academics section are weighted higher in the total results. In Figure 4-12, as you can see, College A received the most *total* points of 360, while College D received the most *weighted* points of 73.5.

# Collaboration Goes a Long Way

We're sometimes asked, who makes this important decision—the students or the parents? We think it needs to be a collaborative effort. Parents can use this decision worksheet to work with their child in selecting the best college. One successful approach is to work together to determine the relative weightings for each category. Is Cost three times more important than Social Life? How do you distribute the 100

**FIGURE 4-12 Simplified Assessment**

| | | | | College A | College B | College C | College D |
|---|---|---|---|---|---|---|---|
| Location | 10 | % | Score | 80.0 | 70.0 | 50.0 | 50.0 |
| | | | Weighted | 8.0 | 7.0 | 5.0 | 5.0 |
| Academics | 40 | % | Score | 50.0 | 50.0 | 50.0 | 80.0 |
| | | | Weighted | 20.0 | 20.0 | 20.0 | 32.0 |
| General Characteristics | 15 | % | Score | 70.0 | 80.0 | 90.0 | 60.0 |
| | | | Weighted | 10.5 | 12.0 | 13.5 | 9.0 |
| Costs | 25 | % | Score | 70.0 | 80.0 | 80.0 | 90.0 |
| | | | Weighted | 17.5 | 20.0 | 20.0 | 22.5 |
| Social Life | 10 | % | Score | 90.0 | 50.0 | 80.0 | 50.0 |
| | | | Weighted | 9.0 | 5.0 | 8.0 | 5.0 |
| | | | Total score | 360.0 | 330.0 | 350.0 | 330.0 |
| | | Overall weighted assessment | | 65.0 | 64.0 | 66.5 | 73.5 |

percent weighting across all of the categories? In Will's case, his parents wanted to increase the importance of Cost since they were paying much of his college tuition, and the financial aspect would be somewhat of a hardship for them. Parents and children together can discuss the criteria that go into each category. What should be added? What are the most important criteria? In the end, the student can use the parents' input to help them determine the weightings for each criterion. The parents can let the student determine the values for each of the colleges. After all, the student's opinion on each college is the most important.

The value of collaborating is that the relative weighting frames the overall decision, so the parents can help shape the decision while still leaving the final decision up to the student. Following the Decide Better! worksheet increases the chance for a positive outcome and reduces the risk of a poor choice.

# To Sum Up

Making a decision about what college to go to is one of the most difficult and important decisions of your life, and you should take advantage of all of the resources that you have at your disposal to help you make this decision. Many students make their decision about which college to attend by focusing too much on their emotional desires and not enough on a rational understanding of which college would meet their needs the best. The process laid out in this chapter is an attempt to add value to your decision-making process and help you to choose the school that will enable you to get the most out of your college experience. Following this structured process and using the worksheet will help you to decide better! It will also help you and your parents understand why you reached the decision you did.

To obtain a version of the Decide Better! worksheet that you can download on your computer, visit http://www.DecideBetter.com/college.html.

# Chapter 5

# The Gap

## Deciding Whether to Take a Year Off

Recently while traveling, we met a 28-year-old from Connecticut named James. He seemed to be a bright person, as he was very knowledgeable about a wide range of topics. When we spoke to him about writing our college decision-making book, he related the mistakes he made when it came to his college education—or lack thereof. James acknowledged that his biggest mistake was his decision to take a year off between high school and college. He graduated from a college-prep school in Connecticut and had been admitted to a big university in the Northeast. He decided that he wasn't ready to go yet and asked for—and received—a one-year deferral from the school. While he knew this could potentially be a good move for him, he didn't spend the necessary time or energy creating the best possible gap-year program he could. He didn't prepare ahead for his year off and ended up missing the deadlines for many of the best-organized gap-year programs. Instead, he decided that he would simply work for one year and then go back to college.

James got a decent job working for a landscaping company and moved out of his parents' house and into an apartment with one of his friends. Since his job was 25 miles away, he had to buy a car, for which he got a loan. Throughout the year, he wasn't making enough

*Note to Parents*

*Taking a year off isn't always a bad decision. Sometimes it can provide rewarding and important experiences for your children. But the decision needs to be made based upon the facts and weighing the pros and cons of the options.*

to cover all of his bills, so his credit card debts increased. After a little while, he decided that he should take a second year off before returning to college. When it was time for him to reapply to schools after taking a year and a half off, he found it much more difficult to pull together the necessary information, including the recommendations, his test scores, and other requirements. He was convinced that he would not be able to afford college while also paying for his car and his growing credit card debt. In the end, he decided that it just wasn't the right time to reapply. Now, at 28 and sitting next to us waiting for a flight in an airport, James still hadn't returned to school and continued to regret it. He put the blame squarely on the fact that he accrued too many debts during his time off that he wouldn't be able to repay while in school. Had he either gone straight to college or enrolled in a more structured program that might possibly have included a time limit, subsidized college costs, or housing or living expense assistance, he believed that he would have been able to complete his education.

This story illustrates another important decision that many people face when considering college: whether to go right after high school or to take one or more years off. Known as taking a "gap" year, the term describes the decision many students make not to go straight to college for one reason or another, and it is a legitimate option to consider. But it is not a decision that should be made lightly. In fact, the question is not, "Should I go to school next year or not?" The real question is "Should I go to school next year or should I take a year off to do either X, Y, or Z?"

A wide range of reasons could be listed for why students might consider taking a gap year. These reasons might include being uncertain about whether you can afford college or what you want to do with your life; being too worn out from tough junior and senior years in high school to be able to dedicate the necessary energy to college academics; being admitted at your top-choice school for enrollment only in the following year; having a desire to increase your knowledge of a particular subject matter, language, or region of the world before entering into college; being rejected from every school you applied to; or gaining work or internship experience before college starts.

Before you jump into taking a year off because you're unsure what you want to do with your life, you need to assess what you're getting into. Again, as with the decision about whether to go to college at all, money is often a big issue for students who are considering taking a gap year. Some decide that they want to work for a year or two to save money for college. Others decide they want to become involved with some type of program that will subsidize some or all of their college education after the program ends. These are all legitimate options, and all of them have their own strengths and weaknesses.

# Play Fair When It Comes to the Gap

Because no pre-determined program is laid out for gap-year students, the sky is the limit. But if you're thinking that you just need some rest before college, a gap year shouldn't be the option you consider. You need to think very carefully about your reasons for taking a gap year, and you need to be very specific about what you're trying to achieve during this time. If you want to sit at home and play video games for 12 months between high school and college, you will be losing out on a huge opportunity that a gap year can provide for you to achieve goals above and beyond those available to many students who do go straight to college. We often counsel students who are considering taking a gap year to think about it as an extension of their academic and personal life goals. It is an opportunity to achieve something special— something that will help define who you are for the rest of your life. Some of the most interesting students we've met have used a gap year to achieve some amazing experiences. Then they've gone on to very successful careers in college and beyond. Other students, however, seem to have wasted their time and don't gain anything substantial by taking this time off from school.

# Giving Back During the Gap

**Is College Right for Me Now?**

- Are you ready to continue your education?
- Are you burnt out from high school?
- Do you think you will do better in college if you have some real-world experience first?
- Do you think you will get into a better school if you have nonacademic experience?
- Do you want to accomplish something in particular outside of school before going to college?

We see many people who make excellent decisions about taking a gap year—or even two gap years. For instance, if you know that you want to become involved in a particular program that would be better for you to do straight out of high school before you jump into a four-year college commitment, then you should consider doing it. Joining the military is a common example of this. While potentially dangerous—especially during a war—it is also a great way to gain valuable personal life skills, to make wonderful friends, to learn a lot about yourself, to give back to your country, to show responsibility, and, last but not least, to subsidize your college education. Similar programs that don't involve the military can provide valuable experiences and opportunities for personal development and community service. AmeriCorps, for example, offers several options, including programs through organizations such as City Year, which place you in a major city for one year of civil service that includes teaching, working in poor neighborhoods to reduce crime, and contributing other essential services in impoverished areas. Moreover, they also provide financial assistance for college after you complete your one-year program.

In addition to providing amazing life experiences and money for college, other potential benefits can be reaped from being involved in an organized and meaningful program or the military. We know several students who have joined City Year after high school. The vast majority of them went on to have stellar academic careers. One of these students found that being in City Year truly benefited her academic standing. While in her senior year of high school, Natasha, a very good student with many extracurricular activities, applied to a wide range of schools, including top Ivy League schools. While she was accepted to some very good schools, she wasn't accepted to any of the top ones she applied to, and she knew she could do better. She also knew that she wanted to give something back to her community, which prompted her to join City Year instead of saying yes to one of her college offers. After working with the organization throughout the summer and fall following graduation, she reapplied to a few of the top schools that had rejected her, hoping that her experiences working with underprivileged students in inner cities would help her chance of being accepted. She was right. That spring, she was thrilled to learn that she was admitted to Harvard University, her top school that had rejected her only one year earlier. She enrolled there and ended up having a very good academic career.

> Some of the most interesting students have used a gap year to achieve some truly amazing experiences.

Now that you know a little more about the positives and negatives of taking time off between high school and college, if you are still considering this as an option, you need to be sure that you make the best decision possible. Gap years are not for everyone, even some people who think they would benefit from them. Here's a relatively straightforward framework to help you make a good decision about taking a gap year.

## Do You Need a Year?

If you are considering taking a year or more off from school, you need to first clearly lay out for yourself exactly why you are contemplating taking a year off. We presented many valid reasons for taking a gap year earlier in the chapter, as well as some that are less valid. Perhaps you're not ready, you don't have enough money, or you simply want to increase your knowledge of the world before you commit to attending more classes every day. You should be able to directly connect your reasons for considering a year off to a goal that you hope to accomplish during the time you're

**FIGURE 5-1  Gap Year Objectives**

| Rank | Objective |
|------|-----------|
| 1 | Gain leadership skills |
| 2 | Travel abroad |
| 3 | Travel in the United States |
| 4 | Refresh my desire to study |
| 5 | Earn money for college |
| 6 | Be more marketable to schools |
| 7 | Gain professional skills |

out of school. If you can't do this, you haven't thought about your motives enough. By the end of your gap year, what goals will you have completed? What activities and experiences will you have gained? What new knowledge or information will you have learned? Where do you want to be financially?

All of these valid questions should help you to better understand why you're considering this option. If you don't know the answers to them, then you probably haven't identified the true underlying reason you're not ready to go to college. You should write out your reasons for wanting to take a year off. Allison, who wasn't sure that she was ready for college and wanted to gain valuable skills, preferably while traveling, is a perfect example. She spent several hours thinking about exactly what she wanted to accomplish that would be better than what she could gain by going straight to college. Allison's reasons, with their priority rankings, can be seen in Figure 5-1.

The second step is quite probably the most important component of your decision: what are your options for the gap year? Take a sufficient amount of time to consider your choices. Be realistic. Most likely, your options are not laid out in front of you. Some students may already be dedicated to one particular option, such as joining the Air Force, while others are vague as to what activities or programs they think will best help them achieve their gap-year goals. Before committing to not attending college, however, you should be aware of all of your options.

Some of the most common activities in a gap year include traveling independently, with family, or friends; traveling as part of some type of exchange program, educational program, or other learning program; doing an internship; working in an area that will give you needed experience; participating in a leadership program, public service program, civil service program, volunteer program, or other program run by a nonprofit organization, governmental entity, corporation, or other establishment; or joining the military. Some options may be ones you need to create, while some already have an existing structure with set application and participation requirements. If you are not committed to one particular program already, spend a few weeks researching your options—you may discover some you hadn't thought of yet. Once again, you should write down all of your options after completing your basic research. You should also try to prioritize them based upon how much you think you would enjoy them and how much you would get out of each option by the time you're finished. Our sample student, Allison, put together her list after much research, tentatively ranking each option. Her analysis can be seen in Figure 5-2.

## Think Through the Options

The third step is to carefully consider each of the options, comparing all of them to each other. This is a very important, although somewhat more difficult, step in the process. The best way to do this is to compare all of the activity options for the gap year to each other using criteria that you develop yourself. In the second step of the process, you laid out your objectives for the gap year—what you wanted to accomplish were you to take a year off. Based on those objectives, you should determine the criteria to use when comparing the activity options that you came up with in step two. (You may need to add additional criteria that are not directly related to those priorities, however, so that you can pinpoint some of the drawbacks of your choices as well.)

To better understand this part of the process, let's look once again to our sample student, Allison, who has compared her eight activity options to each other by using the seven objectives for her year off. You'll notice that she also added two more criteria to her objectives for comparison so she could see not only the benefits of each option but also some of the drawbacks that could come into play. Her analysis can be seen in Figure 5-3.

**FIGURE 5-2  Prioritize Your Activity Options**

| Rank | Activities |
|------|-----------|
| 1 | Join City Year |
| 2 | Participate in an international volunteer program in Africa |
| 3 | Do an Outward Bound program |
| 4 | Travel independently in Europe |
| 5 | Join the Peace Corps |
| 6 | Join the army |
| 7 | Do an internship at the local newspaper |
| 8 | Work as a freelance writer |

**FIGURE 5-3   How Do the Activities Achieve Your Objectives?**

| Options | Leadership Skills | Travel Abroad | U.S. Travel | Study Interest | $$ for College | More Marketable | Professional Skills | One Year | Danger Level |
|---|---|---|---|---|---|---|---|---|---|
| City Year | Yes | No | Yes | Yes | Yes | Yes | Maybe | Yes | Low |
| International volunteer program in Africa | Yes | Yes | No | Yes | Maybe | Yes | Maybe | Yes | Moderate |
| Outward Bound | Yes | Maybe | Maybe | Yes | No | Yes | Maybe | Yes | Low |
| Travel independently | No | Yes | No | Yes | No | Maybe | No | Yes | Low |
| Peace Corps | Yes | Yes | No | Yes | Yes | Yes | Maybe | No | Moderate |
| Army | Yes | Yes | Yes | Yes | Yes | Yes | Yes | No | High |
| Internship | No | No | Maybe | Yes | No | Maybe | Yes | Yes | Low |
| Work as free-lance writer | No | No | No | Yes | Yes | Maybe | Yes | Yes | Low |

As you can see from Allison's completed list in Figure 5-3, she assigned a judgment to each activity as to how well it would achieve the goal she set. Along the top of the worksheet, she listed her potential achievements, adding two to the list: spending only one year on the activity and the level of danger associated with the activity. This made sense since some of the possible activities required a time commitment of longer than one year, and some of them—particularly joining the Army during wartime—inevitably had risk associated with them. She wrote a "yes" if that option enabled her to achieve that goal, a "no" if it did not, and a "maybe" if either she wasn't certain the option would achieve her goal or if it could potentially achieve the goal, depending upon which program she selected. The "maybe," for example, was assigned to Outward Bound for both international and domestic travel since the organization offers programs both in the United States and in Canada. "Maybe" was also listed for being more marketable to schools after both traveling internationally on her own and completing an internship, since some of the outcome depends upon what type of internship she would do and where she would be located. In terms of the danger level, she simply used a rough estimate of what that would be for each option, assigning "high," "low," and "moderate," accordingly.

# Make Sure the Options Meet the Goals

The final step is making your decision. We can't tell you what to decide. You need to evaluate for yourself what the best option is. It may well be that, after spending weeks trying to come up with alternatives to going straight to college and evaluating these options, you say to yourself that taking a year off isn't right for you. Or you may say that you've found the absolutely perfect option that is so good that college can wait a year. At least now you know that's true. The decision making process is not a waste of time. It's your decision to make—but the outcome will be much better if you've analyzed it correctly. This decision is very complicated. In fact, it involves making two interrelated decisions somewhat concurrently. The first is whether to take a gap year; the second, which is related in various ways to the first, is what you would do were you to decide to take a gap year. For example, you may decide that you're better off taking a gap year only if you can do one of options A, B, or C, but that you would be better off *not* taking a gap year if you could do only option D, E, or F. This is where your analysis of the worksheet you made in the previous step comes in.

After completing the worksheet, Allison went through and circled each of her responses as to whether the gap year option she was considering met her needs in terms of the goals she laid out. Let's examine her decision-making process based upon Figure 5-4. As you can see, she ruled out the following four options because they didn't accomplish enough of her goals: Outward Bound, traveling independently, doing an internship, and working as a freelance writer. While these all originally seemed like good options for her, she came to believe that, since they didn't allow her to achieve many of the goals she envisioned for her potential gap year, she would prefer to go straight to college rather than implement these options. Each of the remaining four options—joining City Year, participating in a volunteer program in Africa, enrolling in the Peace Corps, and enlisting in the Army—would enable Allison to achieve many, but not all, of the objectives she set out for herself.

Starting at the top of Allison's remaining list of objectives, you can see that all four options enable her to gain valuable leadership skills. All except for City Year will enable her to travel abroad, while City Year and the Army will both enable her to travel domestically. All four will strengthen her desire to go back to school and study, and all four of them, with the possible exception of volunteering in Africa, would provide her with assistance toward paying for college—some with more money than others. All four would most likely make her more marketable for colleges, which would enable her to get into better schools. They would all provide some level of professional skills, although the types of skills would vary depending upon which activities she was involved in during her service for each option. City Year and volunteering in

Africa would both enable her to defer college for only one year, while joining the Peace Corps or the Army would require a two-year commitment at a minimum. Finally, in terms of the level of danger, the Army certainly has the highest potential for danger, while the Peace Corps and volunteering in Africa have moderate levels, depending upon where she would go, and City Year would generally have a low level of danger.

**FIGURE 5-4   How Do the Activities Achieve Your Objectives?**

| Options | Leadership Skills | Travel Abroad | U.S. Travel | Study Interest | $$ for College | More Marketable | Professional Skills | One Year | Danger Level |
|---|---|---|---|---|---|---|---|---|---|
| City Year | (Yes) | No | (Yes) | (Yes) | (Yes) | Yes | Maybe | (Yes) | (Low) |
| International volunteer program in Africa | (Yes) | (Yes) | No | (Yes) | Maybe | (Yes) | Maybe | (Yes) | Moderate |
| Outward Bound | Yes | Maybe | Maybe | (Yes) | No | Yes | Maybe | Yes | Low |
| Travel independently | No | Yes | No | (Yes) | No | Maybe | No | Yes | Low |
| Peace Corps | (Yes) | (Yes) | No | (Yes) | Yes | Yes | Maybe | No | Moderate |
| Army | (Yes) | (Yes) | (Yes) | (Yes) | (Yes) | (Yes) | (Yes) | No | High |
| Internship | No | No | Maybe | (Yes) | No | Maybe | Yes | Yes | Low |
| Work as freelance writer | No | No | No | (Yes) | Yes | Maybe | Yes | Yes | Low |

# Watch Those Deadlines

As you are in the process of making your decision, don't forget to consider the deadlines for each of the options under review, as well as the timing requirements. Another student we spoke with, Rick, neglected to think about deadline time lines when he was making this decision, and he paid a very high price for his mistake. He knew from the time he was a freshman in high school that he wanted to take a gap year so that he could spend a year in China learning martial arts. Thus, he didn't apply to college during his senior year. Rick reasoned that later on he could apply for admission for the year following his gap year. Instead he applied in April to the three martial arts academies he wanted to attend in September. By the time he received the responses from each of the three martial arts schools, it was mid-June. To his shock and amazement, he was rejected by all three programs! With less than two months before he had planned to start his martial arts training, he had no opportunities for his gap year. Because of the timing of the deadlines and his lack of advance planning, he

ended up spending the year following high school working at the same local arcade that he had worked at for the previous two summers. Had he pursued both college and gap year options, he wouldn't have run into this problem. He made the assumption that he would be admitted into one of the three martial arts academies and made no backup plan, so his gap year did not help him to achieve any of his goals.

Allison, on the other hand, knew her deadlines were backward. In other words, her college application deadlines were due prior to the deadlines for her gap-year options. She didn't make the same mistake that Rick did. She proceeded during the fall semester of her senior year in high school as though she were not going to take a gap year. She went through all of the steps of visiting schools, interviewing, getting recommendations from teachers, deciding which schools to apply to, and completing and submitting her applications—all on time. After all, she knew she didn't have to make the final decision about taking a gap year until the spring, so she didn't want to be left with less-than-perfect options. Moreover, even if she did end up deciding to take a gap year, she still wanted to have a college lined up for the year after her year off, assuming she could get a deferment from the school. In other words, she kept her options open.

# Forget Me Not

One additional important decision you need to make before committing to taking a gap year is to determine what your relationship with your college is going to be while you are taking your gap time. If you're planning to take more than one year off, you probably can't have any ongoing relationship. But if you're truly planning to take only one year off, you should consider whether you're going to apply to colleges during your senior year, just as you would if you were not taking a year off. You could wait for your acceptances, enroll in your top choice, and then request a one-year deferment from that school. While there is no guarantee the school will give you the deferment, if it does, you will not only be much more likely to attend school there the following year, you will also save yourself much of the headache of having to reapply after you're out of school and into a different routine.

As for Allison—in the end, she decided that she would take a year off only if she could do a City Year program in a location of her choice. Unfortunately, she was not offered the city she chose. Instead, City Year offered her a position in a city she deemed unacceptable. Thankful that she had planned ahead and met all of her deadlines when they needed to be met, she went to college the next year, foregoing a gap year. She was glad that she had undergone the process and planned accordingly so that she was able to make an informed and correct decision.

> Don't forget to think about how you are going to stay in touch with your future school while on your gap year.

## To Sum Up

Deciding to take a gap year between high school and college could be good for you, but be sure you do it for the right reasons. The purpose of a gap year is not to delay going to college. It's commitment to do something useful in the year or two you delay your education. We provided a structured process for deciding what to do, and we recommend that you evaluate your gap year options in conjunction with applying to college in order to give you flexibility.

# Chapter 6

# Does the Early Bird Get the Worm?

## Making Your Decision about Applying for Early Admission

One student we advised a few years back, Rose, made her early admission decision a little too hastily. Instead of looking at all of the positives and negatives of applying early, she simply stated right from the outset that she was committed to attending her top choice school and that she was going to apply for early decision. Her friend who was a year older attended the school already and, after visiting a few times, Rose was certain it was the right choice. After applying early and before she received her admission notification from the school, Rose went with some of her other friends on a college visit tour. Much to her chagrin, she realized that some other schools would have been a better fit for her. She began hoping that she wasn't admitted to the school she submitted her early application to. Unfortunately, when the letter came, she was admitted and subsequently had to enroll in the school. We had the chance to reconnect with Rose a few years later, and she told us that after her freshman year she decided she actually did like the school she had applied to and stayed there through graduation. So Rose's

*Note to Parents*
*Applying early can be a great option for your children, as long as they are completely committed to attending the school if they're admitted. Be aware: it could be binding!*

decision worked out fine, but if she had to do it over again, she told us that she would have visited more schools before making a hasty decision to apply early.

As you're wading through the college admission process, you will discover many new terms and phrases. Two phrases in particular that you need to fully understand are *early decision* and *early action*. These aren't options to decide early that you're sick of high school and then act on this decision by ceasing all school activity before you graduate, so don't get too excited. Basically, early decision and early action are admission options that enable applicants to apply early and receive admission decisions early. This is a terrific plan of action for many students, but it's definitely not right for everyone, and it's important to know exactly what you're getting into before opting for either one. As with all decisions, pros and cons are associated with all three of your options—early decision, early action, and regular admission.

Be sure that you are clear about the differences between these admission options before determining whether to participate in early admission. It is always best to check with admissions offices to clarify policies if you have any doubts or questions. *Early decision* entails applying to one school only on an early admission basis and committing to attend that school if accepted. Be aware that early decision is a binding agreement—you are required to attend the school if accepted. *Early action* does not require you to attend if accepted. Instead, early action allows applicants to apply early, yet still provides the advantage of early notification. The first of two types of early action is the *single-choice early action program*. Single-choice early action programs do require that an *early* application be limited to *one* school but allow applicants to apply to any number of other schools under regular admission programs. The other type of early action program is an *open early action program*, which does not limit the number of schools to which you can apply under early action. Acceptance in any early action program is nonbinding.

The decision whether to apply early action or early decision is pretty straightforward—you either do it or you don't. The options are clear and concrete; however, the process surrounding this decision may not be as simple. Around 400 schools offer some type of early admission, but when you do the math, those 400 comprise only 10 percent or so of U.S. colleges. So, if your first-choice school doesn't offer an early action or early decision process, then by all means, move along to the next chapter.

## Is Your Action Binding?

The first and most important consideration is whether the decision is binding. If it is, then you definitely need to do all of your research before you make this decision. Remember, all schools that refer to the *early decision* process are offering binding agreements. You are going to that school if you're accepted to it. Some schools will give you the option to back out of the binding agreement if they don't offer you the financial aid package that you need in order to attend, but that is the only reason for being able to break your agreement with them. Even then, you bear the burden of proof when claiming financial duress for negating the attendance commitment. Don't fool yourself—these schools have thought of everything. Even if you elect to take a year or two off, that's fine, but once you decide to enter the world of academia, you are still bound to that early decision school. Be sure you adequately understand the ramifications of this before rushing into applying for early decision. You would not want to apply for early decision and change your mind about which school you want to attend before you hear back from the early decision school about whether it's going to accept your early application. By that point, it's too late to change your mind. Early action schools provide more flexibility than early decision schools, so you should base your decision about whether to apply early upon which one of these processes you are facing.

**Early Decision**

- Binding—If you get accepted, you have to go.
- One choice—You can only apply to one school early.

**Early Action**

- Nonbinding—If you get accepted, you don't have to go.
- One or more choices—Under open early action, you can apply to as many schools as you want; under single-choice early action, you can only apply to one school early.

Approach your decision by making a pros and cons list. Give yourself some time to address the values and hazards of each option. To make this pros and cons list, simply draw a line down the middle of a sheet of paper so you have two columns (or you can do this on your computer), and write "pros" on the top of the left column and "cons" on the top of the right column. Then write down each of the positive features of applying early and each of the negative aspects of applying early. As mentioned above, you should give yourself some time to think of them all. One good way to do this is to keep your list with you at all times so when you think of another pro or con, you can add it to the list wherever you are.

To understand whether you should apply early, you need to ask yourself, "Why do I want to apply early?" These are some common reasons why students consider taking this step:

❶ They are completely committed to attending their first-choice school and are ready to apply today

**Reasons to Avoid Applying Early:**

- All of your friends are doing it
- It's easier than applying to multiple schools
- You are not sure you will still want to attend the school if you get accepted
- You plan to evaluate your admissions to many schools and their financial aid packages
- You want to stop working at your studies as early as possible
- You are someone who changes your mind often

- They want to avoid having to go through the process of applying to six or eight schools, reasoning that it would be easier to complete one single application
- They believe that their chances of getting into one of their Reach schools is improved by applying early
- They're applying early because everyone else is or because they have been advised to

These are all viable reasons for making this decision, but are any of them the right reason for you? Don't be impulsive and don't be a follower. You need to make this decision for your own reasons and only after thinking about it carefully.

# Double-Check Your Commitment

The first question to answer is, are you 100 percent committed to attending the school you're considering sending an early decision or early action application to? This may sound simple, but if you're applying early to a school that mandates enrollment if you get in, then you had better be completely certain that you want to go there. Have you visited the school? Have you attended a class? Have you met and spoken with students? Have you read the campus newspaper? Have you researched several other schools to determine if this one is the best fit for you? Have you spoken with a financial aid officer to make sure that you can afford the tuition and fees or that you will have help doing so? Have you talked with your family and your college counselor about this school? If you have any doubt whatsoever about your choice, then you should consider making the decision not to apply early decision, but rather to apply either early action if the school offers it or during the regular admission process.

# Analyze Your Strategy

You should also find out whether you are more likely to get accepted by your first-choice school if you do apply early. Finding this out is actually very simple; just ask an admissions officer for these three pieces of information:

🕐 What proportion of the freshman class is admitted early?

🕐 What is the percentage of early applicants who are admitted?

🕐 What is the percentage of regular applicants who are admitted?

By determining this information, you will know if your chances of admission are indeed increased by applying early. If they are significantly increased, you may decide that it is in your best interest to apply to the school early, particularly if it is a school you think you have a lower chance of being accepted to during the regular admission period. Even if the school has a higher rate of acceptance in the early decision period, you may still be better suited for regular admission if you believe that your academic level will increase significantly between the fall semester and the spring semester. When applying early, you will likely have to send the school your grades through your junior year, but when applying regular admission, you must also send your fall-semester grades from your senior year. If you believe that your fall grades are going to be significantly higher, you may want to consider waiting.

Are you 100 percent committed to attending the school you're considering sending an early decision or early action application to?

An additional risk to applying early is that schools sort their early applicants into three categories:

🕐 *Admitted*—Students they will admit early

🕐 *Deferrals*—Students who will not be admitted early but whose applications will be considered during the normal application period

🕐 *Rejections*—Students whose applications are rejected outright and who will not be considered for admission during the normal application period

If you're considering an early application option, but you're worried that those bumps and blemishes on your transcript may hinder your route to an acceptance letter, then you also need to consider the fact that some colleges have a policy that a rejection during early action or early decision constitutes a full-blown rejection. This means that you're out of the game before it's even started. Some schools, however, will reject or accept you during the early application period with no bearing on your chances during the normal admission time. You may want to find out the policy of the school you're applying to before you get benched during the warm-up.

We have assembled a series of questions for you to go through to determine whether to apply early, based upon the most common factors that lead to that decision. The questionnaire in Figure 6-1 is designed to make you think about the best course of action for you, but is not designed to tell you that you should or shouldn't apply early. Use the Decide Better! questionnaire and then make your best decision.

## To Sum Up

Early admission is not for everyone, but it may be for you. Making a decision about early admission requires the specialized decision-making process and the careful scrutiny of the particular considerations that we outline in this chapter. Be sure you really want to attend that school if you are accepted.

**FIGURE 6-1 Is Applying Early Right for You?**

1. Have you identified one school that you think is absolutely perfect for you?

   • If Yes, go to question 2.
   • If No, you should probably not apply early.

2. Does your first-choice school offer the option to apply early?

   • If Yes, go to question 3.
   • If No, you cannot apply early.

3. Does your first-choice school offer early decision or early action?

   • If early decision (binding), are you prepared to attend the school if you get accepted?
     —If Yes, go to question 4.
     —If No, you should probably not apply early.
   • If early action (nonbinding), are you restricted to applying to only one school early?
     —If Yes, is this the only school you want to apply early to?
        — If Yes, go to question 4.
        — If No, you should probably not apply early.
     —If No, you may want to consider applying early.

4. Are you prepared to complete your SATs, your recommendations, your writing samples, your financial aid forms, and other required application materials earlier in the year?

   • If Yes, go to question 5.
   • If No, you should probably not apply early.

5. Is the percentage of early applicants admitted to this school higher than the percentage of regular applicants who are admitted?

   • If Yes, you may want to consider applying early.
   • If No, you should probably not apply early.

# Chapter 7

# Maybe

## Help, I've Been Waitlisted!

Jack had dreamed of attending an Ivy League school for as long as he could remember. Throughout high school, he did everything he could to make himself as desirable to those schools as they were to him. He had his heart set on one—it was perfect. But when acceptance season rolled around, Jack received a blow to the gut—he'd been waitlisted. Rather than picking himself up, dusting himself off, and pondering his next move, Jack did nothing. He spent the afternoons staring at the mailbox waiting for a letter congratulating him on being taken off the waiting list and accepted. But that letter never arrived. As August came, Jack's friends were packing up and heading to colleges, but he had no plans. He ended up living at home and taking classes at the local university. The worst part was that Jack had been accepted to an array of other top-notch schools but became so consumed by his waitlisted status that he missed the enrollment deadlines and never bothered to find out if one of those might have been a comparable or an even better fit for him.

If you've been waitlisted, you may be wondering what it is, what you are going to do about it, or why it happened. Colleges today use their waitlists in a way that they've never done before, and it's important that you understand that as an applicant. For the most part, schools are putting more students on the waitlist and accepting a smaller number of students, relying on their waitlist to fill out the remainder of the class that they

### Note to Parents
*Being waitlisted isn't the end of the world, but with only a 20 percent chance of being admitted, you should work with your children to look into accepting admissions at a backup school.*

didn't subsequently admit and enroll. Now chances are higher than ever that you, as an applicant, will be waitlisted.

You may be asking what *waitlisting* means. The short answer is that colleges are playing it safe. A waiting list (waitlist) is simply a list of applicants deemed acceptable by the school, but who may not be automatically accepted for enrollment. Thus, students on waitlists wait to hear their fates until the school makes final decisions on their applications. Let's say one particular college has 10,000 applicants for a class of 1,000 students and decides that it doesn't make sense to admit 2,500 students (an acceptance rate of 25 percent) and only enroll the 950 students who accept admission. Instead, the college chooses to accept the 1,500 students who are *more* likely to attend the school, and of those, roughly 800 to 850 will likely actually enroll. Of the 1,000 it didn't admit, some were at the top and some were at the bottom of their acceptance criteria in terms of GPA, SATs, and other criteria. After receiving the enrollment letters from the students who were first granted admission, the college still needs to fill the ranks of the upcoming class. In this case, the college needs to accept and enroll 150 to 200 students—a full 15 percent to 20 percent of its incoming class! At that point, the college turns to its waitlisted applicants to fill these openings.

> Chances are higher than ever that you will be waitlisted.

But why would colleges do this, and how does it affect you if you have been waitlisted? Frankly, more colleges are using waitlists this way because it's better for them. The two main reasons schools use the waiting list are: 1) schools cannot predict with total accuracy how many of the students that they accept will actually enroll and 2) they want to prevent both underenrollment and overenrollment. Moreover, they know that other schools are waitlisting, so it is a competitive practice. As an example, students who are admitted to school A and who send in the deposit to indicate that they're planning to enroll may also be offered admission to school B after being on school B's waiting list. If school B is a higher choice for the applicant than school A, the applicant may prefer to withdraw from enrollment in school A and instead enroll in school B. Admissions officers have come to call this phenomenon the "summer melt." By using a waiting list, the school can prevent having a class that is less than full come September.

**College Waitlist Statistics from the National Association for College Admissions Counseling:**

- Roughly 1/3 of colleges used waitlists from 2005 to 2006.

- An average of 10 percent of applicants to colleges who use waitlists are placed on the list.

- An average of one out of five students will be accepted off of the waitlist.

Another reason schools employ a waitlist process is to fill out the incoming class with a desired and specific demographic. Schools try to enroll a well-rounded group of freshmen, and waitlists can aid that goal. Schools have no way to ensure that the exact type of students they are seeking will accept admission. For example, the admissions personnel go through the profiles of students who plan to enroll and discover they need more diversity. The school might want more musicians, more students who intend to study physics, more students who will pay full tuition, more of a specific minority, or more students from a specific region of the country, for instance. Admission officers will go to the waitlist to find these students.

Being waitlisted may not be such an unfortunate prospect. Many schools accept a very high percentage of students off of their waitlist. Being waitlisted does not mean you won't get in. You still have a pretty good shot at being accepted and enrolling at one of the schools that you are waitlisted at.

## Do Something, Not Nothing

What can—and should—you do to enhance your prospects at being accepted once you are waitlisted? According to admissions officers from around the country, you shouldn't sit at home doing nothing. Admissions counselors will tell you that if the school that put you on a waitlist is your first-choice school, and you haven't heard from them before the deposit deadline, look down your list to the next school you've been accepted to and send that school an enrollment deposit. That's an easy decision. You don't want to be left without a school to attend come fall, and you have no guarantee you're going to be accepted off the waitlist. Moreover, you're more likely to be able to transfer into that top-choice school at which you were waitlisted than you are to be admitted to it if you take a year off between high school and college.

**Common Sense Dos and Don'ts for the Waitlister:**

- Do: send updates with your most recent grades or other achievements.
- Do: send them a brief note expressing your continued interest in the school.
- Do: consider any other options the school may give you, including later enrollment or admissions to other affiliated schools.
- Do: enroll somewhere—even if the school you enroll in is not your first choice, and even though you may lose your deposit—it's worth it.
- Don't: contact the school admissions personnel in an obsessive manner.
- Don't: involve your parents in the process—this is a chance to show your independence and to demonstrate that you won't go back to your parents for help.
- Don't: send new recommendations, new essays, etc. to the school admissions personnel unless they ask for the information or you clear it with them beforehand.

So what do you do now? Your best course of action is to assume you're not going to get into the school that waitlisted you. The prudent decision is to take the next steps toward going to your second-choice school. In addition to sending in your deposit, you may want to mentally prepare yourself for going to your second-choice school. This preparation would include getting ready to move in with the new roommates to whom you've been assigned, researching and signing up for your fall courses, and picking out what clothes and other items you're going to pack.

## There's Always That Chance

For some of you, though, we realize your mind may be set on attending your first-choice school, and you have no intention of budging from that goal. And, yes, while you have only a slim chance of being admitted off of the waitlist to the school, that doesn't mean that you have zero chance. Roughly 20 percent of students on a college waiting list are accepted—a one in five chance—so your admission is not completely out of the question. Now is your chance to decide: are you going to wait, or are you going to do everything you can to increase your chance of admission? If the school is truly your first choice, it's probably worth your extra effort to give it all you've got to boost your chances of acceptance. If that's what you decide, you need to make a series of important decisions. The first is to determine how you will walk the fine line between being proactive and enthusiastic versus being annoying. Thus, you need to consider your actions wisely. College admissions personnel are very busy so you probably shouldn't go visit their office unannounced, bringing 16 new recommendations, four new writing samples, and your parents. You should, however, remain in contact with someone from the admissions office. If you have previously been in touch with an admissions staff member, stay in contact. Let that person know you're still very interested in the school, that it remains your first choice, and that you would absolutely enroll were you offered admission. College advisors acknowledge that schools are more likely to admit you from their waiting lists if they think you will attend.

> If you find yourself waitlisted, you certainly shouldn't sit at home doing nothing.

## No May Not Always Mean No

Since college admissions personnel are busy, they may tell you not to contact them and not to send them any additional materials. If that's the case, there are still two things you should consider doing. First, in lieu of being in direct contact with an admissions officer, ask the college counselor from your high school to call the admissions office to indicate your intention to enroll if admitted. Your high school counselor might also be able to get information on any specific actions you could take to enhance your acceptance prospects. Second, while you may have been told not to send any additional materials above and beyond what they've already received, that doesn't mean they don't want to receive pertinent updated materials, such as new grade reports. And, of course, you can't send any information without a cover letter, so be sure to write a very concise and creative letter to include with your updated grades. Carrying out these steps carefully might be the difference between being placed in the "no" pile or being catapulted to the "yes" pile!

If all goes well, you will have one more major decision to make. If your proactive actions result in an acceptance letter, you must decide—and usually very quickly— what you're going to do. Do you already know that you're going to accept the admission to the school for which you were waitlisted and change your intent to enroll in the school you sent your deposit to? If so, this is an easy decision. If you're still uncertain, you should once again review all of the positives and negatives of attending each of the schools. You may also find it useful to return to chapter 4, which focuses on how to select a college once you've been accepted. You can use that exercise to examine whether you want to stay with the college that already has your deposit or whether you're going to attend your dream school that kept you waiting. Repeating these steps will help you gain renewed clarity to make your best decision. You should also note that by choosing the school you were waitlisted at you will lose your deposit that you already sent into the other school.

## To Sum Up

You may very well be waitlisted to one of the colleges you applied to. Waitlisting is a technique that is now being used more often by colleges to allow them to have additional flexibility, both to complete class size and to achieve the mix of students they want. If you are waitlisted, you need to decide if you want to be considered on the list and if you will go if you are eventually accepted. The chance of being accepted is about 20 percent, although it varies by school and year. Regardless, be sure to enroll at the college that is next on your list to secure a spot for the fall.

# Section II.

## Academic Decisions

olleges exist for academic purposes. You will have a lot of other experiences when you're at college, but you're there to obtain that degree. Your academic career is important. It will help to determine a lot of outcomes in your life, possibly including your career, your salary range, what you will and will not be able to accomplish, and many other events and opportunities. Don't panic—you're going to be able to succeed in school. But you will be more successful if you approach the important decisions that you will face in a structured and conscious manner. This section discusses how to make the best possible academic decisions while you're in college.

The first chapter in this section, chapter 8, is designed to help you make the best decisions when it comes to managing your time. You will have a lot to do while you're in college, including going to classes, studying, doing homework, hanging out with your new friends, going to parties, being involved in extracurricular activities, and participating in many other activities. Don't forget you also need to sleep and eat. Far too many students fail to realize that they have a limited amount of time every week in which to cram all of their activities. Inevitably, when something suffers, it's their academics. If you look at your time wisely and make a conscious

> **Note to Parents**
> *Academics are the most important part of your children's experience in college, though your children may not think so. Remember, however, that they need to determine for themselves how they will proceed with their academic careers once in college.*

decision to plan accordingly, you will ensure that your academics—the real reason you're at college—won't get the short end of the stick.

Chapter 9 helps you to accurately decide how long you're intending to stay in college. Are you hoping to get out in four years? If so, then you need to make that decision and make all of your decisions about courses, extracurricular activities, your major, and other issues with that central decision in mind. If you fail to make that a priority in your decision making, you will be more likely to find yourself in the unfortunate position of not graduating on time.

Chapter 10, which is perhaps the most important chapter in this section, is designed to help you make the most structured and accurate decision possible about what you're going to major in. So many possibilities for majors are available when you're in college, and you need to determine which one will help you accomplish your college goals. We compare your decision about a major to a game of chess. The first moves that you make in the game will largely determine which future moves are possible and which ones are not. A good move early in the game will ensure you're on the path to success. This chapter will help you make good decisions before you declare a major—and hopefully prevent you from experiencing the problems associated with changing majors later on in your academic career.

Chapter 11 and chapter 12 deal with making decisions about how to use your summers wisely and whether to study abroad, respectively. These chapters lay out similar decision processes that will help you determine the goals you're hoping to accomplish with your summer or study abroad program and to map how well each of the possibilities will help you to achieve these goals. With only three summers and only one likely chance to study abroad, you're going to be glad you took this approach and made the best possible use of this time.

The final chapter in this section, chapter 13, provides an approach for making a good decision if you're considering transferring to a different school. We all make mistakes, and many students make a mistake when it comes to deciding which school to go to. If you're considering transferring to another school, you must keep a variety of factors in mind. Moreover, you should approach this decision in a structured manner, not simply make it on a whim. While it's bad enough that you have to go through the entire application process again and start at another school as a new student, having to do so again after that would be even worse. By making the best decisions possible about whether to transfer and where to transfer to, you'll be thankful you avoided a bad decision.

This section covers a lot of material, but it's important material. While in college, you will face a huge number of decisions that will make a big difference in your life. We provide you with information to help you understand these decisions and a number of frameworks you can use to help you make these decisions well so you will be ready to have the best academic career possible.

# Chapter 8

# The Balancing Act

## How Can I Balance Academics and Everything Else?

Jerome, a student at a large university in Texas, had reasonable intentions but lacked a realistic game plan. He was a star football player in high school and received a full scholarship to play college football. He knew, however, that he was unlikely to be a professional football player after he graduated. While he certainly enjoyed it, he didn't think he was good enough to make it to the NFL, so he decided that he needed to make academics a high priority. Of course, he also wanted to have fun—that's a big part of college life.

*Note to Parents*

*College is about academics —but it's also about many other things. Balancing these is a challenge, so encourage your children to decide how to allocate their time wisely.*

As Jerome began his freshman year, the time requirements placed on him by his football obligations were high—as many as four hours a day of practice and most of the weekend hours during the football season. He also felt a lot of pressure to socialize with his teammates, something he admitted he enjoyed. And while he was serious about his studies and had signed up for a full load of classes—including several classes in economics, the department he envisioned majoring in—he could almost immediately see his academics slipping.

He knew he needed to spend hours studying and in class, but he simply couldn't find the time. Jerome's problem wasn't a lack of desire to do well in classes or an unwillingness to spend the necessary hours to get good grades. His problem was a lack of planning. He simply didn't allocate his time intentionally, and his approach to accomplish everything by "winging it" backfired.

> There are so many activities and events going on in college that it's physically impossible for you to do everything you want to. That's why you need to prioritize.

You'll have a lot to do: going to class, studying at the library, reading all of the assignments, writing papers, taking exams, eating, sleeping, writing for the student newspaper, playing sports, joining a fraternity or sorority, going out with friends, going shopping, going to parties, and more. How are you ever going to do everything? And, more importantly, how are you going to do everything well?

The short answer is: you're not. The more detailed answer is: if you plan correctly and make careful decisions about your time, you can make it all work perfectly or close to it. College is a multifaceted experience. It's not all studying and taking exams (although that is the most important part of it). And yet it's also not all about going out with friends and having fun. Where you find the equilibrium will determine whether you graduate in four years, what your GPA will be when you graduate and, therefore, which options will be open to you after graduation and which ones will be closed. It will also determine what you will think when you look back at your time in school, in terms of whether you had fun or whether it was an experience you hope to soon forget. You will have new friends, new knowledge, and new skills. But if you can't manage your time correctly, you won't have the right balance for success.

# Winging It

You can use the following process to decide how to allocate your time effectively in order to accommodate your multifaceted activities. Only you know how much time you want to spend socializing as compared to studying, sleeping, playing sports, or participating in other extracurricular activities. But the worst option is to just wing it. The best approach is to decide how you will incorporate all aspects of college life into your schedule.

Winging it, as we saw with Jerome, is not going to work. Simply choosing to study randomly is unlikely to allow enough time to complete everything required of you. When you start a semester, virtually the only aspect of your time that is going to be mandated is your class time. That's easy. The courses that you signed up for have

Winging it just isn't going to work. You need to intentionally plan your time if you're going to accomplish everything.

a built-in structure and time frame. Everything else can slide. (Of course, you probably want to sleep at some point, but those hours are flexible.) But winging everything else is only going to lead to problems and, like most students in college, when you run short of time, academics suffer. That's why it's so important to plan your time accordingly.

# Deciding How to Allocate Your Time (Four-Step Process)

Using this four-step decision-making process will help you get everything you imagined you would and more out of your time in college. This process helps you decide how to allocate your time successfully. The first step involves a broad top-down allocation of how much time you envision spending on each of four categories of activities: Basic Needs, Academics, Extracurricular Activities, and Social Life. The second step involves estimating from the bottom up approximately how you're going to distribute your time to each of the individual activities within each of the four broad categories. The third step involves a reconciliation of the top-down allocation and the bottom-up estimates. The final step involves producing a rough distribution of your time based on each day of the week and shaping this plan to fit your changing needs as your semester progresses. As part of this process, we have also created a worksheet that you can use to help you complete these steps. You can either reproduce the worksheet on your own or download it from the Decide Better! Web site at http://www.DecideBetter.com/college.html.

To understand how this process works, we're going to use a specific student who used the worksheet as an example. Joshua was about to begin his sophomore year at a liberal arts college in the western United States and had recently completed his rather rocky freshman year. He loved all aspects of school, including his classes—he was majoring in English literature—as well as his social life and his extracurricular activities. He had a great group of friends, and they spent a lot of time hanging out together. He also was extremely involved in a wide range of activities outside of classes: he wrote for the school newspaper, was the secretary of his class in the student government, was an active member of the honor society, and he represented the student body on three administrative committees (the curriculum committee, the speaker's bureau, and the honors committee). In addition to this, he was on the intramural soccer team and loved to go running in his spare time. As you can tell, his schedule was packed, and he didn't know how to fit everything in.

During his freshman year, Joshua simply tried to wing it. He attended classes, went to his committee and student government meetings when they were scheduled (missing some, of course, when they overlapped), and played his weekly intramural game of soccer. He also spent almost every Friday and Saturday night—and even some Thursday nights—hanging out with his friends (going to movies or to parties, or doing other activities). His studies ended up getting the short end of the stick and, as he learned at the end of his second semester, his grades suffered. Joshua was capable of getting straight As, as he had achieved in high school, but after his first year in college, his GPA was below a 3.0 (less than a B average). Now that his sophomore year was about to start, he knew he needed to change his approach to managing his time. He decided that he needed to allocate his time intentionally, not haphazardly.

Joshua used the following decision process with the worksheet provided to ensure that he would be able to accomplish the most each day according to his priorities for the activities that were important to him. Using Joshua and his worksheet as an example, let's go through the process step by step to see how to accomplish a successful and intentional allocation of time.

## Step 1: Rough Top-Down Allocation

As we mentioned, the first step in the process is to decide on a rough top-down allocation of how you envision your priorities. If you have 100 percent of your time to allocate to your basic needs, your academics, your extracurricular activities, and your social life, what percentage of your time would you assign to each one? To do this step, prioritize your various activities and determine a very rough idea of how to break down your time. This step is simply a rough allocation—don't feel like you need to be too accurate yet. You will have the opportunity to evaluate your priorities and hone a more detailed plan in subsequent steps. For now, just make a basic breakdown.

Looking at Figure 8-1, you can see how Joshua initially assigned his time to these four categories. This shows how he envisioned prioritizing his time on a weekly basis: Academics would be most important, requiring 40 percent of his time; followed by ensuring that his Basic Needs were met, which required 35 percent of his time; with his Extracurricular activities

**FIGURE 8-1  Top-Down Allocation of Hours Available**

| Basic needs | 35% | 58.8 hours |
|---|---|---|
| Academics | 40% | 67.2 hours |
| Extracurricular activities | 15% | 25.2 hours |
| Social life | 10% | 16.8 hours |
| **Total hours allocated** | | **168 hours** |

trailing behind at 15 percent; and finally his Social Life filling in the smallest portion of his time at 10 percent. He believed that these proportions represented a basic view of how he prioritized the 168 hours he had each week.

## Step 2: Bottom-Up Estimate

The second step in the process involves estimating how many hours you think you will need to spend on each activity within the four broad categories. This is more of a bottom-up estimate compared to the previous top-down allocation. While you will need to determine which activities are ones that you will spend time on, in general these should be included within the four categories:

- *Basic Needs*—Sleeping, eating, preparing yourself (showering, getting dressed, putting on makeup, etc.), exercising, commuting (walking to class or elsewhere, driving, etc.), and relaxing
- *Academics*—Class time, routine homework and studying, special projects (including papers or other major projects), and preparing for exams or other tests
- *Extracurricular Activities*—Meetings or activities (such as sports), preparation for events or activities, and other extracurricular requirements
- *Social Life*—Going out, staying in with friends, and other social activities

Let's look at how Joshua completed his worksheet initially, as shown in Figure 8-2. All students have the same 168-hour week in which to squeeze all of their activities. As you can see, Joshua doesn't seem to have enough time in the week to complete all of the activities he envisions for himself. One total listed at the bottom of the figure shows the total hours allocated as the 168 hours in a week. The other total, the total hours estimated, listed directly above it signifies the total number of hours that Joshua estimated he would spend on his combined activities—a whopping 212.5 hours. That's 44.5 hours more than there are in a week, or almost two full days more. He would need the week to be 27 percent longer to accomplish the goals he has set out for himself. This is how Joshua arrived at the total of 212.5 hours he thought he would need each week to get everything done.

**Basic Needs:** Joshua estimated eight hours of sleep per day for a total of 56 hours of sleeping. He liked to sleep closer to 10 hours per night on the weekends, although he knew that he usually slept more like six-and-a-half or seven hours per night

**FIGURE 8-2   Bottom-Up Estimate of Hours Required**

| Basic Needs | 35 | % | Hours |
|---|---|---|---|
| Sleeping | | | 56.0 |
| Eating | | | 14.0 |
| Preparing (showering, etc.) | | | 7.0 |
| Exercising | | | 5.0 |
| Commuting (walking, driving, etc.) | | | 3.5 |
| Relaxing | | | 14.0 |
| Basic needs hours estimated | | | 99.5 |
| Basic needs hours allocated | | | 58.8 |

| Academics | 40 | % | Hours |
|---|---|---|---|
| Class Time | | | 15.0 |
| Routine homework/studying | | | 45.0 |
| Special projects | | | 5.0 |
| Exams | | | 5.0 |
| Academic hours estimated | | | 70.0 |
| Academic hours allocated | | | 67.2 |

| Extracurriculars | 15 | % | Hours |
|---|---|---|---|
| Meetings/activities | | | 14.0 |
| Preparation | | | 10.0 |
| Other | | | 2.0 |
| Extracurricular hours estimated | | | 26.0 |
| Extracurricular hours allocated | | | 25.2 |

| Social Life | 10 | % | Hours |
|---|---|---|---|
| Going out | | | 10.0 |
| Staying in with friends | | | 5.0 |
| Other | | | 2.0 |
| Social hours estimated | | | 17.0 |
| Social hours allocated | | | 16.8 |

| Total | 100 | % | Hours |
|---|---|---|---|
| Total hours estimated | | | 212.5 |
| Total hours allocated | | | 168.0 |

during the week. He estimated that he spent roughly 14 hours per week eating, which consisted of one hour per dinner and 30 minutes each for breakfast and for lunch. It took him about an hour to get ready for each day, including showering, getting dressed, and having coffee before going to have breakfast, so that accounted for an estimated seven hours per week. He also liked to exercise for about 45 minutes every weekday and spent about 15 more minutes showering after a run on the treadmill. (He played soccer on the weekends, so he didn't need to work out otherwise on the weekends.) Joshua's exercise time accounted for an additional five hours per week. Since he lived about a mile and a half off of campus, he spent about 30 minutes per day walking to his classes and back to his apartment, or about three-and-a-half hours per week. At night, he liked to take about two hours to relax, playing video games, watching television, or going to a movie with his friends, so that accounted for 14 hours per week, something he thought was a reasonable amount of time. He was very surprised, however, to see that the total for his Basic Needs was 100 hours per week, while he had only allocated 58.8 hours per week total for these activities. "Hmm, this could pose a problem," he thought, but he moved on for now to the next set of activities: Academics.

**Academics:** The class time for the 15 credits he was enrolled in was easy to figure—15 hours per week. In terms of routine classwork, Joshua knew that each professor planned for three hours of work per credit hour per week, meaning that overall, he should expect 45 hours of routine homework per week. In addition, he expected to need roughly five hours per week for special projects and an additional five hours per week to prepare for exams, tests, and quizzes. In total, this gave him 70 hours for Academics per week, although he had only allotted himself 67.2 hours when he had considered 40 percent of his time to be about right. Once again, he had estimated more time than he had allocated for this category of activities.

**Extracurricular Activities:** Joshua's extracurricular involvement was extremely important to him. If you remember, Joshua was a writer for the college newspaper, the secretary of his class, an active member of the honor society, and a member of three committees—the curriculum committee, the speaker's bureau, and the honors committee. In addition, he was a member of the intramural soccer team, which meant one practice per week and one game per week. For these activities, he estimated that he needed to spend about 14 hours weekly in meetings and playing games, and an additional 10 hours per week preparing for all of these activities, including writing articles for the newspaper. He also added another two hours for additional time to meet with his newspaper editor, the class president, and to attend other outside meetings. This brought him to a total of 26 hours, just barely over the 25.2 hours he originally allocated in the first step of this process.

**Social Life:** In terms of his social life, something Joshua obviously enjoyed, he had allocated a minimum amount of his precious time to these activities—10 percent. He figured that he would spend about four hours on both Friday and Saturday nights going out and possibly two hours on Thursday night, for a total of 10 hours per week. He also figured he would spend about five hours per week just hanging out with his friends at his apartment or just relaxing on campus, as well as an additional two hours doing other activities. This totaled

*Note to Parents*

*If your children are active in many areas, including academics, social life, and extracurricular activities, not only will they come away from college with a well-rounded education, they will also gain time-management skills that will help them in their future professional and personal lives.*

only 17 hours per week, which was approximately the same as the 16.8 hours per week that he had allocated.

## Step 3: Reconciliation

So, wait a minute, going back to the totals, if this is the ideal amount of time that Joshua envisioned spending on each activity, how could he possibly do it? He couldn't magically find an additional 45 hours in the week. Fortunately, he had decided to tackle time management early on rather than simply assuming that he could wing it and somehow spend as much time as he wanted to on each activity. Most importantly, he realized that he couldn't do everything he wanted to. He was either going to have to give up an activity, reduce the amount of sleep he got every night, virtually stop hanging out with his friends, or stop doing as much school work. None of these seemed like very good options to him, but he still needed to figure out a plan to reconcile the differences.

He decided that his solution would be to reduce the amount of time he spent on everything except his academics—especially since he might get more or less work than he had estimated in any given week. After thinking more about his situation, he decided to roughly maintain the allocated percentage breakdown from the first step of the process and make the bulk of the changes in his estimates for the time to spend on each activity from the second step. He did, however, change one of those allocations. He decided to give up his participation on two of the administrative committees that he was on—the speaker's bureau and the honors committee. He decided to stay on the curriculum committee because he believed representing the student body in the process of determining the courses that the university would offer was very important. He therefore reduced his breakdown for Extracurricular Activities from 15 percent to 10 percent of his time, adding the additional 5 percent to his Basic Needs, which was the category with the highest discrepancy between the allocated time and the estimated time.

His overall changes can be seen in Figure 8-3. As you can see, he decided that he could probably live on six hours of sleep per night, not eight, at least for the time when he was in school, and he also figured out he could read while eating breakfast and reduce his time spent on lunch and dinner, so he needed to spend only an hour a day on meals. Likewise, he would spend only 30 minutes per day, instead of an hour, getting ready in the morning and reduce his weekday workout time from an hour to 45 minutes. Finally, he would also minimize his relaxation time from two hours a day to one.

**FIGURE 8-3   Reconciliation of Allocated Hours and Estimated Hours**

| Basic Needs | 40 | % | Hours |
|---|---|---|---|
| Sleeping | | | 4.2 |
| Eating | | | 7.0 |
| Preparing (showering, etc.) | | | 3.5 |
| Exercising | | | 3.8 |
| Commuting (walking, driving, etc.) | | | 3.5 |
| Relaxing | | | 7.0 |
| **Basic needs hours estimated** | | | **66.8** |
| **Basic needs hours allocated** | | | **67.2** |

| Academics | 40 | % | Hours |
|---|---|---|---|
| Class Time | | | 15.0 |
| Routine homework/studying | | | 45.0 |
| Special projects | | | 5.0 |
| Exams | | | 5.0 |
| **Academic hours estimated** | | | **70.0** |
| **Academic hours allocated** | | | **67.2** |

| Extracurriculars | 10 | % | Hours |
|---|---|---|---|
| Meetings/activities | | | 7.0 |
| Preparation | | | 7.0 |
| Other | | | 2.0 |
| **Extracurricular hours estimated** | | | **16.0** |
| **Extracurricular hours allocated** | | | **16.8** |

| Social Life | 10 | % | Hours |
|---|---|---|---|
| Going out | | | 10.0 |
| Staying in with friends | | | 5.0 |
| Other | | | 0.0 |
| **Social hours estimated** | | | **15.0** |
| **Social hours allocated** | | | **16.8** |

| Total | 100 | % | Hours |
|---|---|---|---|
| **Total hours estimated** | | | **167.8** |
| **Total hours allocated** | | | **168.0** |

In terms of his academics, he decided to leave them as they were, but as already mentioned, he reduced the time he would spend on extracurricular activities by removing himself from two of the three committees he was on. This saved him a total of 10 hours per week of meetings and preparation for meetings—a huge savings. He also reduced his socializing time by 2 hours, bringing him to a total of 15 hours, down from 17. These changes brought him within sight of his goal: 167.8 hours estimated to be spent in a week with 168 hours of time.

# Step 4: Distribute Your Time and Manage Your Semester

Using these techniques, you can determine approximately how much time you will need to spend each week on your academics, your basic needs, your socializing,

**FIGURE 8-4   Daily Allocation of Time (in hours)**

| Basic Needs | 40 | % | Total | Mon. | Tues. | Wed. | Thurs. | Fri. | Sat. | Sun. |
|---|---|---|---|---|---|---|---|---|---|---|
| Sleeping | | | 42 | 6 | 6 | 6 | 6 | 6 | 6 | 6 |
| Eating | | | 7 | 1 | 1 | 1 | 1 | 1 | 1 | 1 |
| Preparing | | | 3.5 | 0.5 | 0.5 | 0.5 | 0.5 | 0.5 | 0.5 | 0.5 |
| Exercising | | | 3.75 | 0.75 | 0.75 | 0.75 | 0.75 | 0.75 | 0 | 0 |
| Commuting | | | 3.5 | 0.5 | 0.5 | 0.5 | 0.5 | 0.5 | 0.5 | 0.5 |
| Relaxing | | | 7 | 1 | 1 | 1 | 1 | 1 | 1 | 1 |
| **Hours estimated** | | | **66.8** | **9.8** | **9.8** | **9.8** | **9.8** | **9.8** | **9.0** | **9.0** |
| **Hours estimated** | | | **67.2** | **9.6** | **9.6** | **9.6** | **9.6** | **9.6** | **9.6** | **9.6** |
| **Academics** | **40** | **%** | **Total** | **Mon.** | **Tues.** | **Wed.** | **Thurs.** | **Fri.** | **Sat.** | **Sun.** |
| Class time | | | 15 | 3 | 3 | 3 | 3 | 3 | 0 | 0 |
| Routine homework | | | 45 | 6 | 6 | 6 | 6 | 6 | 7 | 8 |
| Special projects | | | 5 | 1 | 1 | 1 | 1 | 0 | 0 | 1 |
| Exams | | | 5 | 1 | 1 | 1 | 1 | 0 | 0 | 1 |
| **Hours estimated** | | | **70.0** | **11.0** | **11.0** | **11.0** | **11.0** | **9.0** | **7.0** | **10.0** |
| **Hours estimated** | | | **67.2** | **9.6** | **9.6** | **9.6** | **9.6** | **9.6** | **9.6** | **9.6** |
| **Extracurriculars** | **10** | **%** | **Total** | **Mon.** | **Tues.** | **Wed.** | **Thurs.** | **Fri.** | **Sat.** | **Sun.** |
| Meetings/activities | | | 7 | 1 | 1 | 3 | 0 | 0 | 1 | 1 |
| Preparation | | | 7 | 1.25 | 1.75 | 0 | 0 | 0 | 2 | 2 |
| Other | | | 2 | 1 | 0.5 | 0 | 0.5 | 0 | 0 | 0 |
| **Hours estimated** | | | **16.0** | **3.3** | **3.3** | **3.0** | **0.5** | **0.0** | **3.0** | **3.0** |
| **Hours estimated** | | | **16.8** | **2.4** | **2.4** | **2.4** | **2.4** | **2.4** | **2.4** | **2.4** |
| **Social Life** | **10** | **%** | **Total** | **Mon.** | **Tues.** | **Wed.** | **Thurs.** | **Fri.** | **Sat.** | **Sun.** |
| Going out | | | 10 | 0 | 0 | 0 | 2 | 4 | 4 | 0 |
| Staying in | | | 5 | 0 | 0 | 0 | 0.75 | 1.25 | 1 | 2 |
| **Hours estimated** | | | **15.0** | **0.0** | **0.0** | **0.0** | **2.8** | **5.3** | **5.0** | **2.0** |
| **Hours allocated** | | | **16.8** | **2.4** | **2.4** | **2.4** | **2.4** | **2.4** | **2.4** | **2.4** |
| **Total** | **100** | **%** | **Total** | **Mon.** | **Tues.** | **Wed.** | **Thurs.** | **Fri.** | **Sat.** | **Sun.** |
| **Hours estimated** | | | **167.8** | **24.0** | **24.0** | **23.8** | **24.0** | **24.0** | **24.0** | **24.0** |
| **Hours allocated** | | | **168.0** | **24.0** | **24.0** | **24.0** | **24.0** | **24.0** | **24.0** | **24.0** |

and your extracurricular activities, and you can plan your week more carefully. While this step will take some time to accomplish and will be difficult to stick to, it will help you realize how precious your time is. Using your worksheet from steps 1 and 2, you can now attempt to distribute these requirements by day of the week. We know, this sounds like it's impossible, but give it a shot. This part of the step brings time management planning from a theoretical exercise to a reality.

As you can see from Figure 8-4, Joshua spent some time trying to do this part of the process, and after a little finagling, he saw that he really had to be cautious about which activities he spent his time on every day if he was truly going to accomplish everything he had set out to. While he knew he didn't need to stick to this schedule exactly, it helped him to have a rough estimate for how much time he could spend doing each of his desired activities. As you can see from Figure 8-4, the goal of this step is to get the hours in each day to add up to 24 hours and to get the hours spent on each activity to add up to the number of hours that you've indicated you will spend on it in the previous step.

Moreover, you need to be aware that all of these requirements will fluctuate as the semester proceeds and will need to be readjusted with a new semester or as you change the activities you're involved in. For example, if you stopped playing soccer and you wanted to take up skiing, you're going to need to readjust your time accordingly. As your semester progresses, so will your requirements. During midterm exam week, for example, you will need to spend a lot more time studying and a lot less time socializing or doing extracurricular activities, and possibly spend a lot less time sleeping. The week after midterms, however, you may be able to catch up on some of that sleep and spend a little extra time socializing with your friends. But you will at least have a basic framework to help you schedule all of your activities and to increase the likelihood that you will be able to succeed at them all.

## To Sum Up

College is a busy time. It's very easy to overextend yourself but doing so will almost inevitably lead to neglecting your studies or else not meeting other commitments. This four-step process helps you break down your schedule so you can better determine two key components of time management: first whether you can be involved in all of the activities you think you can and second how you need to spend your time to be able to accomplish them all. While you won't need to stay mindlessly committed to the rigid schedule that you set from completing the process in this chapter, you will need to stay committed to your awareness of how you spend your time and when you think you can relax with friends or when you need to spend that time more productively. It's the only way you'll make it out of college with the best all-around experience. You decide!

# Chapter 9

# Four and Out

## You Need to Decide How Important It Is to Graduate in Four Years

Peter really enjoyed his early college years. He made good friends, took interesting courses, and to his delight, he had a great social life. College was as much fun as everyone said it would be. He was able to take classes only a few days a week and none before noon—that was "Peter's Policy." But by his junior year, he realized that he had a problem. He was going to be 12 credits short by the time he finished his fourth year, and he couldn't possibly complete his core curriculum requirements by then either.

When he talked with his parents about his problem, they were angry with him. They told him that they refused to pay for more than four years of college, and he realized the financial aid he received would be gone, too. His fourth year of college (he couldn't call it his senior year any more) wasn't much fun. While most of his friends were enthusiastic about their next steps after college, he had no idea what he would do. On the day of graduation and celebration for his friends, Peter was waiting tables at a local restaurant back home. He realized that the fun he had in his first two years came at a great cost. He hadn't thought about graduating in four

**Note to Parents**

*Pay attention! This is important to you. You want your children to graduate from college in four years, so don't take it for granted.*

years until it was too late. He had just never made that decision. Peter attended a local college at night over the next two years and eventually completed enough credits to get his college degree, but it just wasn't the same.

Do you want to graduate from college in four years? For most students, the obvious answer is "yes—of course." Yet only 37 percent of college students in a four-year college graduate within four years from the time they started! That's fewer than four out of every ten! Hang on, we're not done—only 63 percent of students in a four-year college graduate within six years of the time they started. How many years are you going to take to graduate?

Why is it that so many students take longer to earn their diploma than the four years they envisioned it would take when they enrolled? In general, students have accumulated fewer credits than they need by the time they reach their fourth year because they weren't able to balance everything to finish the necessary coursework in the allotted time. But the underlying reason that students take longer to earn their degrees is that they never decided that graduating in four years was a priority. We'll recommend the decision process for this, but first you should understand the impact of taking longer than four years.

## More Than Four

The range of students who take more than four years to graduate is universal. No particular characteristics indicate whether one student or another will graduate in four years. But the unfortunate fact is that a higher proportion of those students who do fail to earn their degree within four years—or even six, for that matter—are low-income and minority students.

The Education Trust, a nonprofit organization that produces studies and advocates for improvements in the education system in the United States, has studied the rate of college graduation and, since the four-year graduation rate is so low, the Trust focuses primarily on six-year graduation rates rather than four. Even giving this leeway for the sake of studying the numbers, a study from the Trust found that "among students most likely to succeed—those who begin their college career as full-time freshmen in four-year colleges and universities—only six out of every ten of them, on average, get a B.A. within six years. This translates into over half a million collegians every year . . . who fall short of acquiring the credentials, skills and knowledge they seek."

**FIGURE 9-1 Too Few Students Graduate**

| | 6 Year Graduation Rate |
|---|---|
| Total | 63% |
| Low-income | 54% |
| High-income | 77% |
| African American | 46% |
| Latino | 47% |
| White | 67% |
| Men | 59% |
| Women | 66% |

*Source: The Education Trust

As you can see from Figure 9-1, the six-year graduation rate is lower for low-income and minority students, but the rate is still far from high for high-income and white students. (The entire report can be found on the Education Trust Web site at http://www.edtrust.org.)

Differences in graduation rates are stark when you compare one college to another. For example, graduation rates vary significantly if you look at the selectivity level of colleges. According to the U.S. Department of Education, the six-year graduation rate at four-year colleges that are considered to have "very selective" admissions policies is 74.9 percent. Schools with selective policies generally include those colleges that enroll students who were in the top 10 percent of their high school classes. For "moderately selective" schools, the six-year graduation rate falls to 54.5 percent, and for "minimally selective" schools, the rate falls even more dramatically to 35.7 percent.

In *Decide Better! for a Better Life* we brought up the lesson of the frog in boiling water. As the lesson goes, if you put a frog in a pot of boiling water, it will immediately jump right out. If you put that same frog into a pot of water at room temperature, however, and slowly bring it to a boil, the frog will simply sit there, simmering away until it dies. While we've never tested the accuracy of this assertion, the lesson is a useful one. Some decisions, if left unmade, will be made for us. The decision about whether to graduate in four years is one of these decisions. If you don't intentionally decide to graduate in four years before you begin college, you will sit in school as your academic water slowly comes to a boil. Only when it's too late will you realize that you've boiled away your four years without earning your degree.

# The Cost of More Than Four

The cost of taking more than four years to complete college can be very high. First, consider the direct costs. If tuition, room, and board cost $40,000 per year, then each additional year it takes to complete college could be an additional $40,000. A five-year college education costs $200,000—a whopping 25 percent more than the $160,000 it costs for four years. Typically, students who take more than five years will take college courses part time, so expenses are less than $40,000 per year, but dragging out your education is still a lot more expensive. Even if you take classes only part time, which may be charged by the credit hour, the school still charges the required expenses that are above and beyond tuition. All schools charge other administrative fees that are payable regardless of the number of credits you're enrolled in, so bear that in mind.

For many students, the cost can be much higher. In most cases, financial aid and other forms of financial assistance end after four years, so the net cost for the fifth year can be much higher than the previous year. Moreover, financial aid may not cover more than 15 credits, so if you fall behind and need to make them up, you must spend more money which may translate into borrowing more money. In some cases, parents may be unwilling to pay for the additional cost for the extra years a student takes to earn a college degree. This is an important point to resolve with your parents early on. Are they paying for only four years of college or as many as it takes?

The other cost to consider is the opportunity cost for the additional time you spend at college. You could be starting your career instead. Even if you go on to graduate school after taking more than four years to earn your undergraduate degree, you would still start work a year later than you could have. Consider the opportunity cost of a year of lost wages as part of the total cost of taking more than four years to graduate. For example, if you assumed you would have made $40,000 a year working instead of paying $40,000 for that fifth year of college, then your true cost for that fifth year could be as much as $80,000—half of the original cost of college! Moreover, consider the opportunity cost of your time—what else could you have done with your life if you didn't have to remain in college for that extra year or two?

> Will you really decide to make graduating in four years a priority?

On the nonfinancial side, if you take more than four years, you won't graduate with many of your classmates. When they are celebrating their graduation, you will be at home working or taking classes to make up for being behind. You may also have to live with the disappointment of others, such as your parents, relatives, professors, and friends, who naturally expect that you will graduate in four years.

## Reasons for More Than Four

If it's so expensive, then why do so many students fail to graduate in four years? In order to graduate in four years, you need to take a sufficient number of credits, generally 15 per semester. If you take fewer than this, then you need to make them up somehow in order to graduate as planned. This could mean that you need to take classes in the summer. It could mean that you need to take more than 15 credits for one or more semesters. And it could mean that you need to take an entire extra semester or two (or more).

Students take fewer credits in a semester than they should for several reasons. The mix of courses they take may work out to fewer than 15 credits. Some courses, such as those with laboratory requirements, could be more than three credits each. Some courses, such as specialized lectures, or other courses without the same work requirements, may be fewer than three credits. So in any given semester, you might have a course load, for example, of only 13 credits. After only a couple of semesters like this, you may find yourself further behind than you had expected.

Another reason students take fewer credits may be that they think that a full 15-credit course load is too demanding for them so they take a lighter workload. They may take 12 credits, or even fewer, in order to make school easier. If you do this, unless you consciously plan to make the deficit up by taking a semester of more than 15 credits or by attending summer school, you have just made the decision to take more than four years to earn your degree.

Sometimes students either fail a class or drop out of a class and need to take it again or lose the credits. This also means that it will take them more than four years to graduate unless they find some way to make up those credit hours. This happened to Kerri, who found that she was falling behind even before the end of her freshman year. She enrolled in a course that was not right for her during her first semester. She had been convinced to take the class by her parents, but it was much too difficult, and she could already predict the poor grade she would have received if she remained in the course. After much thought about it, she withdrew during the third week of classes. Unfortunately, it was too late into the semester to add another class so instead of 15 credits for the semester, she was only registered for 12. Then, in her spring semester, largely due to the configuration of her classes, she was enrolled in only 13 credits, and when it came time to select classes for the following fall semester, she once again was enrolling for 13 credits. This meant that after only three semesters in college, she would be behind by seven credits—almost half of an entire semester. At this rate, in four years she would be behind by almost 19 credits!

Fortunately, Kerri realized what was happening, and she picked up another three-credit course for her sophomore fall semester, bringing her to 16, which meant she would be only four credits short by the end of that semester. She decided to take the same course load for the spring semester of her sophomore year, and then she proceeded to take one class for three credits at the small community college near her house during the summer. With these decisions, she was back on track and ended up graduating in four years. She recognized her situation early and was able to recover due to her dedication to that goal and her decisions to catch up.

In some college programs, it's tricky to fit in all of the classes you need to complete your major. You need prerequisites that are only offered at certain times, and these classes may be full when you want to take them. Other courses that are more interesting may compete with the times that these courses are offered, or the courses you need may only be available in the early morning or on Fridays. You may reason that you can wait and take these required courses later. Navigating through all of the prerequisites as well as the classes needed for your major can be tricky.

The following are other reasons that students fall behind, take a semester off, or otherwise have to make up credits or face graduating late:

- They suffer from educational burnout.
- They are academically unprepared for the amount of work required to earn the necessary number of credits.
- They have chosen the wrong major and have to make up credits.
- After realizing the school was a bad academic fit, they have transferred schools.
- They have spent too much time having fun and not enough time on academics.
- They experienced high levels of stress that discouraged them from taking a full load of courses.
- They were balancing school and external demands, such as a full-time or a part-time job, which interfered with taking a full load of courses.
- They faced changing financial conditions that made it more difficult to pay for classes, including changes in tuition, personal financial changes, and changes in the amounts of scholarships or financial aid.
- They were struggling with personal or family issues, including sickness or death in the family.

While some students simply fall behind in credits, many others end up taking one or more semesters off because of academic or personal problems. This action, known as "stop-out" in higher education circles, automatically puts students behind in terms of graduating in four years, although it can sometimes be necessary to get back on track for graduating in the minimal number of semesters.

# Decide on Your Priorities

You need to decide if graduating in four years is your priority. After you've made the easy part of that decision, now comes the hard part. If graduating in four years is an important priority for you, then the following should also be priorities when necessary:

- Taking early morning classes (before noon is generally considered early morning for most college students)
- Taking required courses first, in order to get them out of the way, before taking more interesting courses
- Studying harder in order to make sure you don't fail a course
- Taking courses in the summer in order to make up credits, or even to get ahead of credit requirements
- Taking at least the minimum number of credits each semester (usually 15) even if the course mix isn't as interesting
- Making sure you selected the right major since changing majors could require more courses and delay graduation

It may help to mention just a few of these in more detail. You may not be a morning person, for example, so you make it your priority not to have any morning classes. Or you decide that you really would like to have a three-day weekend every weekend, so you're not going to sign up for any classes on Fridays. Or you only want classes two days a week, so you only take classes on Tuesdays and Thursdays. While these sound like sweet schedules, they're not going to be part of any strategy that will ensure you graduate in four years. Many required courses for your degree, including for your major or minor, won't fall into these rigid requirements you have arbitrarily set for personal, not academic, reasons. Is your priority to sleep late and have a long weekend? Or is it to graduate in four years?

# Stay Focused on Reality

What about being sure that you always take the number of credits you need to ensure you graduate in four years—typically 15 per semester? You will always want to participate in many other activities at school in addition to keeping up with your academics. Maybe you're involved in a leadership role in your fraternity or sorority. Or maybe you're running a major event or a big student organization. Or maybe you're highly involved in the student government. These are all great ways to be involved while you're in college, but remember that you're at college primarily to graduate, not to do these other activities. To the extent that you're able to accomplish your academic requirements *and* your extracurricular activities, being active is great. But if you need to prioritize competing activities, your coursework has to come first.

Likewise for your summers. Backpacking in Europe or spending the summer relaxing at the beach sounds wonderful. But if you're behind in school, is that what your priority should be for your summer?

Jim is a student who can provide us with some good insights into prioritizing your education. In high school, he was a very good student, earning mostly As and only a few Bs. In his freshman year of college, he also did very well in his classes. When it came time to register for courses for the fall semester of his sophomore year, all of his friends were talking about the comfortable schedules they had set up for themselves. Some of them only had classes on Mondays and Wednesdays or only on Tuesdays and Thursdays. And virtually none of them signed up for any morning classes. They were already talking about how much partying they would be able to fit into their second year in college. Jim was swept away in this tide.

As an engineering major, the requirements for his program were very strict, and he had to take many courses to complete the major, each of which also had their own prerequisites. While planning his schedule for the fall semester of his sophomore year, two courses that were prerequisites for other courses were offered, and he was strongly urged by his advisor to enroll in them both. Jim was told that if he didn't, he would be behind schedule for completing his major requirements. Both of them met three days a week—Monday, Wednesday, Friday—and one started at 8:00 a.m. and the other at 10:00 a.m. That was going to throw off his plan. He also was hoping to get one of his core requirements—a foreign language requirement—out of the way that semester, but that class, too, was only offered at 8:00 a.m. on Tuesdays and Thursdays. How could he possibly take classes five days a week, let alone having classes at 8:00 a.m. all five days?

After thinking it through briefly, he reckoned that he could always take them another semester, and he proceeded to register for five elective courses—none of which would count toward his major, his minor, or his core curriculum requirements. He thoroughly enjoyed the fall semester of his sophomore year, especially since he was enrolled in easy courses and had a really great schedule. When it came time to register for his spring semester, however, he learned a hard lesson. The prerequisite courses were not available that semester—they wouldn't be available until the next fall. He immediately felt a huge weight on his chest. How could he have been so irresponsible? For the spring semester, Jim had no choice but to register for five courses, only one of which would count toward any of his requirements. After he finally took the courses he needed in his junior year, Jim found that he was not going to graduate on time. He couldn't take all of the courses he needed for his major in his fourth year. He ended up graduating with his engineering degree after five years instead of four. While he was happy with his accomplishment, he never really forgave himself for not prioritizing his plan of study over his social life.

## Some Tips

If you have decided that graduating in four years is a priority, then here are a few tips to implement that decision. First, be sure to take a least the minimum number of credits (usually 15) each semester. You need to enroll in a sufficient number of courses, and if you drop one, be sure to enroll into another of equal credit hours and that applies to your degree requirements. It is also good to create a little cushion by taking more than the required number of credits early on. Having earned a few extra credits at the end of your first year gives you some flexibility later on.

It can be a little tricky to schedule in all of the basic required courses and the course requirements for your major and possibly your minor. Seek out help from your advisor. Come up with a plan of action. Anticipate what courses you will take in subsequent semesters, not just the current one. Your advisor knows what you need to take and how to work through the course requirement process but be sure to remind him or her that your primary objective is to graduate in four years.

If you run into trouble taking a course, work hard to correct it. If you can't get enrolled into a course that you need, especially if it's a prerequisite for another requirement, go to the professor or to the department head and ask for help. Ask your advisor to help, too. Tell them all that it's important to you to graduate in four years. Do whatever you need to do to get into the courses you need.

If you get behind, be willing to take on a bigger course load than normal in the following semester or the last few semesters. You should always be aware of the number of credits you have and how many you need to take to complete school on time. If necessary, go to school in the summer. Make sure in advance, though, that the courses you take in the summer will be recognized for credit and will apply toward your graduation.

Most of all, be proactive in creating and following through with your plan of action. Most colleges require you to file a plan of action for how you will complete your major with the department so they can be sure that you're going to take all of the required courses. Following your plan is crucial—not that you need to take every course you plan for yourself when you're a freshman. But you do need to ensure you meet the specific course requirements as well as credit hours. In addition to your major (and minor), you also need to have your own personal plan of action for your entire *four years* at college. This should be an estimate of the courses you're planning on taking each semester from your freshman year through graduation, including the requirements of your major, the requirements of your minor, the core curriculum requirements, and an accounting of the number of credits required for graduation. While you shouldn't feel obligated to take every specific course you've planned to, you should make it a point to achieve all of your requirements *and* credit hours in the time frame you set—four years.

> ### Note to Parents
> *If you remain active in your children's choice of classes and work with them on creating and sticking to a plan of study, your efforts will go a long way toward helping them stay on track to graduate in four years.*

The overwhelming majority of students who fail to complete their degree in four years don't sit down one day and say, "I'm going to finish my degree in six years, not four." What happens is that they gradually fall behind here and there, and before they realize it, six years have passed, and they're just getting around to completing graduation requirements. How can you avoid this position? By making the decision ahead of time to prioritize your time line for graduation and by implementing that time line.

One trick that students can do is to take an 8.5-inch by 11-inch manila folder and open it up. Then take forty sticky notes and place them in eight groups, with five notes in each group. Each note represents a course you will take for graduation, and each group of five notes will represent the courses you will take in a given semester. You will have two semesters per year (unless you have trimesters, in which case you will have 12 total groups). Write your courses on these sticky notes, starting with the core curriculum requirements, moving on to the courses for your major, then your minor, and finally your electives. While you may not have all of your electives or even the courses for your major or minor picked out yet, you can simply leave these blank or indicate "major course #6" or "elective #2" on the notes. Once you have them written, you can begin to rearrange them, moving this course to a different semester and that course to a different semester. The placement can depend on your preferences, but it should also depend upon which courses are offered during which semesters. This may sound like a very simple exercise, but you will be pleasantly surprised how useful it is in helping to visualize how you plan to complete all of your required courses and finish your program on time.

## To Sum Up

Many students take more than four years to complete college, so don't take it for granted that you will somehow magically graduate in four years. You need to decide up front if completing college in four years is a priority for you. Is it a high enough priority that you would sacrifice other conflicting desires? If it is, then decide to do it, live that commitment, and work hard for "Four and Out"!

# Chapter 10

# Major, Major Decision

## Choosing Your Major Is Like Making a Chess Move

Haley was a student at a small liberal arts college in New England. She was very talented and excelled in all of the courses she took. In addition, she loved music and theater. When she was a freshman, she immediately began taking classes in both the music department and the theater department, loving all of them. After only one semester, she decided to declare her major in music and proceeded to sign up for all of the music courses she could in the spring semester and the following fall. During the fall semester of her sophomore year, she had to take a course in political science to complete one of the core curriculum requirements. She wasn't looking forward to it, but not long into the semester she realized that she absolutely loved it—even more than either music or theater. She just hadn't known anything about political science before taking a course in it. How could Haley have overlooked the idea of majoring in political science for so long?

> ### Note to Parents
> *Choosing a major is a decision that has to be made by your children because it will determine their futures, but you should play a role in this decision. Your experience in the real world and your understanding of your children will make a valuable contribution to the decision.*

Well, she missed it because she didn't take the time to adequately examine her options before declaring her major.

College brings all kinds of new opportunities to the academic table. It brings completely new subject matter and the option to learn topics and concepts that you had no idea existed. High school is much more limited in the breadth of subject matter, and college can often bring you to new places. But if you don't take the time to examine the various departments and courses that are available, you will be certain to miss something. Instead of rushing into the decision, Haley should have explored her options at greater length before declaring her major. In the end, she decided it was worth it to change to political science as her major, but she was required to pick up an extra 15 credit hours above the minimum required for graduation. Haley completed her major in political science, but it took her four-and-a-half years to graduate instead of four, making her college education 12.5 percent more expensive than it would have been if she had made the right decision to begin with.

"So, what's your major?" That's the most common question you'll be asked while in college. Deciding what you're going to study for your major and your minor are possibly the most important decisions you will make in your entire college career. Your decision about a college major will significantly influence your future, perhaps even more than where you go to school or what grades you achieve. Deciding a major shouldn't be a haphazard process. You shouldn't choose a major because it has easy requirements or because your friends chose it. You need to choose the major that's best for you—taking into consideration what your interests are and the possibilities your major holds for your future professional career.

Maybe you decided your course of study before you even moved into your dorm room the first year of college. We still suggest you read this chapter to make sure you understand the implications of your decision. The information in this chapter will help to confirm your decision, or perhaps it may cause you to rethink your decision. In either case, it's useful. If you're still undecided, dig in and get to work on your decision. We want to stress right from the beginning that you're not alone in this process. Many schools provide a lot of resources to help you with this decision. Your faculty advisor should be able to help you navigate these resources, but we'll examine that idea later.

The decision technique for selecting your major is similar to a strategy used in the game of chess. Thinking several moves ahead is critical in chess and also very useful in selecting your major. The technique uses *decision mapping* to help you visualize several moves ahead in your decision on a major. But first, who makes the decision about what major to choose, and when should the decision be made?

# Who Makes the Decision

The decision on selecting a major should be made by you, the student, since it will determine the course of your life. But let's look at the role your parents should play in the decision. You can benefit a lot from parental advice and help. Parents have useful insights about careers, jobs, and future opportunities. Parents can research some of the potential career opportunities based on their knowledge of your interests and talents. Parents are great resources for you on this matter. Of course, it's still your decision. But take the time to sit down and talk about this decision with your parents. Set some quiet time aside specifically for this conversation. It will probably take several discussion sessions. First talk about your alternatives. Then discuss how each of these alternatives may determine your future moves. Finally, apply the mapping technique we recommend in this chapter—even if you only do it on your own.

One parent we know told all of his children that they could major in anything they wanted, as long as it helped them get a job when they graduated. His logic was that he was paying for college and didn't expect to keep supporting his children after they graduated. To him, college was an investment in the transition from his support to their independence, and it needed to be a good one. He didn't make the decision, but he established the criteria for it.

Though a little harsh, this approach has some merit. Too many parents invest a lot of money to send their child to college and then have a "failure to launch." Their child comes back home to live with them just like they had before going to college. This may be okay with some parents, but it's a big surprise and disappointment for others. It's worth discussing your parents' ideas about the amount of independence they expect from you as you move into your next phase of life.

# When to Declare Your Major

When do you need to make this decision? You may feel like you're being pushed right from your first day of college to make a decision about your major, but you don't have to make the decision right away. Resist the pressure and take some time to make a sound decision. Declaring your major at the last possible moment may not be worse than declaring the wrong major and then being forced to switch—possibly too late to be able to complete your course requirements within the four years you've hoped your studies will take. So take your time and do your research. Or at a minimum, don't feel pressured to rush into this decision. You should think carefully about your interests, your strengths, your plans for your life after graduation, your desire to continue your studies with graduate school, the majors that are available at your college, and which of these majors are particularly strong at your college.

Determining the right major for you is probably the most important decision you will make in college, and if you've erred, even if it means that you have to stay in school for an extra year or even two, changing your major still could possibly be the best decision to make. You need to major in the subject that best suits you and your needs. Keep in mind that choosing it too late can be very expensive. The goal is to avoid that expense by making the right decision the first time.

> Rushing into a decision about your major could prove to be disastrous. Take your time and choose right the first time.

While the majority of colleges don't require you to declare a major in your first semester, some universities do require you to select one of the *schools* within their university before you get there. These may be the School of Arts and Sciences, the Engineering School, the Education School, the Business School, or the School of International Affairs, for instance. If that's the case, don't fret too much—you can usually change out of that school if you decide later that you want to major in something that isn't offered in that school. At one university for example, many of the students who begin to major in premed transfer to the business school after the first year. (The easiest course to follow, however, is to choose the school that you are most likely going to want to major in when you enroll as a freshman.) Not every school offers the option to transfer, though, and it's not always a simple or automatic process. It's therefore best to find out right from the beginning how easy or difficult it is to change colleges within your school.

Figure out when you are required to make your major decision before you make it. One strategy that works well is to give yourself more time by using your first year to focus on courses that meet your general academic requirements regardless of your eventual major. That way, you can put off making the decision and not be held back in your graduation time line because you wisely took classes that apply to your degree in any case.

# A Chess Move

As we mentioned, deciding on your college major is like making a move in chess. Choosing your major is not your final move, but it sets up your next move and, therefore, subsequent moves. The decision also limits or restricts these next moves. A good chess move puts you on a winning path and gives you good options for your next move and the one after that, while a poor move makes it difficult for you to win because it limits your subsequent choices. Good chess players will think four to five moves ahead before they make their next move. Apply the chess move analogy to your decision by anticipating the next moves in your life. Fortunately, you will usually only need to think one to three moves ahead.

First of all, you need to anticipate what you want to do next when you graduate from college. Some questions to consider might be: Do you think that you will end your education at that point or go on to get a master's degree or maybe even a doctorate? If so, do you want to commit to that much school before you can launch your career? Are reasonable career opportunities available for your area of interest and are those opportunities available in the geographic area where you'd like to live? If you are planning on working after college then you should anticipate how your college degree will help you get a job.

Deciding on your major is like a chess move—it sets up the options for your subsequent moves.

Lois failed to analyze her decision this way. She majored in sociology because she thought that major would be easier for her than other majors. She worked hard enough to graduate but was in the lower part of her class. She definitely didn't want to continue further in her education after college, but she couldn't find a job that enabled her to use her degree and that paid her enough to cover her student loan payments. After looking for a job for several months during the end of her senior year and into the summer, she took a job working as a waitress. Many college students end up as Lois did, at least temporarily working in similarly low-paying, service-oriented jobs after they graduate because their college education didn't prepare them for a career. While this may the desired career course for some people, for others the failure to decide on the right major may cost them a better opportunity.

## Map Your Decision

We recommend a technique called *decision mapping* to help you make this decision. It's simple. You write down some of the alternatives you would like to have available to you when you graduate from college and then map how different potential majors help you with these next moves. Just like a move in chess, the move you decide to make with your major will either create opportunities or restrict your next moves. It's easiest to understand this with a few examples.

Martha enjoyed art and was especially intrigued by computer art. She envisioned being a famous artist with people seeing her work in art galleries and buying it. But she was also realistic. She didn't have the financial resources to support herself while developing a career as an artist right out of college. Aspiring artists often find it difficult to make a living based solely on their art right away. She needed an income as soon as she left college, even though she knew she would still pursue a career as a famous artist concurrently. She was determined that she wasn't going to move back in with her parents after college, no matter what.

Martha put together Figure 10-1 to map out the alternatives for her major and their impact on the next step in her life. If she majored in art, it would help her to be a better artist, but there was still a big risk that she couldn't afford to do this. It was unclear if majoring in art would help her to get a good job. She might be able to get a job at an art gallery, but she didn't think that it would pay very well. She was also interested in computer science as a way to have a profession as a graphic artist. Majoring in computer science would allow her to combine her interests in art as well.

**FIGURE 10-1 Martha's Game of Chess**

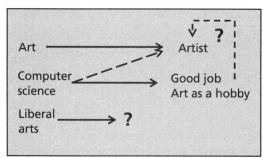

If she worked as a computer graphic artist, she could still pursue art as a hobby, and maybe over time she could become a professional artist. She also had an interest in a broad liberal arts degree because she would enjoy exploring her other interests in literature and history, but she couldn't map how this major would help her with her next step.

In the end Martha decided to major in computer science. She believed it was more practical and less risky than majoring in art because her first priority coming out of college was to get a good job. She decided to carry an extra course load and make art her minor. And she didn't give up her dream of turning her hobby in art into a second career. Martha thought ahead one subsequent move—or two, if you consider that she set up a potential move from art as her hobby to becoming an artist later in life after she established herself financially. Her example shows that you may need to think more than one move ahead.

Here's another example. We advised a recent graduate, Shauna, on what to do after college. She graduated first in her class from a small liberal arts school and was president of the student body so she should have been extremely marketable. She decided that what she truly wanted was to go to business school to obtain her MBA (Master of Business Administration) so she could work in investment banking or consulting, and she understood that every top MBA program requires their applicants to have a minimum of two or three years of job experience before they have a chance of being admitted. With her grades, her stellar performance, her achievements in extra-curricular activities, her intelligence, and her excellent communications skills, this shouldn't have been a problem.

**FIGURE 10-2 Shauna's Game of Chess**

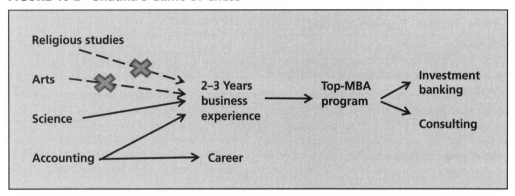

But after applying for a wide variety of jobs, she still hadn't been hired at any of them six months after graduation. Much of the reason was due to the fact that she decided to major in religious studies—a discipline that the top corporations generally don't see as providing useful skills. If she decided that she wanted to pursue a doctorate in religious studies, she most certainly would have been accepted to a prestigious school. Obviously, she hadn't thought about the fact that her choice of major would open certain doors and close others. As illustrated in Figure 10-2, if Shauna had thought ahead a couple of moves, she would have realized that majoring in religious studies wouldn't lead to a job that could position her for a good MBA program. At the time she chose her major, she had also considered majoring in a science—probably chemistry—or in accounting. If she had done this, she would have been positioned well to get a job that would lead to a good MBA program and then a career in investment banking or consulting. Majoring in accounting also would have provided the opportunity for her to get started in a long-term accounting career if she didn't get into a good MBA program. In addition, if Shauna had considered double majoring, she could have solved her problem by taking coursework that she was interested in while concurrently taking coursework to prepare her for her career.

Robert provides another good example. He had always been very ambitious throughout high school and was called an overachiever, which he didn't mind. When he started college, he wasn't completely certain what he wanted to major in or what he wanted to do with his career. After his freshman year, he began to think that he wanted to be either a lawyer or a doctor. The two completely different career paths were both paths he thought he would be interested in and that would provide a lot of personal satisfaction. The problem that he noticed, however, was that each of these possible careers would require him to take completely different courses (and majors) in college. The prelaw program at his school would prepare him for law school and the required courses would introduce him to all of the various types of law (property, family, contracts, environmental law, etc.), as well as various types of professions in law (public defender, prosecutor, corporate law, etc.). This background would help him get the two to three years of legal experience that law schools typically look for when accepting applicants. The premed program would help him with all of the necessary coursework and background to go into a medical school program directly from his undergraduate degree. Alternatively, he could choose to major in either chemistry or biology, both of which would help him pursue the route to become a doctor. He was unsure which route to take.

After speaking with his parents, his advisor, and some of his friends who were in the prelaw and premed programs, Robert sat down and mapped out his options. The map helped him determine what each route would enable him to do and what each would prevent him from doing. Looking at the map he created, you can see he considered a number of options. First, if he majored in prelaw, he would be limited to becoming a paralegal and then going to law school. Were he to decide that law wasn't right for him after choosing prelaw as a major, he believed his career options would be limited. In terms of premed, he had a similar realization. A student who majored in premed and didn't then follow through with medical school would not have very many career options. At this point, since he was only at the end of his freshman year, he wanted to keep his options open. He believed that majoring in chemistry or biology would enable him to go to medical school as long as he took all of the additional prerequisite courses that medical school requires that are outside of either chemistry or biology. He also believed that if, for some reason, he decided later on that he didn't want to go to medical school, he could still transition these majors into a good career. Many jobs are available for people with a background in chemistry and biology other than becoming a doctor. In addition, he was also advised by a professor in the prelaw department that many law schools place a high value on students who apply with an undergraduate degree in the sciences. While he may have a harder time getting the two to three years of legal experience before going to law school, he was told this certainly wasn't impossible.

This chess-like process helped Robert to think clearly about which options would be opened up for him and which ones would be closed as a result of the choices he made. He decided to major in chemistry and to minor in prelaw, enabling him to strengthen his ability to go either the lawyer route or the doctor route, all the while keeping open the option of doing neither of these and instead having a career in chemistry. You can see his game of chess in Figure 10-3.

**FIGURE 10-3   Robert's Game of Chess**

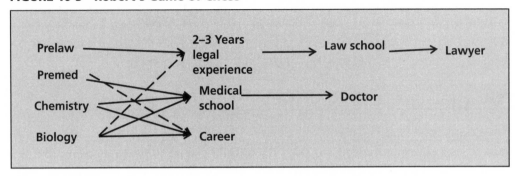

## Your Major Is a Major, Long-Lasting Decision

It's important to remember that, while your major may not define the rest of your life, it is something that can have an impact upon the number and types of options you will have after you graduate. If you major in accounting, for example, you're unlikely to be admitted into a PhD program in history. Likewise if you major in acting, it's unlikely you'll be admitted to medical school. Of course, these are not hard-and-fast rules. If you major in accounting but minor in physics and perform internships in physics labs and other physics-related activities, you may be admitted into a physics graduate program after all. If you major in acting, you may in fact become a doctor, either because you've decided to take the required premed courses anyway or because you spend an additional two years after college going back to take these courses (a costly, but not impossible, scenario). In other words, your major doesn't have to be directly related to what you want to do after college, but it certainly helps.

> You have time to make your best decision about your major—so use it.

Not completely understanding your interests and goals can often be detrimental to a successful education. But it's something you can prevent if you think about it ahead of time. Let's look at one student, Zachary, who had declared computer science as his major by the spring of his sophomore year. He knew that he wanted to make a lot of money, and he also knew that computer science was a great way to do this. After taking the required courses for several semesters, he finally admitted to himself that he didn't like computer programming at all. He realized that he had blindly chosen to follow money rather than working toward some combination of financial stability while pursuing a career that interested him. In the end, he switched his major to physics, which required him to take a very high course load and to earn credits during the summer to get back on track to graduate in four years. It ended up being a good move for him. He worked for three years after graduation, then went to business school at Harvard, and is now very successful. And he loves what he does, something he may or may not have been able to achieve with his original major.

# An Alternative Approach: Follow Your Passion

An alternative approach to deciding on your major is to follow your passion, even if it means ignoring how it may affect your future career. Juan did this. He had a passion for music, and although he didn't know what he would do in the future, he knew that music would be central to his life forever. Because of this, Juan decided to major in music, and his college days were the happiest of his entire life. He learned so much about music that it enriched his life tremendously. He never had a career in music, but he never regretted his choice of major.

You need to examine your interests. To help you understand yourself better, try asking yourself these questions:

- What classes in high school did you enjoy the most and why?
- What classes didn't you take but wish you had?
- What are your favorite nonacademic activities?
- What skills do you wish you had?

All students should consider two specific aspects of their decision about what major to declare: the first is that you choose a major because you want to pursue a career in that field, and the second is that you are so fascinated by the subject matter that you want to learn as much as possible about it. While these are probably the two most important factors to consider when choosing your major, remember that you can take them both into account at the same time. In other words, they are not mutually exclusive. Also, the decision will be different for different people.

You have the time to explore possibilities, so use it. If you know you want to major in American studies, try looking at history as well. You will get very little benefit from declaring your major in the fall semester of your freshman year, and doing so may mean that if you decide to change majors at some future point, you will have to earn additional credits to catch up.

Obviously, you will have to examine what majors are available at your school. You can't major in a subject that isn't offered at your school, so your range of possibilities is already defined. (If you are certain that you want to major in a subject that isn't offered by your school, you may want to consider transferring to a school that offers it. You can learn more about transferring in chapter 13.)

When considering different possibilities, keep in mind that you may not know much about some majors, but that doesn't mean they won't be right for you. In fact, many students explore subject matter that is completely new to them and end up majoring in that subject and even going on to a career in a related field. College has many more disciplines than high school, so don't worry if you don't know about each of them—now is your chance to learn about them. Additionally, you should remember that even if you took one or more courses in high school in a particular discipline and you didn't do very well or didn't like them, that doesn't mean you won't enjoy that topic and do well in the courses in college.

> **Resources Available to Help You Select a Major:**
> - Academic advisor
> - Professors
> - Other students
> - The course catalog
> - The college Web site
> - Outside college guidebook
> - Your parents

## Using the Resources Available to You

Whether you realize it or not, a plethora of resources are available for you to use in considering different majors. The first—and easiest—resource is, obviously, the course catalog. While it won't give you complete depth of understanding about each major, it will certainly give you a basic sense of what you would learn in that discipline. This information is available on your school's Web site, so it requires minimal research effort for you to understand your options.

In conjunction with examining available courses in each discipline, you should also begin to look at the requirements of each major. What and how many introductory courses would you have to take? How many advanced-level courses are required, and are you allowed much flexibility to take the courses that most interest you? Would you be required to do an internship or a thesis? Would you be required to take a certain number of courses in each subdiscipline? What are the other requirements for the major, such as quantitative or lab requirements? This information is also easily obtained on your school's Web site.

In addition to the written materials available to you, other people can provide a wealth of knowledge. Your friends—both those at your school and those at other schools—know you and may have insight about what they think would interest you. Upperclassmen are great resources because of their knowledge about their majors and the courses they've taken. While their interests may be different than yours, they have more experience and can recommend professors, discuss the quality of the courses, and explain the processes they went through to determine their majors.

One of the best sources of information is your academic advisor. Usually a professor, but occasionally a full-time counselor or an administrator, your academic advisor is initially assigned to you randomly or because you expressed interest in a particular department. It's very possible that your advisor won't be from a department that you ultimately pursue as your major, but that doesn't mean the advisor won't be helpful. In fact, the advisor's knowledge of the school in general and his or her ties with professors in other departments can be extremely useful to you. The advisor's goal is to get you into the major that best suits your needs and your interests, and they usually take this role very seriously. Additionally, the Career Center at your college should be able to provide you with valuable information about what you can do with various majors.

> Test-drive your major before committing to it. It will be time well spent and you won't regret it.

One student we advised a few years ago, Ted, entered a liberal arts school not really knowing what he wanted to do. He had been involved in theater in high school, but on the technical side, not the acting side, and had initially listed stage lighting as an interest when he completed the enrollment forms for his new school. He knew he was unlikely to major in theater, but he was assigned an academic advisor in that department based upon his enrollment forms. Almost immediately, his advisor knew he was in the wrong department but didn't pressure him to select a major quickly. He wanted to advise him correctly and helped him sign up for courses in a wide range of departments, including some that Ted had not previously considered. At the end of the fall semester of his sophomore year, Ted finally was convinced that political science was the major for him. He hadn't thought that majoring in political science was even a possibility for him, but he loved it. He is still thankful that his advisor recommended that Ted take a course in political science.

Either in coordination with your academic advisor or simply on your own, you should also meet with professors in other departments where you are considering majoring. Unfortunately, few students actually take this step, even though it often proves to be one of the most useful. All professors maintain office hours, and while they generally are used for students in their classes, they will be willing to meet with you to answer your questions about their discipline, the degree requirements, the course requirements, and any other questions you may have. You should visit with a professor who teaches the classes that you would be most interested in taking. Also, you should prepare questions ahead of time. You don't want to waste their time, but they will be more than happy to help you if you're serious. Professors are there to guide you, so you should take advantage of their availability.

# Try It On for Size

We tell students who are undecided about their majors to test them out. This is a good way to use the information available and to avoid making a mistake in choosing a major. In other words, try on your major before you buy it. You would test-drive a car before deciding to buy it or you would try on clothes to see if you think you look good in them before you buy them, so why not try on your major before you commit to it? After all, it's much more important to you than a sweater.

How do you try on a major before you buy it? The best way is to envision yourself taking the required courses, putting together a plan of study, doing the required assignments, reading the required books, completing the papers or other requirements, working with the professors and students in that discipline, and participating in the outside activities offered by the department. Can you see yourself spending time with the other students in the major? Can you envision yourself completing the requirements? As we mentioned, you should sit down and begin to write out what courses you would take to complete the requirements of the major. Would you enjoy them? Would they provide you with the skills that you're seeking for your college experience? You can also look at the syllabi of many of the courses that are available in the department to see if the materials interest you. Many schools post these online, and for those courses that are not available online, the professors are likely to be happy to provide you with a copy of their course syllabus.

Some people say the best way to learn about whether you would be interested in a particular major is to take a class in it and find out. While that may be true, you should be prudent in implementing this approach. If you take a class in every single department in the school, you will be there for five years before you select your major. But if you implement this tactic wisely, you can benefit significantly. For example, many schools—and pretty much every liberal arts school—have core curriculum requirements that all students have to take. This core usually consists of a wide range of disciplines from math to science to English to arts. Since you have to fulfill these requirements no matter what major you select, use these core requirements to your advantage. Try completing one or more of these requirements in a discipline that you want to know more about. If you have a lab requirement, for example, and you think you may be interested in physics, then take your lab requirement in physics. If you have a general humanities requirement, then take a course in history, political science, sociology, or whichever discipline you think you may like if you tried it.

Colleges mandate these requirements so that their students graduate with a well-rounded range of skills and knowledge. But you can also use them to help you choose your major.

> **Bad Reasons to Choose a Major:**
> - Your parents told you to
> - Your sibling majored in it
> - Your friends are majoring in it
> - The major you really like is too challenging
> - The major has easy graduation requirements and courses
> - The major has few 9:00 a.m. classes
> - Your boyfriend or girlfriend is majoring in it
> - You opened to a random page in the course guide and chose it
> - You threw a dart at a dartboard and it landed on that major
> - You think you could learn to enjoy it

Just as important—or even more so—as trying on your major is trying on your potential career. After all, if you're going to choose your major based on a career you think you want to do, shouldn't you first explore whether that career is really what you would be happy doing? Many students use summer jobs as an opportunity to do this. Think about the different jobs and careers that you currently envision as your goal. To what do you aspire?

Another way to find out more about your interests and possible career is to become involved with an outside activity that is similar to the major and to a particular career. Every college offers a wide range of extracurricular activities for your enjoyment and professional development. If you think you may want to be a writer, work on the newspaper or the literary magazine. If you think you may want to be a doctor, be a volunteer paramedic. If you want to be an actor, act in one of the plays. If you want to be a news anchor, work for the campus television or radio station. The opportunities are endless and, unlike a career or a major that you've already committed to, you can always decide to stop doing it if you change your mind and think it's not right for you. Take advantage of this opportunity to explore a diverse set of options while you can.

# Don't Forget the Minor Decisions

Most colleges offer you the option to choose a second discipline of study as a minor. Why do we consider the extra work and additional requirements to be so advantageous to you? You now have an opportunity to better balance your interests and your goals for your future. You have the ability to hedge your bet on your major. It's not an all-or-nothing decision. Although your major is certainly more important when employers and graduate programs look at your education, your minor also plays a role, especially when it successfully complements your major.

Remember Robert, the student who wasn't sure if he wanted to become a lawyer or a doctor? Choosing to major in chemistry led to one of these future options while choosing to minor in prelaw enabled him to keep other options open. This decision allowed him to avoid having to choose one interest and reject the other early on in his academic career—before he was ready to make this life-determining career decision.

If you're really ambitious, one final choice to consider is to take a double major. A double major allows you to cover a lot more ground and also keeps more options open. It's like taking two moves on the chessboard before your opponent even takes one. The downside is that your workload will be increased, and you may have to make sacrifices to achieve this goal—including spending less time with your friends and on your extracurricular activities. You may also have to sacrifice completing your program in four years if your majors require a higher commitment level, which could lead to a higher total tuition cost for your education. But a double major is definitely a possibility worth thinking about if you want to leave your options open.

## Changing Majors

We all make mistakes in life—and some of them are bigger than others. One common mistake is choosing the wrong major. In fact, a number of studies show that many undergraduates change their major at least once and some students change more than once.

While changing your major during your freshman year may have very little impact on your overall college experience, doing so multiple times or doing so later in your academic career has the potential to cost you dearly. All schools require a minimum number of credits to graduate. These credits are made up of some combination of base (often called core) requirements, the requirements of your major and minor, and the electives that allow you to explore other academic areas. While each school has its own approach to these requirements and each major has its own number of mandatory and elective courses, at some point you will have to focus your efforts more specifically on your major and your minor so you can earn a degree.

When you're considering changing your major, it's important to compare the costs and benefits of continuing on in your current major with the costs and benefits of changing into the new major. If you change your major, how many courses that you've already taken will not count toward your degree? Most won't count for your major, but can you effectively turn your major into your minor and pick up a new major? Are you simply making your minor your major? Or are you picking up a completely new major? By changing majors, will you have enough class time and nonutilized credits remaining so that you can avoid taking additional courses above and beyond the number your school requires? Or will you have to take classes in the summer or stay for more than four years? This extra time in school will cost you financially. You also need to determine how a potential change in major would affect your academic and professional careers. Are you changing because you think you're going to like the subject material better? Are you changing because you think your career will benefit more from the new major?

Perhaps you would be better off making the change, especially if you're in your sophomore year, have taken only a few courses in your major, and can apply the credits you've earned so far in your original major to the overall school requirements, electives, or a minor. On the other hand, you may be better off completing your existing major and either making the new discipline your minor or simply taking a few courses in it to satisfy your interests. This strategy may be best, particularly if you're in your junior or senior year and you would be taking more courses than the minimum your school requires for graduation—costing you both time and money.

We all make mistakes, but choosing the right major the first time can save you a lot of grief, a lot of time and, most importantly, a lot of money.

Choosing a college major is, unfortunately, a decision that many students do incorrectly the first time. It's not the end of the world if you do. But just because you don't think you like your current major doesn't mean that you should necessarily change it at a late date. Early, yes. Late, maybe not. If you're thinking about changing majors, get advice from your parents, your advisor, professors in the department you're thinking about changing into, and even a career counselor. They may have perspectives that you hadn't considered. Once you have evaluated the opinions of others, made an assessment of what the costs and benefits would be of remaining in your major or changing to something else, you can then make an informed decision.

# To Sum Up

How are you going to make your decision about a college major? You could make your decision based only on your interests. Or you could base your decision on the type of job you will get. More likely, and more advisable, is to make this decision based on the goals you've set for your time in college and the effect that your course of study will have on your professional life. Just as you would during a very difficult game of chess, you need to look ahead at future moves rather than moving your piece without thinking. Every single move—and more specifically the early moves in the game—will drastically affect the future moves you can, and can't, make. By considering your college major decision as the opening move in a game of chess and mapping out which options will be open to you and which ones will be closed, you will be able to see the best options for you. You won't regret taking this decision seriously. After all, it is the most major decision of your time at college and most likely the one with the longest-lasting ramifications.

# Chapter 11

# I Know What You Did Last Summer

## Making the Best Decisions to Maximize Your Summers

I n late July, after her junior year in college, Kelly realized she had made some bad decisions. She was reading e-mails from her classmates who described what they were doing in the summer. One friend had an internship in San Francisco, and another was teaching kids in Africa. A third was touring Europe by bike. Kelly was at home waiting tables again for her fourth summer in a row. She came home every summer so she could see her high school friends, some of whom didn't go on to college, but now she realized she was wasting her precious summertime. Like too many college students, Kelly didn't take the time in advance to decide what she should do with her summer.

Ever since childhood, when your parents first sent you to school, you've understood the absolute importance and necessity of summer. The promise of those three months of freedom saw you through some rough times. When you failed that history exam and immediately tore it into pieces, the thought that summertime was coming sustained you.

Through it all, summer break gleamed and shimmered in the near future like a lighthouse guiding you to safety. But now that you're in college, you probably won't need summer vacation the way you used to. College is different, right? It's going to be a constant party with a little studying thrown

Summertime, at last! But will you make it count?

in, right? Plus, you won't have to take any classes you don't want to, so you'll enjoy studying, right? And nobody in college is as stale and immature as those high-school classmates you're leaving behind, right? Everybody is cool, funny, smart, entertaining, and mature, right?

Are you absolutely right on all accounts? College is a magical land where every day is packed with fun and excitement. The word boring will melt away from your vocabulary and your life will become instantly perfect in every way. But for argument's sake, let's say college isn't perfect. Let's pretend that after nine months of 8:00 a.m. classes, 12-page exams, and a hygienically questionable roommate, you find yourself turning to summer for that same support and comfort it provided for so many years before. However, now summer break is filled with even greater promise and opportunity. The resources and options available to college students are limitless. Some will work, while others take classes. Some will move home to reconnect with family and high school friends, while others will spend three months studying abroad in some exotic country. With so many choices, it's easy to get confused and not pursue any real decision. You may not even know where to begin.

## Don't Squander Summertime

A large percentage of students, widely considered to be more than 50 percent don't adequately plan their summer break to their own satisfaction. One of these students, Derek, told us about his mistakes when it came to the summer between his junior and senior years in college. He hadn't given summer much thought, and when he was just one month from the end of classes, he finally began to wonder what he would do. All of his friends were telling him about the exciting experiences they were planning for the coming three months: One was going to intern for a senator on Capitol Hill in Washington, D.C. Another was going to travel to Eastern Europe with his family. And yet another had decided to live with his parents for the summer and work for a family friend as an assistant at a marketing firm. These all sounded very exciting to Derek.

He hadn't found time to think about his summer, mostly because he was so caught up in his current six courses and three time-consuming extracurricular activities. Derek was clearly an outstanding student, but now it was nearly too late for him to plan a summer that would maximize his time, energy, and excitement. Fortunately, one of his professors asked him to fill in for the summer doing research for a book that the professor was working on, since the student assistant he had previously hired for the summer had to refuse the job unexpectedly. Derek was lucky to find this last-minute option. Most students probably wouldn't be this fortunate.

As this example indicates, when making your decision about what to do with your summer, you should start this decision-making process early. Don't wait until the last minute to throw together a haphazard plan. Start considering your options and your goals around the middle of the fall semester and try to start the ball rolling when you come back from winter break. This vague time line does vary, however, depending on what specific activities you want to do, but we'll get to that a bit later.

# Expand Your Horizons

Whether you have one or two ideas about what you want to do this summer or you're overwhelmed by the dozens of options available to you, the best way to achieve what you want is to approach the decision rationally. One student, Christina, didn't necessarily use the process outlined in this chapter to the maximum effectiveness, yet she used her creativity and commitment to achieving her goals to find a way to be involved in exactly the types of activities she wanted to do. Let's use her experience as an example.

## Step 1: Determine Your Objectives and Priorities

The first step is to determine your priorities. What do you want to get out of your summer experience?

🔹 Do you want to make money?

**_Ø_**  Do you want to travel to another country?

**_Ø_**  Do you want to experience life in a big city?

**_Ø_**  Do you want to get professional career experience through an internship?

**_Ø_**  Do you want to spend time at a summer camp?

**_Ø_**  Do you want to spend time back home?

You have to make these decisions for yourself. Not all of these priorities are mutually exclusive—you may actually be able to achieve several of these goals simultaneously, depending upon how you implement your decision. Start the process of deciding how to spend your summer by making a simple list of your priorities in the order that you think you are interested in them. Don't think about feasibility at this point in the process—think only about your hopes and dreams for what you will achieve during the summer. Later in the process you will have the chance to change the order of these priorities and to examine the feasibility of them. Our sample student, Christina, set her priorities in the order shown in Figure 11-1.

Christina had always dreamed of living in New York City and performing on Broadway. (Unfortunately for her, that dream vanished when, after every single time she would sing, she would find her dog cowering under the bed in the room farthest away from where she practiced.) Even though her Broadway bubble had burst, her Manhattan dream still tugged at her. So in December and January of her freshman year—still early enough to keep her options open—she started contemplating what she would do the following summer. Moving back home with her parents lacked appeal. After tasting the freedom of college, she did not want to return to living under parental supervision with curfews and restrictions on watching television. The idea of spending those three months in New York City sounded fabulous to her, but she foresaw a few problems. Where would she live? How would she support herself? She knew her parents weren't going to simply pay for her to live there. In spite of the difficulties she foresaw, she made her list of prioritized objectives before moving on to step 2.

**FIGURE 11-1  Prioritize Your Objectives**

| Rank | Objective |
|------|-----------|
| 1 | Live in New York City |
| 2 | Travel abroad |
| 3 | Travel in the U.S. |
| 4 | Earn college credits |
| 5 | Make or save money |
| 6 | Don't live at home |

# Step 2: Consider All of Your Options

As you begin to mull over your options, you need to recognize the importance of your summer break. It's a gift—three months to accomplish everything you couldn't squeeze into your busy school-year schedule or to take advantage of other opportunities that you don't have available to you during the school year.

When considering your summertime possibilities, remember that this is not a narrow, black-and-white decision. Not only are the options close to limitless, but you can find ways to combine your realistic options with your ideal choice to make a realistically ideal plan. So, let your mind flow. If you restrict your ideas to the traditional options (work, go to school, travel, intern, etc.), you may miss out on other, even more inventive experiences. Also, this list can evolve as you add and delete ideas from it as you work on it.

As Christina began to determine her options, she knew that while she had some difficult logistics to figure out, New York City was still her top choice. She realized she should not rule anything out ahead of time, so she ordered her list from her most favorite to her least favorite. She created a list of options for her summer in a rough order of how she would prefer them, which can be seen in Figure 11-2.

**FIGURE 11-2  Prioritize Your Activities**

| Rank | Activities |
| --- | --- |
| 1 | Live in New York City and don't work or take classes |
| 2 | Take courses at school in New York City to gain credit |
| 3 | Intern in New York City |
| 4 | Work to earn money in New York City |
| 5 | Take courses at current college to gain credit |
| 6 | Work at summer camp I used to attend while in high school |
| 7 | Get an internship somewhere other than New York City |
| 8 | Travel in Europe for the summer |
| 9 | Work with a professor at my college for the summer |
| 10 | Live and work at home for the summer |

As you can tell from her options list, her overriding goal was to be in New York City. In order to actually achieve this, however, she would need to be creative. That's why a large number of her options involved being in the city. After thinking long and hard about it, it suddenly dawned on her that education was a priority for her parents. When it came to Christina furthering her knowledge and progressing in her academic career, they would stop at nothing to help her. So, what if she took summer classes at a school in New York?

After much research, she devised her ideal plan. With financial help from her parents, Christina could attend New York University and take two classes—both of which would transfer to her regular college and gain her eight credit hours. And since she would be a student, she would be eligible to live in New York University housing and receive a meal plan. With a little creativity and research, she had turned her New York City dream into an actual possibility that wouldn't involve living in a run-down apartment and waiting tables to afford to do it. This plan also helped nudge her along the path to her college degree. Obviously, Christina was fortunate that her parents agreed to help her—an advantage that may be unavailable to many students. A similar plan could still be possible for someone who lacked this financial help but other decision steps need to be made to get to this conclusion if you lack your parents' help. At this time in your life you will have more resources at your fingertips than you do after you graduate from college. You should take advantage of the scholarships, grants, and financial aid that are waiting for you in your financial aid office.

## Step 3: Determine How Well the Step 2 Options Meet Your Step 1 Goals

Christina's case may have been a little simpler than it would be for other students since she was very committed to one option—going to New York City. If you are less sure of the goals you want to accomplish, step 3 is actually the most important step, and you should spend some time on it. Christina placed all of the options she designed along one side of a piece of paper, ordering them from her most favorite to her least. She then created one column for each desired accomplishment, in the order from the most important to the least important, from left to right. Once she did this, she then determined whether each of the options would achieve each of her goals by simply going down the list. Her chart looked something like Figure 11-3.

As you can see, she went through all of her options and matched them up with all of the goals she set previously. The first four options enabled her to live in New York City so she put a yes next to all four. The six other options did not so she filled in no for those. The only option allowing Christina to travel abroad was the one to travel in Europe, and while she didn't have a specific option enabling her to travel in the United States, being in New York City involved travel, so she listed the first four as both a yes and a no. The two options that would allow her to earn college credits

**FIGURE 11-3 Match Your Options to Your Goals**

| Options: | Live in NYC | Travel Abroad | Travel in US | Earn Credits | Make $$ | Don't Live at Home |
|---|---|---|---|---|---|---|
| Live in NYC | Yes | No | Yes/No | No | No | Yes |
| Take classes in NYC | Yes | No | Yes/No | Yes | No | Yes |
| Intern in NYC | Yes | No | Yes/No | Yes/No | Yes/No | Yes |
| Work in NYC | Yes | No | Yes/No | No | Yes | Yes |
| Classes at current college | No | No | No | Yes | No | Yes |
| Work at summer camp | No | No | No | No | Yes | Yes |
| Intern not in NYC | No | No | No | Yes/No | Yes/No | Yes |
| Travel in Europe | No | Yes | No | No | No | Yes |
| Work with professor | No | No | No | No | Yes | Yes |
| Live and work at home | No | No | No | No | Yes | No |

(the second and fifth options) both involved taking classes so she put a yes next to them. The two options for internships might or might not grant her college credits—depending upon the type of internship she got and whether she could convince the department at her school to allow her this option—so they rated a yes and a no. In terms of making money, working in New York City, working at the summer camp she used to attend, working with a professor at her school, and working at home all enable her to earn money, while some of the internships she would be considering also offered small stipends for her time. And finally, since she really didn't want to live at home in the summer, none of the options she had come up with placed her at home except for what she considered as her "option of last resort," which was to live and work at home.

By analyzing how well her goals could be achieved with each of the options she had devised, she could then reprioritize her list of options. She decided that her first four options were still her favorites and in the correct order since living in the city was by far her top priority. But she did decide that interning somewhere other than New York City was probably a better option than taking classes at her current college or working at summer camp, so she made that option her new number-five option. She kept all of the others where they were originally. Her list was already very well considered when she began this step; you may need to reprioritize more than Christina did. If you have enough time, put the list aside for a few days and then revisit it to see if you've changed your priorities.

# Step 4: Pursue Each of Your Options

Since not all of your options may be possible, you can't simply choose your top option and pursue it exclusively. You may need to pursue multiple options concurrently to ensure that you have a suitable backup plan. Moreover, just because you have prioritized your options in a particular way doesn't mean that you can pursue your first option first, your second option only if you don't get the first, and so on down your list. Your prioritization has nothing to do with the time frames for pursuing the options, almost all of which are imposed on you by someone other than yourself. A good way to handle the deadlines and be sure that you stay ahead of them is to maintain them in a list that indicates the date for submitting applications or other requirements to achieve that option, as well as the date when you have to accept—and at least tentatively commit to—that option.

Christina's deadlines can be seen in Figure 11-4. As you can probably guess, the deadlines for some of her options were easier for her to indicate than others. For example, taking classes in New York City would require a formal application to New York University, which had both application and acceptance deadlines that were set by the school. Similarly, her current school had its own deadlines. She reviewed the work and internship deadlines and recorded the dates that represented the earlier end of those deadlines. Living at home, working in New York City, traveling and other options had more flexible deadlines, so the dates she set for those largely represented her self-imposed deadlines based upon how long she believed it would take to secure these options. While many of these deadlines were either estimated or flexible, getting these down on paper made it easier to track so that none of her options were ruled out by her lack of timely action on them.

Some of your options may simply be less viable for you than others, and if you know that, you can focus your energies accordingly. For example, if you don't have any money saved, and your parents have told you they won't give you any, backpacking for the entire summer in Europe is pretty unlikely. You should keep it on your list, though, in case you stumble into enough money for the plane trip and food while you're there. If it's your first option and the one that you would do anything to achieve, however, you may want to put all of your energy into achieving this option. Can you work this semester to raise the money? Can you go with some type of organized school or volunteer group that may provide some subsidy or scholarship? Determining the feasibility of your options can help you decide how much or how little effort to put into achieving a particular summer activity.

As you can imagine, pursuing as many of the options as she deemed necessary meant that Christina needed to work on several of them simultaneously. The first one

**FIGURE 11-4   Deadlines**

| Options: | Deadline for Applying | Deadline for Accepting |
|---|---|---|
| Live in NYC | May 1 | May 15 |
| Take classes in NYC | February 1 | March 30 |
| Intern in NYC | March 15 | April 30 |
| Work in NYC | May 1 | May 15 |
| Take classes at current college | April 1 | April 30 |
| Work at summer camp | April 1 | April 30 |
| Intern not in NYC | March 15 | April 30 |
| Travel in Europe | May 1 | May 15 |
| Work with professor | March 15 | April 30 |
| Live and work at home | May 15 | May 30 |

on the list just wasn't going to be feasible. She wouldn't be able to go to New York City without getting credits, getting an internship, or working, so at this point she simply stopped dedicating her energy to that option. She could dream that she could move there without having any responsibilities, but when it was time for her to make a real decision, she stopped dreaming and started planning. She sent in her application to take classes at New York University first and, while waiting for her response, she prepared applications for several internships both in New York City and elsewhere. She also researched jobs in New York City and prepared an application to work at the summer camp.

# Step 5: Make Your Decision

If your first option is feasible logistically and has been offered to you or you qualify for it if you choose it, then take it. If not, you should analyze the remaining options. You've correctly prioritized your list, so you can simply go down it, selecting the first one on the list that's feasible and that you qualify for. If at this point you're starting to think that maybe you're prioritization was wrong, don't worry, it's not too late to revise it. Luckily enough for Christina, she was accepted to her preferred choice, to take courses at New York University, so she stopped working on the other options and enrolled in courses there.

In addition to helping to make the best decision about what to do with your precious summer, using this decision-making process can also help you if you need to "sell," or rationalize, your decision to someone. This process can be especially helpful if you need to convince your parents of the benefits of the option you hope to pursue by showing them that you have put an adequate amount of time, effort, and thought into the decision. Moreover, if you intend to ask for their financial assistance for your options, they will see that you have actually researched the possibilities and have attempted to maximize your goals. By getting their input earlier in the process, you can also solicit their advice, but be careful because they may have different ideas for what constitutes a good summer activity, and if you're not prepared to consider these, you may not want to ask them for their opinions.

> *Note to Parents*
> *Whether it's taking classes, doing an internship, working, or traveling, your children should be prepared to make the most of the limited time they have in the summer.*

## To Sum Up

While it takes more time to use this process than simply choosing one option to pursue or simply moving back in with your parents, this objective approach will ensure you get the highest returns for your time. By expanding your ideas beyond typical summer activities, you may discover a situation that would never have occurred to you had you not devoted the time to follow our recommended five-step process. Don't diminish your best summers yet.

# Chapter 12

## Leaving on a Jet Plane

### Making Good Decisions about Studying Abroad or at Other Colleges

Phil was majoring in international studies at an Ivy League school with the hopes of having a career in either industry or government that would deal with global finance. After a few years of work experience, he planned to get an MBA from one of the leading programs. In his junior year, he arranged to do a semester of study at a college in Shanghai, China, which proved to be invaluable. It gave him an understanding of Chinese culture and helped him master the Chinese language. When Phil graduated from college, he was able to get a great position working in Shanghai for an investment firm.

One of the most exciting and rewarding times that you can have while in college is actually not even at your college—it's when you're studying abroad or even studying for a semester at another school in the U.S. through an exchange program. Never again in your life

*Note to Parents*
*You may think that studying abroad is a waste of time and money, but it can often prove to be one of the most memorable and exciting—not to mention enlightening—parts of college. And it doesn't have to be expensive either!*

are you going to be afforded the opportunity to travel as you would as an undergraduate—living out of your backpack, staying in someone else's house, and eating as cheaply as you possibly can. More importantly, you're unlikely to ever again have the opportunity to travel for the sake of learning and gaining valuable experience, let alone do it for an extended period of time.

Outside of college students, few people are afforded this chance at extended travel, and those who are spend the majority of their time trapped in business meetings, stuck at airports, or confined to military bases. Needless to say, college students are very fortunate to have this option at their disposal. If your college years are something that you wish to cherish forever, you will want to consider studying abroad and learning what it's like to be in, live in, and study in another country, experiencing the country and its culture, people, language, and customs only as someone who stays there for an extended period can. It can prove to be one of the defining events of your entire academic career.

Many decisions go into this process, however. The first and most important of these decisions is, obviously, whether or not you are going to take this step and leave your campus for this great adventure. It is often an exciting opportunity, but one that is full of uncertainty and even some anxiety. In addition to that basic decision, however, other decisions will also need to be made in conjunction with your ultimate yes or no to studying abroad. You'll need to make decisions that answer these questions:

- Where are you going to study?
- How long are you going to stay there?
- What courses are you going to take while there and will they transfer fully to your college?
- What goals in terms of academics, culture, travel, and language do you want to accomplish before returning?
- Do you want to go alone or with someone else from your class?
- Do you want to play it safe in Europe or take a chance in a more exotic location?
- Do you want to arrive early or stay late so you can travel?
- Will you work while there?
- Will you take an internship while there?

The opportunities are enormous. Unfortunately—or fortunately—so are the magnitude and the number of decisions that you need to make.

# Deciding Whether (and When) to Study Abroad

Let's start from the top. If you're absolutely certain that you're going to study abroad or absolutely certain that you're not, go ahead and skip this section of the chapter. But if, like the vast majority of college students, you haven't decided whether a program like this is the right move for you, read on. Most students who study abroad do so in their junior year. The reason for this is that the freshman year is designed to integrate you with your classmates and get your initial course requirements completed. The sophomore year is designed to get you integrated more with your major by beginning to take the foundation courses that will lead you to a degree in a particular field. And your senior year is designed for you to finish all of your course requirements and to have fun while doing so. But what about your junior year? It's perfect for studying abroad.

Is studying abroad really all it's cracked up to be? Oui, oui.

But just because the timing works out doesn't mean that studying abroad is right for everyone. Here are some basic questions that you should ask yourself to determine if you're going to get what you need on a personal level out of your time abroad:

- Am I interested in learning another language?
- Am I interested in learning about another culture?
- Do I like traveling to strange places with people I don't know?
- Am I willing to stay in a stranger's house or foreign dormitory as an exchange student?
- Am I comfortable entering new situations where I won't know anyone?

In addition to these questions, however, you need to ask yourself some specific questions to determine if studying abroad is right for you on an academic level:

- Will I still be able to complete my academic requirements if I study abroad, including my major requirements and my minor requirements?
- If I am involved in extracurricular activities in a leadership role, will I be creating problems for the other leaders of these activities by leaving?
- Will I miss out on opportunities that I am extremely interested in by not being on campus?

These are all questions that you must answer for yourself. You need to prioritize your college goals and define how studying abroad is going to affect these priorities.

One student, Chris, provides us with a good example. During the fall of his junior year, many of his friends were making decisions to go to different places throughout the world for their spring semesters, but Chris was still uncertain. He really wanted to go to an exotic country for a semester to study, but he had a number of other requirements that he had to consider when making his decision. He was very active in the student government and was planning to run for student body president the following year. In addition, the president of the college was retiring, and he was one of the top contenders to serve as the student representative on the college's search committee to find a new president—an extremely prestigious position.

In the end, he decided not to go abroad and stayed at his college, becoming one of the most involved students in both the student government as well as in working with the administration. He was elected as the student body president and was also selected to be a member of the presidential search committee and ended up being happy that he had stayed on his campus instead of going abroad for his spring semester. Several years after he graduated, we had the opportunity to reconnect with him. When we asked him about studying abroad and his decision to stay and increase his involvement with college activities, he still was confident that he made the correct decision to stay on campus that spring. He did, though, express remorse that he hadn't studied abroad during another time—for example, one summer or semester of his sophomore year. His friends who had studied abroad talk about their experiences to this day, and he wishes he had been able to both study abroad and be as involved as he was on his campus. But he knew he had to choose one or the other at the time, and he still stands by his decision.

> **Advantages of Studying Abroad:**
> - Learning a new language
> - Traveling
> - Meeting new people
> - Learning about a new culture
> - Getting a break from your school

Look at what you hope to accomplish in college and determine if studying abroad outweighs the other activities that you would be sacrificing. Whether you decide to study abroad or to stay on campus, not making a decision would be worse than either of those *conscious* decisions.

# Benefits of Studying Abroad

It's also important to understand some of the benefits, both short term and long term, of studying abroad before you make your decision. Many students—and parents—simply dismiss studying abroad as a waste of time and money. But consider the advantages that will stay with you forever. People who have studied abroad talk about the people they met, the culture and languages they learned, their travels, and the overall experience they had. In addition, a lot of benefits will stay with you for the long run and could even impact the rest of your academic and professional careers. These benefits include not only intercultural development but also personal development, academic development, and career development.

In 2004, the Institute for the International Education of Students (IES) completed a study of 3,700 students who participated in study abroad programs from 1950 through 1999—a 50-year period. The study asked these alumni a series of questions about the long-term benefits of their experiences studying abroad. Here is a short breakdown of what respondents said about studying abroad:

Personal development:

- 96 percent of respondents said it increased their self-confidence
- 97 percent said it served as a catalyst for increased maturity
- 95 percent said it had a lasting impact on their world view

Academic commitment:

- 80 percent said it enhanced their interest in academic study
- 87 percent said it influenced subsequent educational experiences
- 86 percent said it reinforced their commitment to the study of a foreign language

Intercultural development:

- 98 percent said it helped them to better understand their own culture, values, and biases
- 90 percent said it influenced them to seek out greater diversity and friends
- 94 percent said it continues to influence their interaction with people from different cultures

Career development:

- 76 percent said it enabled them to acquire a skill set that influenced their career path

❶ 62 percent said it ignited interest in a career direction they pursued after the experience

Complete study results can be found at the IES Abroad Web site (http://www.ies abroad.com).

As you can see, the long-term benefits of studying abroad are significant. Pushing it aside as an option simply because it seems to be a waste of time and money doesn't sufficiently take into account the important impact studying abroad may have on your personal, academic, and professional life.

## But There's No Way I Can Afford It

Some of the greatest resistance to participating in a study abroad program is its associated cost. Before you rule it out as an option because of cost alone, however, investigate it a little further. Many study abroad programs are remarkably affordable. In fact, programs can cost as little as $3,000 per semester or as much as $20,000 per semester for tuition. Compared to the amount your school costs, some programs could actually be a pretty good deal. But, don't forget the associated costs, many of which have the ability to add a much higher price tag to this total. For example, many programs don't include the costs of room and board in the tuition costs. In fact, some don't give you the option to stay in a dorm, and if that's the case, then you need to consider the costs of renting an apartment. If you're going to be staying in a home with a family, you won't have to foot this bill. In addition to the housing costs, don't forget that, being in a new city with new and exciting sites to see, you're going to want to go out with friends, go to the museums, and travel around the city and the country. All of that will cost money. But at least those expenses can be budgeted based upon what you can afford. You must pay for the tuition, and you must pay for housing and for food. Everything else is just a bonus.

Another consideration is the cost of travel to and from your destination. Depending upon where you go, what time of year you fly, and how far in advance you buy your ticket, these costs can add up. Moreover, if you're going to spend an entire year abroad or even an extended semester (which many countries have), you may need to consider whether you're going to plan on coming back home for any holidays or special events.

Also be sure to find out how studying abroad is going to affect your financial aid and your loans. Your college may be willing to continue your existing loans for your study abroad program, but you need to work with them to determine if this is possible and how any expenses above and beyond your tuition costs at your home institution will be handled. Likewise for any federal or private loans that you may have. Most programs that are completed in coordination with your college are set up so that you pay your existing college tuition, and the program administrators, in turn, pay the college where you're going to study abroad, so your overall loan structure will remain intact. Again, you'll need to work with your study abroad office to determine the specifics at your school.

Not all study abroad programs are actually more expensive than your tuition, however. One student, Kevin, who attended a liberal arts college in upstate New York, decided to study abroad in London during the spring semester of his junior year. London is a very expensive city, and tuition at the universities there is also expensive. Kevin decided to participate in a program that was administered through his own school, which meant that he paid his regular tuition to the school for that semester, and his school paid the school in London. His regular tuition costs (not including room and board) actually covered both his tuition and his room and board at the school in London. Even more shocking, though, was that when it came time to leave for London, the program coordinator told him and the other students in the program that the school had opened bank accounts for each of them in London and deposited £1,500 into each of them. Kevin was amazed. He suddenly had money to do some of the activities that he didn't think he would be able to afford. Moreover, they also had a separate fund that each student could draw from for any cultural activities they wanted to do, including going to museums, plays, certain local travel, and other activities.

So, like Kevin, you may be surprised that you could actually pay less for a study abroad program than you would for staying at your own college for the semester. If you're concerned about the costs of studying abroad, before making a decision without determining the costs, talk with the advisor in your study abroad office. He or she will be able to help you figure out the program that makes the most sense for you.

## So Many Options

Once you've decided that you want to study abroad, you have to make the important decision about where to study. The options are limitless. You can study in one of the more commonly selected places such as England, France, Germany, Italy, Spain, or Mexico. You can study in one of the more exotic places such as any of the countries in Africa, Asia, and the Middle East. Some study abroad programs are offered by sister schools in other countries. Some programs are through major universities in the United States that specialize in study abroad opportunities. Some are less-traditional programs that combine some level of work, internships, independent study, volunteerism, and traditional study. The downside to having so many options is that you really need to sift through them all to find which one is right for you. It can be a lot of work. But given the large number of options, you can rest assured that you will be able to find a program that is perfect for you.

> **Three Reasons Not to Choose a Study Abroad Program:**
> - Because a friend is going to the same program
> - Because you knew someone who went to that country and liked it
> - Because you've heard they party a lot there

Here is a more in-depth look at the various program options. Keep in mind, however, that not all of these will be available through your school's study abroad office, and some of them may not be accepted for credit by your school. While you may be able to convince your school to accept credits from any of a number of options, you need to pay careful attention to that before committing to something that is going to cost you money and prevent you from reaching your graduation goals in the time frame you had laid out for yourself.

Essentially two types of programs are available, each with its own variations. The first are traditional academic programs, which consist of coursework that you would transfer into your school as credits toward your graduation. The second are programs that have a more experiential component to them, including but not limited to internships, immersion programs, and volunteer programs that are usually completed in coordination with some type of academic study as well.

The most common study abroad programs are those that can be considered more traditional. These programs essentially consist of taking courses at an accredited university in another country. These generally include three types of programs. The first type includes programs that are offered in direct coordination with your college, usually through a formal agreement between the two schools. The benefit of these programs is that all of the courses that you could possibly take—or at least the vast majority of them—would be eligible for credit at your institution. This is a very important advantage, and it can definitely make your life easier. If you have to convince your school that the classes you take when you're abroad are substantially similar to the ones you would take at your own school, the process will likely involve a lot of paperwork.

The second type of traditional university study abroad program includes those that are very well-established programs but are not directly affiliated with your college. You can usually get your credits transferred very easily, but the process will be less automatic than if you use a program that has an agreement with your home institution. The benefit of going to a program that is unaffiliated with your college is that the diversity of programs available to you will be significantly higher. If you're looking for a program that is less traditional or in a less well-traveled area, you may have to seek out programs that aren't the most readily available ones in your school's study abroad office.

If you're looking for something that's even more exotic or in a location that is remote or much less traveled, you may have to look a little farther away from the more established programs that are available. You can probably study at any school in the world that offers a similar level of coursework as your college. If you want to study in a remote location in China or in Siberia, for example, you probably can. But you're going to have to do a lot more work to make it happen. You're going to have to work with the institution you want to attend to be accepted, and you're going to have to convince your college to accept the foreign credits you earn. Foreign colleges operate differently than American ones, and credit transfers are anything but automatic. But some of the best study abroad experiences can come from these more exotic schools, so if you think this is what you want to do, be prepared to do more work to make it happen.

In addition to the typical academic programs, a wide variety of nontraditional programs are available to you. These programs, which range from internships to volunteer opportunities to other completely unique immersion programs, are usually specifically designed to provide you with some type of experiential education, be it for professional career purposes, your own satisfaction, or to help you specialize in a particular academic field of study. These programs can actually be some of the most exciting and rewarding programs. For example, a great program in Washington, D.C., is called the Washington Semester. While not actually a study abroad program, it will provide you with many great experiences. It offers an internship in the U.S. Congress, the White House, or a government agency while concurrently requiring you to take one or two courses related to U.S. government. This program is very popular because it really helps you to gain insight into working in the federal government and in politics. For most institutions, the credits are all directly transferrable back to your school.

There are other similar programs throughout the world that work to increase your professional and personal skills while also enabling you to continue your academics. These are too numerous to list, but they include specialized programs in the sciences, including physics, chemistry, biology, and others; language immersion programs of every possible language you could imagine; programs specializing in art history in Venice; marine biology specialization programs that enable you to spend a semester at sea on a boat; and specialized programs in engineering, music, astronomy, computer science, or theater. You can find programs for almost anything else you can possibly imagine, most of which are located in areas famous for their field of study and with resources that cannot be matched elsewhere.

Since so many programs are available, you should use the resources at your disposal to find the perfect fit for you. Start your research at your school's study abroad office. Also, online resources are extremely helpful in locating programs, especially because you can search by country, length of the program, requirements, and academics. (A very good resource we recommend is http://www.StudyAbroad.com.) In addition, you should talk with your parents, with other students, with your professors, and with your academic advisor to find out information either about specific programs or about the types of countries or institutions you should consider.

# Know Yourself and Your Goals

How do you sort through all of these thousands of program options? Before you start considering which study abroad program you should choose for yourself, look at the goals you're trying to accomplish. Once you determine these, you will be able to sift through the options and come up with the one that is perfect for you.

The first questions to ask yourself are: Why do you want to study abroad? What are you hoping to accomplish while you're there? What do you need to do to make it align with your academic and personal needs and wishes? Answering the following questions will provide you with a starting point from which to look at programs and countries:

- Are you interested in learning a new language? If so, what is your current level of understanding of the language you seek to learn? (Remember, classes for many programs—even countries where English is not typically spoken—are taught in English, so don't rule these out yet.)

- Are you interested in gaining professional experience to help with your career, to help you get a job, or to help you get into graduate school? If so, are you hoping to have a job or participate in an internship or a volunteer program while studying abroad?

- Are you interested in learning about another culture?

- Are you hoping to obtain academic breadth or specialization that you can't get at your school?

- What do you like to do in your spare time (go to museums or plays, hike, be on the water, etc.)?

- Are you the type of person who would prefer to live in a big city, a small city, or a more rural area?

- What is your level of independence? Would you feel more comfortable spending a lot of time with other Americans or would you feel comfortable being one of only a few Americans in your study abroad program?

- What type of living situation would you find most comfortable? Would you be comfortable staying in a home with a local family? Or would you prefer to live in a dormitory or an apartment?

- Do you need a program with courses that will satisfy specific academic requirements in terms of your major, your minor, or your basic college core requirements?

These questions will start you thinking about who you are, what you want to accomplish, and how to approach your evaluation of the different study abroad programs.

## Choosing the Right Option

Now that you've begun to understand the goals that you're hoping to achieve while you're studying out of the country, you need to begin to evaluate all of the different options available to you. Like many of the other decisions that you make in college, this one will require you to look at a number of options and assess their strengths compared to your needs. Based on some of the questions posed above, you should be able to evaluate what you need in a program and what you want to take away from your time studying abroad.

The next step is to do a basic, preliminary evaluation of the available programs. Speak with your advisor, your parents, your friends, and—most importantly—the study abroad office. Tell them what you're looking for and what you want out of a program. Discuss possible countries that you think you may enjoy. Ask them to suggest other countries you hadn't considered and ask them to tell you about various programs with which they're familiar. Study the ideas they give you and search out other options online. Find out more about the countries that you're considering and the opportunities to travel there. Try to imagine what it would be like to live in these locations for an extended time frame. If you've never been there before, you may have a difficult time imagining this, but you should be able to get some sense of what it will be like. Even though you're not going to be moving there forever, you should still be working to find a location where you will feel comfortable and be able to enjoy yourself.

After compiling the information about the programs that interest you, narrow your choices to the top programs you're considering. Talk again with your parents, your friends, your advisor, and your study abroad advisor. Discuss with them why you're thinking about these particular programs as your finalists. Once you've established your finalists (we think it's easier to make a decision if you have fewer than five finalists), analyze how well each of them will help you achieve your personal, academic, cultural, and professional goals. Put the options side by side to see which goals you will be able to accomplish with each of them.

Let's use an example. During the spring semester of his sophomore year, Ben decided that he wanted to spend his entire junior year studying abroad. He determined that studying abroad would be a great experience and an excellent opportunity for him to spend some time in another country while learning about its culture and traveling. But he was having a difficult time prioritizing what he wanted to accomplish and analyzing the benefits and drawbacks of his many options. After extensive research, he refined his program choices to five very different locations: London, Paris, Sydney, Amman, and Beijing. He just couldn't decide yet whether he wanted a more traditional location, such as London or Paris, or a more exciting location, such as Sydney, Amman, or Beijing.

Once he had his five finalists, Ben began to research the qualities of each of them based upon what he was hoping to get out of his experience. In Figure 12-1, you can see how he evaluated each program according to the same criteria. These criteria include: the opportunity to learn a new language; whether the courses would be taught in English; the ease of transferring credits back to his college; his level of interest in the coursework; whether the courses he would take would satisfy his major, minor, or core curriculum requirements; the living arrangements associated with the program; whether housing options were guaranteed; how much the program would cost; whether the program provided opportunities to develop professional or career skills; whether the program provided opportunities to travel in surrounding areas, and the ease of doing so; his general level of excitement about the location; the size of the city where the program is located; whether he had an opportunity to do an internship while there; whether he had an opportunity to do independent research for credit while there; the relative level of safety of the area; and the distance from home.

Here's a quick breakdown of how he assessed each program. He would have the opportunity to learn a new language in Paris, Amman, and Beijing, but not in London or Sydney. (Because he wasn't certain about his ability to pick up the languages very quickly, though, his concern about this factored into his considerations about whether to go a location where people speak a different language.) Luckily, though, all of the programs had courses taught in English since the programs were all associated with some type of organized study abroad program, rather than being universities to which he was applying on his own. The one exception was the program in Paris, which required him to take a portion of his coursework in French, a language he had taken for two semesters already. The London and Paris programs were directly associated with his college so the credit transfer process was automatic, and the program in Sydney was associated with a sister school so the credit transfer process was still pretty easy. While he was confident he would be able to transfer his credits from the programs in Amman and Beijing based on discussions with the study abroad advisor and the registrar at his college, he would be required to complete some additional paperwork to do so.

In terms of his living arrangements, Ben was uneasy about doing a home stay since he valued his independence and didn't like working around someone else's schedule. But he also was concerned about being responsible for finding an apartment, which he would have to do in Sydney, as housing wasn't guaranteed. The coursework at the programs in Amman and Beijing was by far more interesting for him since he could study Middle Eastern or Eastern cultures and history, topics that intrigued him, but the work in the other programs was also of interest. All of the programs, additionally, would provide him with credits to satisfy requirements for his major, which was history, as well as some of the core requirements for his school.

Looking at the costs, including tuition, room and board, and personal and transportation expenses, the programs in London, Paris, and Amman were moderately expensive, while the programs in Sydney and Beijing were higher. He believed that all of the programs would provide him with professional and career skills, either by helping him gain an understanding of the country, the language, the culture, or by other means. In terms of travel opportunities, the only limitations were associated with the programs in Amman and Sydney. Travel opportunities were limited in Sydney because of the need to fly anywhere he would want to visit. His travel opportunities in Amman were limited because some travel barriers existed in the Middle East and because he felt reluctant to go on his own to some of the places he wanted to visit. The programs in London and Paris were only moderately exciting for him. Although he did like both cities, he had already been to both on a number of occasions. The prospect of living in Sydney and Beijing definitely excited him, but he seemed to be the most excited by the prospect of living in Amman. While he wasn't certain if a city's size was a limiting factor for him yet, he decided that it would be prudent to take city size into consideration anyway. Likewise, he wasn't certain that he wanted to do either an internship or perform any independent research, but he decided to include these opportunities on his breakdown to keep his options open. In addition to these primary considerations, he thought it was a good idea to add two more categories: the safety of the area and the distance from home. These two wouldn't be primary factors in his decision, but if all other aspects of the programs were equal, he thought they could play some role in his decision.

After he compiled this information on a sheet of paper, as seen in Figure 12-1, he spent about two weeks considering the different options before making a decision. He tacked the list on the wall above his desk as a reminder. He also took the sheet with him when he met with his advisor one day, and he e-mailed it to his parents.

**FIGURE 12-1   Matching Your Options to Your Goals**

| Goals: | Program in London | Program in Paris | Program in Sydney | Program in Amman | Program in Beijing |
|---|---|---|---|---|---|
| Learn new language | No | Yes | No | Yes | Yes |
| Courses taught in English | Yes | Yes/No | Yes | Yes | Yes |
| Easy transfer of credits | Very Easy | Very Easy | Easy | Less Easy | Less Easy |
| Living arrangements | Dorm | Home Stay | Apartment | Dorm | Dorm |
| Guaranteed housing | Yes | Yes | No | Yes | Yes |
| Level of interest in courses | Medium | Meduim | Medium | High | High |
| Courses satisfy requirements | Yes | Yes | Yes | Yes | Yes |
| How high will the costs be | Medium | Meduim | High | Medium | High |
| Develop career skills | Yes | Yes | Yes | Yes | Yes |
| Opportunity to travel | Yes | Yes | Yes/No | Yes/No | Yes |
| Excitement about location | Medium | Meduim | High | Very High | High |
| City size | Large | Large | Medium | Large | Very Large |
| Internship opportunity | Yes | Yes | Yes | No | No |
| Independent research | Yes | No | No | Yes | Yes |
| Other factor #1 (safety) | Very Safe | Very Safe | Very Safe | Less Safe | Less Safe |
| Other factor #2 (distance) | Close | Close | Very Far | Far | Very Far |

The thorough and analytical approach the list represented signaled to them that Ben was making his decision in an informed way, which encouraged them to support his decision. Ultimately, after getting more advice from his parents, his advisor, and his study abroad office, he selected the program in Amman. He continues to believe this was a good choice, and he's glad that he spent the extra time and effort to make the decision using this process. He had indeed moved away from his initial thought that he would simply go to England because it offered an easier program without a language barrier. He was so thrilled with his Amman experience, the program, his travels, and the amount of Arabic he had picked up that he credits the program with changing his life and his future career goals.

## To Sum Up

When you're considering whether to study abroad and which program to pick, it's important to do thorough research and spend the necessary time evaluating each of your options. Taking the easiest programs, while requiring the least amount of effort, quite often also provides smaller rewards. Nobody can tell you what your priorities are or how to weigh the different aspects of each program. But that doesn't mean that you can't—or shouldn't—do so for yourself. It will make a world of difference.

# Chapter 13

# It's Not You— It's Me

## Should You Divorce Your University and Transfer to Another?

Juan was unhappy during his first year at college. He hadn't made any good friends, the school was too far away from home to visit his old friends, and he didn't enjoy the courses he was taking. He looked back on how he made his application and acceptance decisions and realized he just didn't take enough time to make a good decision. By spring he realized that he wanted to transfer to another school, but it was too late to apply. So, still unhappy, he started his second year. His grades began to suffer as he wasted time playing video games and talking with his friends back home. After that semester, Juan decided not to go back, but again he was too late to apply for a transfer. For the next six months, he was indecisive about applying to another school, so he moved back home and worked for a while. When he realized that he needed to reapply to go to another school, the process was

> ### Note to Parents
> *You may think that your children are overreacting about wanting to transfer. Maybe they are. But maybe they have valid reasons for considering it. Listen to what they have to say and advise them as to what you think will be best for them.*

overwhelming so he decided to simply take some night classes at a local junior college. Juan may never complete college because he missed his opportunity to be decisive about transferring to another college when he should have embraced it.

"I can't take one more semester at this place." Most college students have that feeling at one point or another. But whether that feeling is so strong and poignant that it merits transferring to a different school is another matter altogether. Academic stresses and social pressures are common at all colleges. But, we all make mistakes, and choosing the wrong college can be one of these. Nonetheless, transferring may not be the best solution. Before you decide, it's important first to very seriously analyze why you think you want to change schools. Second, define the ramifications of changing schools. And finally, pinpoint the circumstances that would make a transfer be preferable to remaining at your school.

Believe it or not, studies show that up to 30 percent of U.S. college students transfer at least once, including some students who transfer multiple times. In fact, as many as 2.5 million students change schools in any given year. (Keep in mind, however, some of the data can be misleading since the numbers can include students who simply take one or more courses at a different school—not students who actually transfer from one institution to another.) Some of those changes are warranted. Others are capricious. It is important for you to understand that transferring schools is unlikely to solve all of your problems and may create more for you. In this chapter we summarize some of the good and bad reasons to decide to transfer and give you a process for making that decision.

# Good Reasons to Decide to Transfer

How do you know if your reasons for transferring are good ones? The following are some viable reasons to decide to transfer, along with some factors to consider in your decision.

## 1. Upgrading

One very good reason to decide to transfer schools is to upgrade academically. If you didn't get into your top choice school when you originally applied, or if you've suddenly had an academic epiphany and have been getting straight As in college, in contrast to your less-than-stellar performance in high school, you may be a candidate for an academic upgrade. A portion of your future career could depend on what college you graduate from, especially if the difference is between a second-tier school and an Ivy League school.

If you believe that you've simply hit the wall at your existing school, the school is not challenging enough, and it doesn't have enough advanced-level courses for your liking, this may be a reason to consider transferring. But beware that if you're simply looking for a school with a bigger name, be sure that you're not moving from a school that's in the middle range to another that's also in the middle range, but only marginally higher. Moving from a lower-rated school to a highly rated school is worthwhile, but a small change may not be worth the effort. Even if the change is a major upgrade, you should not automatically transfer.

> **Good Reasons to Consider Transferring:**
> - Academic upgrade
> - Academic specialization
> - Family obligations
> - Financial constraints
> - Social issues
> - Academic downgrading

One student, Roger, was considering transferring after his sophomore year at a small liberal arts college. He had very strong grades, was extremely involved in student government and administrative activities at the college, and had a very good social life. It wasn't that he didn't like his school—in fact, he loved it. He was just curious about whether he would get a better education and be more competitive professionally if he earned a degree from a top school. He was intrigued by the possibility of graduating from a great school. He consulted with his parents, friends, professors, and his advisor. In the end, he decided to stay where he was.

A comment from his advisor was the tipping point that persuaded Roger to remain. The advisor honestly explained the benefits of going to a better school, as well as some of the drawbacks, but Roger was ultimately convinced when his advisor said, "If you stay here, you will be a big fish in a small pond, but if you transfer, you will be a small fish in a big pond." Roger thought about this idea. He realized that he was in a unique position at his school due to his involvement in school activities. These activities allowed him to associate with many of the deans as well as the president of the college. Thus, he was already regarded as a student leader, even as a sophomore. He realized that moving to a much larger university, particularly coming in halfway through, offered little hope of gaining a comparable leadership position.

## 2. Academic Specialization

Another valid reason to consider a transfer is if you want to major in a course of study that is more specialized than what your current school offers. Many colleges, particularly smaller colleges, offer a more limited set of options when it comes to majors. Others may have a wide variety of majors but still be relatively limited in terms of the specializations available within a given major. If that's the case, and you feel that you wouldn't be learning what you need to at your current school, then transferring may be the best option. For example, say you now realize that you want to be a doctor, but your college doesn't offer the requisite premed courses. Under such circumstances, you may need to go elsewhere. But if you've decided that you want to major in turf grass science, then you've got some serious thinking to do. Specialized majors can certainly land you a great job after graduation, but you're also going to be extremely limited in your future careers—hence the term specialized. Be sure to consider that before transferring. Would you be better off majoring in environmental science, environmental engineering, biology, chemistry, or one of the other sciences while taking classes for your independent focus and possibly doing independent study in turf grass science?

## 3. Family Obligations

Many students who decide to transfer do so because of family obligations, including changing family situations such as illnesses. If you have a family member who is sick, and you need to move closer to home to help take care of your relative or simply need to be close by, then transferring to a college that's not quite so far away may be a good option for you. Similarly, many students may be attending a school close to home due to family obligations, but then the family is required to move to a different location. If that's the case, and you need to stay with your family, then you may decide to transfer to a different college near the new location. If you think you need to change schools because of family obligations, you need to be very certain that you're not overcomplicating the situation. Are you confusing your *desire* to be closer to home with your actual *need* to be? What do your parents and other family members think?

## 4. Financial Constraints

It's also quite common for students to decide to transfer schools because they can no longer afford to stay at their current school. Financial situations change, and sometimes students overextend themselves financially. Financial difficulties can occur for a number of reasons. For example, your college's financial aid package may have been altered, the amount that your parents can provide may have changed, or tuition may have increased. If any of these are the case, before rushing into transferring to a college that is a more affordable but possibly inferior college, first review your options to stay where you are. Talk to your parents about their ability to keep you on track at your current school. Talk to your school's financial aid officer to see if other options are available for covering the new expenses. Could you find new loan sources? Could you work part-time for a professor, in the library, or elsewhere? Could you get some type of fellowship to cover a portion of your tuition? Before jumping into transferring schools, take into account that you may have other options. But if you can't find a solution, and you really need to go somewhere that isn't so expensive, then this may be a legitimate reason to decide to transfer.

### 5. Social Issues

Many times, students get to college and realize that they just don't fit in. The social situation turns out to be the complete opposite of what they anticipated. Perhaps the other students aren't serious enough about academics and simply party too much, or perhaps it's the other way around, and they could be too serious about their studies and rarely have any fun. Before resolving to transfer in this case, remember that most schools have a wide range of students. Maybe you're not hanging out with the right ones. Give yourself a few more chances to find those friends who are right for you. If you still can't connect with the type of people you enjoy, then consider transferring as a last resort.

### 6. Downgrading

Academic downgrading is one of those dilemmas that could be considered a good reason to transfer or a terrible reason. College is difficult, but it's difficult everywhere you go. If you're simply looking for an easier school because you feel overburdened by your courses, make the effort to find out the underlying reasons you feel this way. On the other hand, if you're absolutely convinced that you're going to fail and not graduate, you may want to consider the options available for transferring to another school that would increase your opportunity to graduate. Finding this type of option is extremely challenging, but not out of the question. No schools will tell you that their coursework is easy—and it shouldn't be easy. But certainly some schools are less difficult and have fewer advanced-level requirements than others. However, before you rush into changing schools without thinking about it, try to get some extra help at your current school. Maybe you simply need different study habits. Maybe you need a tutor. Maybe you need a different major. Talk with your parents if you're concerned, as well as to your advisor. None of them want to see you fail. They all want you to succeed, and they're there to help you do so.

## Not So Good Reasons for Deciding to Transfer

Of course, people cite many other reasons to decide to transfer. Among them are the following bad reasons:

## 1. You're in Love

Love can be great, but it can also be a terrible reason to decide to transfer schools. If you're in love and can't stand to be without your significant other for another second longer, you may have the urge to transfer to be nearby. Our advice is to consider your decision long and hard before packing your bags. Will you be happy at the new school in all other respects outside of being with your boyfriend or girlfriend? What if you break up? If you do break up, would you still be happy at the school without your significant other? Or would you want to be as far away from that person as possible and transfer yet again? What if moving so close to one another makes you realize that your relationship isn't as strong as you thought? Maybe it is strong enough to last, but if that's the case, it's probably also strong enough to last until college is over, when you can finally move close enough together to see each other every day. Remember, you can still see each other during the summers, winter and spring breaks, holidays, and weekends.

**Bad Reasons to Consider Transferring:**

• Love
• Bad roommates
• Bad professors
• Homesickness

## 2. Your Roommates Are Mean

Ask any college student and they'll likely be able to tell you a horror story about a college roommate that happened either to them or to one of their friends. Roommates simply don't always get along. In fact, some end up detesting one another. With any luck, that won't happen to you, but having roommates who are mean is no justification to transfer. Transferring rooms, yes. Transferring schools, no. Once you no longer live with this person (or people), you won't ever have to talk to them again. If you can't change your roommate situation no matter how hard you try, remind yourself that you won't have to live with this person again next year. Moreover, remember that you have no guarantee that you'll get a roommate you're going to like at any other school. Every college has students who make lousy roommates, so changing to another school won't solve your problem. If you're still convinced you want to transfer schools because of a bad roommate, you may actually have another reason that is pushing you in that direction.

## 3. The Professors Are Bad

Every school has professors that specific students don't like and don't think should be teaching. That's part of the diversity of any faculty. And let's face it, nobody's perfect, not even professors. Sometimes they have a bad day—or a bad semester. But if you don't like a particular professor (or two, or three, or six), don't take any more classes with him or her. You're bound to find professors who you do actually like and who are very well qualified to teach you. Avoid using your feelings about a professor as a reason to transfer.

> Transferring schools may be the best option for you, but it will likely include making some difficult decisions and handling some difficult situations.

### 4. The School Is Too Far from Home

Feeling that your school is too far away from your home is another reason that isn't so cut and dried and can serve either as a good or a bad reason to transfer. As mentioned previously, if extenuating circumstances require you to be closer to home, that is certainly a valid reason to transfer. If you're just homesick and miss your parents, you may want to reconsider.

# Kinks in the Road

Transferring is not as easy as just saying, "I want to go somewhere else," and then leaving. The change will likely include a lot of emotion, additional tuition costs and other expenses, personal upheaval, and even uncertainty. The really bad news is that it will also entail repeating virtually the entire process of applying to college. Remember what you endured the first time? Now you have to go through it all over again while you're concurrently doing all of your college-level coursework. Even with all of these downsides, however, transferring may still be worth it. Let's take a quick look at what will change in your life and how a transfer to another school will affect you.

### 1. Leaving Your Friends

While you may be transferring schools because you don't like the social scene or for any of the other reasons that have been discussed, you're going to have to leave people you have come to call your friends. Strong friendships can last through distance, but knowing that won't make leaving your friends any less difficult. You won't realize how tough it could be until it comes to that moment when you have to say goodbye, maybe for good or maybe just for now. We're often told that the most difficult part of transferring is the loss of friendships that have been cultivated during a student's time at college, and we really can't over-emphasize the importance of considering this before you make your decision about transferring.

## 2. Missing Out and Repeating Yourself

Just when you think that you're not going to have to repeat those terrible first weeks at college you experienced when you were a freshman, you'll find yourself reliving that situation if you transfer. It will be even more difficult to try to fit in with students who have already lived, studied, and partied together since they arrived at the school as freshmen. You may think that, as someone who's already completed one or more semesters in college, you're more professional and above the petty issues that arise when students just get to college. Maybe you are. But that doesn't mean that you're going to fit in right away with students who already have established relationships. This is a major do-over—you're going to have to repeat all of your attempts to become close with other students in the new school. While they've already solidified their cliques and friendship bases, you're going to have to try to break into them if you're going to have a good time throughout the remainder of college. And there's no guarantee that you will ever fit in perfectly after you transfer.

## 3. Juggling

You probably remember that applying to college the first time was very stressful and time consuming. The process is only going to be more difficult the second time around. While you may have been in AP courses or other difficult classes as a senior in high school, they probably were not nearly as challenging as what you're experiencing in college. Moreover, you'll need to maintain good grades in order to be accepted as a transfer student, so letting them slide while you're involved in completing the transfer application process is a problem to avoid. You will likely be very stressed for time if you decide to transfer, so you should be aware of that and take it into account in any decision that you make.

## 4. Credits and GPA

Another aspect to consider is whether the new college will accept all of the credits you've earned so far at your existing school. Many colleges will only allow credit transfers for courses in which you've received at least a C. Others set the bar much higher. In addition to this, you may have problems when it comes to transferring the credits for your core curriculum requirements and also the requirements for your major and minor. Even if you're planning on staying in the same major, college admissions personnel typically assume that other schools can't teach the same information as well as their college can. Whether that's true or not, they won't bend their own rules for you. So, if you're a psychology major and want to transfer into the psychology department at your new school, be prepared for the possibility that you may have to take not only introduction to psychology again, but you may also lose the credits that you've already earned in psychology altogether.

Your core curriculum requirements may also be at risk. Most schools have their own very specific idea of what should be required for any basic college education. So if you've already taken those pesky liberal studies courses, don't expect those credits to transfer over completely. The core and major credits may count as credit toward graduation at your new school, but the chances of them counting against specific requirements are lower. In addition, while credits may transfer, the likelihood of your GPA transferring is very small. Make sure to find out if your grades will transfer rather than assuming they will.

> Most schools will accept transfer applications, but not all schools will actually enroll a high number of transfer students.

## The Transfer Process

Schools' transfer rates vary widely—some accept virtually no transfer students, while others accept an enormous number of them. That being said, all schools generally accept transfer *applications*, but they don't necessarily *enroll* all of the students who apply. So if you've got your hopes up for transferring to Harvard or Yale, you should examine how many students they're planning to accept for the semester you're looking into before you cancel your enrollment at your current school.

We've stated that the application process to transfer requires repeating the process that you already completed for acceptance to the school you're attending. That's true, but it's only part of the equation. While you'll definitely have to complete the application, including the essays, the recommendations, and all of the requirements (including possibly having to take the SATs or ACTs again!), you're also going to have to go above and beyond. Consider the following requirements colleges may have as you determine whether to transfer:

- ❗ *A specific number of credits*—Many colleges will only accept transfer students whose number of credits fall into a particular range. For example, you may not be a good transfer candidate if you have completed more than two years of courses.

- ❗ *Good grades*—Colleges don't have to accept you as a transfer student, so if you've only received marginal grades, and you're trying to be accepted to a better school than your current one, you may need to reconsider this plan. While you may have earned straight As in high school, if you don't have excellent college grades, you're going to be much less competitive.

❶ *Extracurricular activities*—You may remember from when you first applied to colleges that many colleges want to see that you're well-rounded and able to successfully manage your time. You are expected to be able to complete your academic requirements while handling involvement in an array of other activities. Don't expect that to be any less important this time around. You need to show that you have a lot going for you and that their institution would be better off with you there. Extracurricular activities are a great way to demonstrate this.

❶ *New recommendations*—While those high school teacher recommendations probably helped get you into your existing college, don't assume that they alone will get you into your transfer school. Instead, you will need to show that you've impressed at least one professor in your current school. Even though you will need to tell your professors that you're planning on leaving them, having recommendations from professors with whom you've studied will let your new school know that you are the type of student it is looking for.

❶ *A good reason, which you make clear to the school*—You may have a perfectly great reason to transfer to a new college, but the admissions staff at your new potential school won't know it if you don't tell them. And if you don't tell them, they may assume the worst. On the other hand, if you are transferring for unfortunate reasons, it's even more important to explain to the new school why you think you—and their school—would be better off with this change. Make sure that this information is a central point you raise in your essay or personal statement. Even better, if you're comfortable doing it, ask the professor who will write your letter of recommendation to briefly discuss your reasons.

# Time Lines and Deadlines

Every school sets its own deadlines for applying as a transfer student. In general, these deadlines are well after those set for general admissions applications for freshman year, but you will not have the opportunity to transfer if you don't abide by the transfer application deadlines. Many of them set their application cutoffs in March or April for admissions for the following fall semester. Deadlines vary even more for spring admissions, but don't be surprised if they're as early as September or October.

Set a time line for your decision process to keep these deadlines in mind and be sure that you don't fall behind. With all of the work you will have to do in your current classes, you don't want to forget one of the deadlines and be forced to rush to complete a portion of the application while you're in the middle of studying for an exam or trying to complete a major project. Even worse, you definitely don't want to forget to approach the professor you're hoping will write a recommendation on your behalf. Asking the professor to write it for you within 24 hours from the time you ask is not a good approach! The professor is demonstrating his or her respect for you and confidence in your abilities by agreeing to write your recommendation, but you will probably lose the professor's respect if you don't give him or her enough time to write it.

Every school will require different submission components, so be sure to check with the schools that you're considering before you assume one or another does or does not have a particular requirement. These are the steps that you should be sure to place on your own application time line, as necessary:

- Writing your personal statement and/or essay (Don't rush this, it's very important as a transfer student.)

- Requesting copies of your transcript from your current institution (Remember that these can take a while to be issued.)

- Requesting copies of your high school transcripts if you are required to provide these

- Approaching and following up with your professor(s) about writing a letter of recommendation

- Requesting copies of your SAT or ACT scores to be sent directly to the new institution or, if required, preparing for and retaking these exams

- Submitting your applications by the required deadlines, including paying the application fees

In addition, many schools will require that you send them midsemester grade reports, which will mean that you have to track down all of your professors and ask them to fill out a form detailing how well you're doing in their current class. Not only does this report tell the school you're applying to how you're progressing at that moment, but it can also serve a different function for you. By asking your professors for these, they will know that you're considering transferring schools, and they may be able to provide you with some advice or some additional information that can either change your mind or lead you to proceed with transferring.

# Make Your Final Decision Final

Clearly, you want to avoid the predicament of transferring once and then transferring again. A high number of students transfer schools more than one time, either because their needs changed after transferring once or because they made a bad decision, again. This is avoidable—at least in the latter circumstance. So before you decide to transfer, do the appropriate research and be certain that the new school you're considering will suit your needs.

Let's walk through a good way to approach and make your decision about transferring. The best way to make this decision is in three steps. First, you need to decide why exactly you think you want to transfer. After looking at all of the reasons discussed, if you think you fit into one of the categories that merits a transfer, you need to examine specifically how you think a transfer will benefit you and meet your priorities at college. Is it worth it to transfer? Or do you think you can get what you're looking for by making some adjustments and staying where you are?

Once you've identified your needs, you should begin to evaluate and prioritize your options and compare how various schools match your desires. The best way to begin this process is to look for the one option that you would rank as your top option. Just as you were able to apply to any of the thousands of colleges when you first applied, the sky is the limit once again. You can apply to any of the colleges that you want to. But now that you've prioritized the goals that you're expecting from your education—whether they include a particular major, a location, a better school—you should begin by looking for the best alignment between your priorities and what schools offer.

What school, if you were able to choose any of them, do you think would have the highest chances of convincing you to leave your current school if you were to get accepted by it? While you may be willing to leave your college if you get into College A, would you be similarly willing to leave it if you were rejected from College A but accepted to College B? In this decision step, figure out which school would be your first choice (or your first two choices if you can't choose one over another) and begin your evaluation from there. Start with your top choice because if you don't think that you would actually leave your current school to go to your top choice, then why would you bother putting yourself through the process of applying and transferring?

A good way to make this decision is to create a pros and cons list. According to your priorities, list the features you're looking for in a new school, the qualities you're missing in your existing school, and the steps you would have to go through in order to transfer. Here are some considerations to include on your list:

- The opportunity to change your major to something more specialized
- The ability to have coursework that is either more or less challenging
- A possible upgrade in terms of the status of the new school
- The ability to have your credits transfer, including:
  - Grades
  - Core curriculum requirements
  - Requirements for your major or minor
- The difficulty or ease you might experience to become involved in the extra-curricular activities that interest you
- The effect a change will have on your social life
- The time it will take to go through the application and transfer process, including:
  - Completing the application, essay, and personal statements
  - Possibly having to complete the SATs or ACTs again
  - Having to get new letters of recommendation

Spend several days putting together your pros and cons decision list. Once you've covered all of the pertinent positives and negatives associated with transferring, it's time to make your next decisions: Are you still convinced you want to submit transfer applications? If so, to how many schools? How are you going to decide which schools to apply to? Would you be willing to transfer only if you get into one particular school or into one of two particular schools?

Other chapters in this book will help you make some of these decisions. To help you decide which schools to apply to, you should use the steps in chapter 2. The process in that chapter will help you prioritize the criteria you're looking for in a college and narrow down the list of thousands of colleges in the United States to a specific few that will fit your needs. As mentioned, some colleges are more or less likely to accept transfer students. If you do your research and find out that the top five schools you would consider transferring to only accept the most qualified students, a label you're uncertain describes you, then you may want to broaden the number of schools you would apply to. If, on the other hand, you have set your sights on one school, then this decision is easy and you can simply apply to that one.

Once you've made your decision about which schools to apply to and you've gone through the transfer application process, you still have some choices to make. We recommend that you review Chapter 4, which is designed to help you choose from among those colleges that accept you. The only difference in the approach for using Chapter 4 now is that it is absolutely essential to use your existing school as one of your comparison schools. Don't simply compare the transfer option schools. You want to be certain that you're not giving up a school that fits your needs well for one that only fits them marginally. If you find, for example, that the academics aren't as good as you thought they were at the schools you've now been accepted to, and that you actually have more and better options where you are, you may decide not to transfer. Only you can make that decision, and by following this process you can feel confident that it will be an informed decision.

# To Sum Up

We all make mistakes or find ourselves in changing circumstances. Sometimes we can actually learn from these situations, and if we're really lucky, we can reverse them. Any mistake that can be reversed is actually a personal learning process— something that you can use to improve your future decisions. If you find that you've made a drastic mistake with regard to the college that you're enrolled in, more than likely you can fix it. But before you rush into changing schools, you need to understand that transferring is not always the best solution. And you need to realize that it's probably not going to be as easy as you imagine it to be. If you believe that you made such a big mistake that you need to transfer, or a change in circumstances necessitates transferring, then make sure you do it well. Don't make this complex move only to have to repeat it. Transferring schools can be very rewarding when it's warranted. But doing so unnecessarily or hastily and having to transfer a second time can be prevented if you prepare and make an informed decision.

*Note to Parents*

*Your children may have many valid reasons for transferring and many less-than-valid ones. But if your children are certain about wanting a change, be sure to help them determine their best options.*

# Section III.

## Social Decisions

**A**cademics are clearly the most important reason for going to college. You're paying for a degree—not for a party. But that doesn't mean you can't have a good time, too. In fact, some of the best experiences that you will have in your entire life may happen in college. Some of the friends you make in college will be life-long friends, and you may even meet your future husband or wife while you're there. The key objective is to achieve the right balance between social and academic life by making the right decisions. This section outlines the primary decisions you will need to make in your college social life and provides you with a set of proven techniques to help you make these decisions.

The first chapter of this section, chapter 14, discusses boundary decisions. Until this point in your life, your parents have dictated (or tried to dictate) your boundaries. You've had to answer their questions: When are you going to study? When are you going out with your friends? What time are you going to be home tonight? Who's having this party and will the parents be home? Are you going to drink? Now that you're in college, you will be released from these parental-oversight boundaries, so you need to make your own boundary decisions. If you simply go to college and don't set any specific

*Note to Parents*
*College life isn't all about studying. New friends, new interests, new responsibilities, amazing experiences—these are all important components of a well-rounded and successful college experience for your children. Encourage them to make their own decisions but also encourage them to make these decisions the right way.*

boundaries for your actions, you could find yourself making a series of disastrous, impulsive decisions. This chapter lays out a method for you to address boundary decisions for yourself so you will find the right balance between academics and your social life that will get you through college with an amazing experience all around.

Chapter 15 pertains to the difficult decisions about drinking and doing drugs. These are decisions that all students will face, and the overwhelming majority of college students drink alcohol at one point or another while they're in college. This chapter encourages you to make responsible decisions about drinking and drugs, intentionally and rationally, instead of making them with little thought while under peer pressure. It also encourages you to anticipate the potential unintended consequences of your actions prior to finding yourself in situations that require you to decide what action to take.

Chapter 16 deals with all of the exciting but time-consuming extracurricular activities that are available to you as a student. Becoming involved in activities outside of class is one of the most important and rewarding parts of college life. Choosing which activities to join is an important decision, since it affects not only your present enjoyment of school but can also have an impact on your future job prospects and career. Beware, however, not to overextend yourself at the expense of your studies. We provide a method for evaluating the various options you are considering while being sure not to overextend yourself.

Chapter 17 addresses Greek life and your decision about whether you should join a fraternity or a sorority. You should be aware of the benefits and the costs that membership in these organizations will mean for you. This chapter provides a framework for making the decision about whether to join a fraternity or a sorority that is based upon what you believe you will gain and what you believe you will sacrifice.

The final chapter in this section, chapter 18, is designed to help you explore your student housing options. Your housing decisions and roommate choices will directly impact your college social experiences. If you live with friends, you may find it necessary to study in the library to avoid major procrastination temptation. If you live with heavy partiers, you may find yourself subject to peer pressure to drink more often than you might want to and to compromise boundaries for quiet hours before exams. Determining the benefits and drawbacks of each option will guide you to a decision that will maximize the benefits you are hoping to get out of any living situation.

# Chapter 14

# Party Time

## Setting Your Own Boundary Decisions

**M**att was excited about going to college. He would be free of his parents and their ridiculous rules. He could do what he wanted, when he wanted, and how he wanted. He wouldn't have a curfew and could sleep as late as he wanted to. He no longer had to hide his drinking. It was about time. Matt had a lot of fun at college, but his grades reflected this. He failed two courses his first semester and was put on academic probation. He also got into trouble a couple of times when he was drunk and was disciplined, but these consequences didn't slow him down. After his second semester he was expelled and had to return home. Matt didn't set his own boundaries, so he had none.

By this point in the book, you probably realize that college is to be taken seriously if you want to make it to graduation. During college, you are establishing the fundamental building blocks to your future. Your behavior in college can help set the stage for the rest of your life—graduate school, jobs, networking, your career, and even the people you call "friends" or "honey." That said, college should not be four years of work, work, work. Likewise, college isn't about drinking seven nights a week and making it to class only if your hangover has cleared.

*Note to Parents*
*You should remember from your college days that you can't spend all of your time studying. Social life at college is one of the most important and unforgettable components of any good college experience.*

College is a unique experience. Life is golden; you are away from home and away from parental restrictions and curfews. You are surrounded with new people, opportunities, unlimited freedom, and limitless possibilities. You are at the verge of adulthood, yet your life lacks most of the worries, stresses, and responsibilities of full-fledged adult life. Your only concern is YOU, and as a college student, you have the chance to redefine yourself. Some students take this freedom to an extreme and turn college into a blurry, four-year-long kegger. We think it would be better if you learn how to make decisions that will provide you with a well-rounded, fun, and memorable college experience. And to do this, you need to set your own boundaries.

In high school, your parents defined your boundaries. You probably rebelled against them, but at the end of the day you knew your parents would make the hard choices for you. They asked about your homework and compelled you to finish it. They determined if you could go away with your friends for the weekend, even though you had an exam to study for. You understood the repercussions of skipping class to go shopping with your friends. Well, hallelujah: Those days are gone!

Now your parents aren't under the same roof, controlling what you can and cannot do. But you may forget that your parents most likely set these boundaries because they thought they were for your own good, even though you may have disagreed frequently. Sometimes the boundaries probably were for your own good, and sometimes they may not have been. You may not have forgiven them yet for forbidding you to go to that once-in-a-lifetime concert to see your favorite musician just because you had a paper due the next day that you hadn't even started! But, if you are completely honest, you were probably also glad they made you more responsible for your actions when it came to completing your work on time.

Whether you take part in the myriad of opportunities to let loose that will be available in college is a personal choice. Yet, realistically, the choice is fraught with very strong influences, the strongest of which is peer pressure. Different students choose different paths, and we would be misleading you if we tried to pretend that social pressure to drink or do drugs was not a part of the college scene. Parents may not want to hear this, and the activities may not be legal, but kids are most likely experimenting with drugs and alcohol anyway. That's the hard truth. Rather than duplicating or discarding their parents' boundaries, students should try to understand the logic behind them and use that logic to make their own decisions about their new boundaries.

> Make your own decisions on what your boundaries will be.

# Movies versus Realities

You're likely familiar with the concept "all work and no play makes Jack a dull boy." The idea isn't to spend your entire time locked in the college library. You need to get out and have a little fun. The real questions are: How much fun is appropriate and when is it a good idea to go out and have this fun? How much fun is too much fun? When should you let loose and relax? When should you refuse invitations to party so you can focus instead on completing an assignment? We've all seen the movies *Animal House* and *Van Wilder* and laughed at the absurdities they portray. Is that what college is all about—toga parties, paying tuition by becoming a party liaison and then, at the last minute, pulling a rabbit out of your hat in order to graduate? Obviously, those plot lines make for hilarious movies, but they don't make for good real-life college experiences. The idea of college is to play hard but work harder. And you need to strike the balance that is appropriate for you. This chapter is all about setting boundaries for yourself and then following them.

At times you may be willing to miss class so that you can have some unbelievable nonacademic experience. But routinely trading your academic responsibilities for partying or sitting around and hanging out with your friends may not be the most beneficial boundaries to set. You don't need to spend all your time working, but you should establish your own boundary lines and understand the consequences if you set these lines incorrectly.

Let's say that you have decided that the party scene is appealing to you and is something you want to experience while in college. Okay, great. How are you going to venture into the college social scene while also maintaining high academic success, participating in extracurricular activities, and finding a few hours to sleep and eat?

# Avoid Impulsive Decisions

The most important message you can take away from this chapter is that deciding to attend a party shouldn't be left until the last minute. This is a boundary decision. Setting your boundaries before you are suddenly faced with this decision is extremely important. Having done that, you can either decide that going to the party doesn't conform to your boundaries, or you can throw aside your boundaries and say you're resetting them. The time to make decisions regarding partying is during the day, when you can clearly consider your options and make the smartest choices.

Here's an example of what not to do. Lilly was in her dorm room on a Wednesday night, frantically typing away in order to finish a paper that was due the next morning. Though she was pushing it, she was pretty much on schedule to finish writing it at a decent hour and then have time to edit and proofread it. Right around 9:00 p.m., her roommate barged into the room, saying "Lilly! There's an awesome party going on down at the Theta house tonight! Get dressed—we're leaving in 30 minutes!" Lilly sat at her desk for a moment, mulling over the decision, despite the fact that no decision really needed to be made. She knew what she should do. She knew this paper had to be finished and turned in by 10:00 a.m. the next morning. But she was so tired. Her brain felt dead from writing for the last three hours, and she had allotted an hour for a break. Before she knew it, she was decked out in her party clothes and was walking across campus with her roommate to the party. She figured she'd stay an hour—which would only push her schedule back by an hour and a half or so—and when she got home, she'd finish it up. She would just go to bed a little later than she'd previously planned to.

> Deciding to go to a party is something you should try to do during the light of the day, not when you're tired of studying or after a long day.

As you can imagine, an hour at the party quickly turned into two, then three, then. . . . At 2:15 a.m., Lilly arrived back at her room, exhausted and with no intention of finishing her paper. She decided she'd set her alarm for 7:00 a.m. and finish it up then. After pushing the snooze button for nearly 90 minutes, Lilly finally woke up and realized she had just over an hour to finish her paper and get it somewhat polished. Needless to say, her paper was far from stellar, and the professor could see how little time and effort she'd put into the assignment. The professor had no problem making the decision to mark a big C- on the top of the front page.

You should not decide to have a night out at the last minute when you have more pressing matters that clearly conflict with going to a party. There will always be another party. Deciding to go to a party should be a premeditated process that takes place during the daytime, when you're thinking a bit more clearly, and you're less likely to be swayed by excitement or the tempting feeling that, "I just need to get out of this room and away from all this work!" We all know people who have partied their way right into academic suspension and possibly even full-blown expulsion, due to the hit their lifestyle inflicted on their GPAs. Partying is not just potentially dangerous to your health and well-being, but it's also potentially extremely detrimental to your academic career when it's taken to an extreme.

## Boundaries

Everyone needs boundaries, and it's time for you to begin to set your own as a responsible young adult. Boundaries are the guidelines you set for yourself on everyday decisions like whether you are always going to attend class, when you will go to bed, whether you are going to get your studies done before you do something else, and so on.

Likewise, in addition to setting boundaries about when you're going to party, you also need to set boundaries for yourself when it comes to how much you're going to party. Are you going to limit yourself to going out one night a week? How about two? How about four? Also, are you going to limit yourself to two drinks? Or four? You have to make these decisions. Your parents won't be standing at your dorm room door when you return, ready to mete out punishment because you missed your curfew. You're the new boundary setter, so start setting them.

At the end of this chapter you'll find a Decide Better! decision worksheet (Figure 14-1) for setting your boundaries. Consider this as a starting point: some of the boundaries may apply to you and others may not, and you may have additional boundaries you need to choose. Work through this Decide Better! decision worksheet when you have time to think about your boundaries and decide rationally; don't make your boundary decisions impulsively when each situation presents itself. That's the point of this decision exercise. By establishing—and sticking to—boundary decisions in advance, you are better prepared to respond to choices that reflect your best interests. This approach is much more effective than just letting a series of spontaneous, individual decisions shape your actions, and therefore your life, by default.

The worksheet poses questions to help you set boundaries. For example, are you going to go out on school nights? If you answer no, then don't go out. If you answer yes but have some restrictions, such as how often, only for a few hours, or when you've completed your work, then list those restrictions for yourself. Are you going to drink, and if so how much? Set your own boundaries and follow them. Similarly set your own boundaries about drugs and sex. Don't leave your decision until you are in a compromising situation and can't think clearly.

If you like, make notes to yourself on your boundary decisions. You can even talk about them to your friends. Some may laugh at you, but others may respect you for acting maturely. You might even find that some friends like the idea, and you can decide to set boundaries together. You might even want to make a pact to support each other in holding to your boundaries.

Another technique to help you make boundary decisions is one we call "changing lanes." Just as you stay in or change lanes when driving your car, you can use the same process for decision making. You want to be in the correct lane for *you* at any given point in your life. That might mean the fast lane at times, and perhaps you'll elect to explore that lane a bit in college. Other times, you'll realize the slow lane would be better for your situation. At times, coasting in the middle lane is perfect. The concept of your driving lane can also be applied to the speed in which you make decisions. In the fast lane, you don't have a lot of time to reflect before reacting, so you make decisions very quickly. This is a good lane to travel in when you already have acquired the resources and experiences to be in the fast lane and can rapidly make sound choices. It's a good lane to be in when you've already established the foundation for how you're going to make these decisions—all you need to do is implement them. In the slow lane, you can take it easy and make decisions over time as you gather more information to support your final choice. In the middle lane, you can stay put, comfortable with the status quo. We recommend that you review the lane you're in periodically. It's desirable to switch lanes from time to time and try new experiences and test your responses to them. Life can come at you pretty fast, especially with all the new freedom you're experiencing in college. Are you in the proper lane and making good decisions at the appropriate pace for that lane?

> **Note to Parents**
>
> *This is where you need to let go. But do it by suggesting that your children take time to decide on their own boundaries in a responsible manner by using this worksheet.*

## To Sum Up

If you want to experience all that college has to offer—including the active social scene—then be smart about it. Don't squander your opportunity to get a quality education that propels you to your future potential. It's okay to get out and have fun—just do so after careful consideration of the consequences. Predetermine your boundaries so that you know when you will party and when you won't. And base these boundaries on your real academic needs. If you do go out, consider whether you're going to do it with the intention of getting drunk or just having fun. If you want to be treated like an adult, then make smart and conscious decisions that reflect your maturity.

**FIGURE 14-1  Make Your Own Boundary Decisions**

1. Are you going to go out on school nights? _____ How often? _____

2. How much time are you going to allocate to studying every night? _____

3. Will you go out at night before an exam? _____

4. Are you going to attend all of your classes? _____ If not, how many classes will you miss and for what reasons? _____

5. How late are you going to stay out when you go out if you have class the next day?_____

6. What are the limits on the types of places you will go out to (bars, parties, etc.)? _____

7. Will you drink? _____ What limits will you place on the amount you will drink (or will you just keep drinking until you get sick or pass out)? _____

8. Who are you going to go out with? _____ Will you go with anyone or only with trusted friends? _____

9. Are you always going to go out whenever someone asks or are you going to assess your own academic and personal needs and make predetermined boundary decisions beforehand? _____

10. Are you going to date? _____ How will you decide who to date? _____

11. Will have sex? _____ What are your criteria for having sex? _____

12. Are you going to do drugs? _____ Are you going to avoid (or leave) situations that put you in a position to be pushed to do drugs? _____ Can you say no? _____

13. How many hours are you going to watch television or play computer games each week? _____

14. How much time are you going to devote to extracurricular activities? _____

# Chapter 15

## Bottoms Up

### Making Responsible Decisions about Drinking

Charlie was generally a responsible college student. But one night his friends convinced him to go out to a bar, maybe because they needed Charlie to drive them. When Charlie wanted to leave early, they convinced him to stay longer and kept buying him drinks. They didn't leave until the bar closed at 1:00 a.m. Unfortunately, Charlie had too much to drink and should not have driven. On the way home, the students were pulled over, and Charlie was arrested for drunk driving. He simply didn't consider this as a potential consequence of his decision before he acted.

> **Note to Parents**
>
> *Telling your children not to drink or not to party isn't going to work. Instead, instilling in them a sense of responsible decision making when it comes to these issues will teach them to understand the consequences of their decisions.*

Drinking is one of the most common activities pursued by college students. College life offers a plethora of drinking opportunities—keg parties, the bar scene, bar crawls, even drinking in the dorms. Drinking can be a big part of college life, and whether it becomes a part of your college life or not (and how big a part of your college life) is something only you can decide. More importantly, perhaps, is that your actions and your decisions about drinking and partying have consequences. As we mentioned in the previous chapter, considering the consequences of your decisions and how they will affect you and other people is critical.

# Consider Unintended Consequences

All decisions have both intended and unintended consequences. We discussed unintended consequences in our previous book, *Decide Better! for a Better Life*. For example, you could park your car at a restaurant and come out to find it damaged or stolen. This is an unintended consequence of parking at a restaurant for which you are blameless. Your decisions, however, sometimes have unintended consequences that could also affect others. For example, you could decide to invite a friend to visit you for the weekend, and she could get into a car accident on the way. This consequence is not your fault, and you should not feel guilty about it.

On the other hand, sometimes you are responsible for unintended consequences. You could drive drunk and have an accident that seriously hurts someone. This unintended consequence is different because you are to blame. You should have considered the possibility of this consequence before you made your decision to drink and drive.

> **Definition: Prudent Person Rule**
>
> Noun. 1. The guideline that states that you will take a rational look at the potential consequences of your actions and then take active steps to mitigate the potential negative results of your actions. 2. The principle that states that it is possible to have fun and be responsible about your actions at the same time.

The rule to use when considering the consequences is called the "prudent person rule." This rule holds that if you could have rationally predicted that a particular consequence would or could result from a decision that you make, and then your actions take this consequence into consideration, you have abided by the prudent person rule. If you know that you risk being hit by a car if you don't look to see if a car is coming as you cross the street, but you still don't look, then you haven't acted according to the prudent person rule. Likewise, if you decide to drink and then get in the car with your friend who has also been drinking, you should be able to predict that a possible consequence of this decision is that you could be injured or even killed in an accident.

Using the prudent person rule is helpful when it comes to decisions about drinking and partying in college. If you use this approach, you will be able to make more responsible decisions about these choices and avoid the pitfalls that can result from the possible consequences of your actions.

# Scary Statistics Show Unintended Consequences

Some statistics from the National Institutes of Health (NIH), a government agency, demonstrate the real-life detrimental effects of excess partying and drinking during your college years. These are actual numbers—and they are striking. They define the likelihood of unintended consequences—and the consequences are serious! You need to see that partying and drinking in excess can lead to many irreparable consequences.

Here is another way of looking at the NIH statistics. If you go to a college with 10,000 students, for example, 2,500 of them will have academic problems as a result of their drinking decisions. Are you going to be one of those who will let your drinking bring down your grades? In your four years at this school, it's statistically likely that two students will die because of actions related to their drinking, whether from alcohol poisoning, drunk driving, or simply doing something stupid. Is it going to be you or one of your friends? Strikingly, 750 students in that same school of 10,000 will be injured as a direct result of drinking.

You can find similar statistics about drugs, which are also prevalent at colleges nationwide. Again, decisions about whether you're going to smoke pot, do cocaine, or use prescription drugs improperly are decisions that you should make before being presented with these opportunities. Also, you should be—and quite likely will be—held accountable for the consequences of your actions.

# Can You Risk Binge Drinking?

Binge drinking is a serious problem on college campuses. What is binge drinking? It is technically defined as consuming five alcoholic beverages in one sitting for men, and four for women. According to college administrative personnel—including deans, vice presidents, and presidents—binge drinking is their number one concern on college campuses! Not fundraising. Not college rankings. Not the football team's ranking. Binge drinking. And the college administrators have good reasons for this.

The media carry many stories of students dying as a result of intoxication. One drunken student fell down a gorge, where he was later found dead. At another school, a fraternity member found his roommate who was already dead from alcohol poisoning. A girl in Pennsylvania was found clinging to life on her 21st birthday with a blood-alcohol level nearly seven times Pennsylvania's intoxication limit. Stories like these are reported from *every single* school in the country. Usually several such tragedies will occur during the course of a typical student's four-year education. You

**College Drinking Statistics**

- **Death**—About 1,700 college students die each year from alcohol-related injuries, including motor vehicle accidents.

- **Injury**—Roughly 599,000 students between the ages of 18 and 24 are injured while under the influence of alcohol.

- **Unsafe sex**—About 400,000 students have had unprotected sex and more than 100,000 students report being too intoxicated to know if they consented to having sex.

- **Academic problems**—Roughly 25 percent of college students report academic consequences of their drinking, including missing class, falling behind, doing poorly on exams or papers,
and receiving lower grades overall.

- **Drunk driving**—More than 2 million students drive under the influence of alcohol every year.

- **Vandalism**—Roughly 11 percent of college students who drink report that they have damaged property while under the influence of alcohol.

- **Police involvement**—About 5 percent of college students are involved with the police or campus security as a result of their drinking and an estimated 110,000 students are arrested for an alcohol-related violation.

This information and more can be found at the National Institutes of Health Web site
(http://www.CollegeDrinkingPrevention.gov).

might ask yourself if this is the type of statistic that you and your parents envisioned for your college experience. The thought of one more student in the morgue should be sobering—especially if that student could be you.

Colleges and universities across the country are cracking down on campus drinking in response to this epidemic. Even "senior week" has proven to be an issue at many schools, regardless of the fact that the vast majority of seniors are of legal drinking age. Senior week is the week between exams and graduation when students' grades are being processed before the official graduates can walk across stage to claim their diplomas. Traditionally, this is also a week of heavy partying and binge drinking. Because of the dangers the schools perceive, many colleges are doing away with senior week altogether. This is unfortunate, considering it's supposed to be a fun-filled, exciting time. It's the last time these students will be undergraduates on campus and it gives them a chance to say goodbye to great friends. It should be spent having fun. If students are proving to be incapable of doing so without actively putting themselves in harm's way and without demonstrating some maturity and re-sponsibility, then colleges are not going to stand by and watch disaster strike.

## Can Pay, So Get to Play

Part of the reason this problem is getting worse, according to a Harvard University survey of students, is that many students have far more money to spend on drinking than they used to. On average, a college student spends $450 on books in a school year, but several times that amount on alcohol. The same study showed that alcohol is responsible for 40 percent of academic problems and 28 percent of all college drop-outs. These statistics, along with the rising number of alcohol-related deaths and injuries, have forced colleges to act. Besides suspending certain events on campus, many schools are launching aggressive antidrinking and antidrinking-and-driving campaigns. Some colleges are offering alcohol-free dorms and sponsoring alcohol-free parties, while others are funding advertising blitzes around campus and through agreements with local bars. Some schools are cracking down on underage drinking by sending out notification to parents when their children are caught drinking ille-gally. Colleges don't want their students to get injured, killed, or suffer academically, and are taking responsible actions to quell this tide.

Dartmouth College students, for example, found ads spread around campus claim-ing that 58 percent of students don't feel alcohol is important at a party, and the Uni-versity of Arizona is using a campus-wide survey to publicize that most students have "four or fewer drinks" when partying, depending upon how much is enough or too much for each individual student. The message colleges are promoting is that most students don't see getting drunk as cool. Some say this is reversed peer-pressure, but schools are doing anything and everything in their power to get the point across.

If you understand the unintended consequences that actions can have, and the prudent person rule, you can see that, while these students don't intend for these unfortunate consequences to happen, the prudent person should be able to rationally predict the likelihood of these potential outcomes and act accordingly. If you don't look reasonably at the possible consequences of your actions, you are not acting as a rational person should. If you do predict these possible consequences and then take steps to mitigate the potential negative outcomes, you are acting responsibly—and you can still have fun in the process. Make a clear decision for yourself about binge drinking: will you or won't you? If you decide not to binge, then determine your own drinking limit and hold yourself to this limit.

Sometimes, the decision to drink is not so cut and dried. You might forget that you have alternatives to drinking—particularly binge drinking—that are still pleasurable and do not amount to social suicide. "Generating alternatives" is a technique we recommend that encourages you to consider what better decisions might look like. Some alternatives take a bit of ingenuity and imagination, but start by thinking of the obvious ones (go to a location where people are not drinking or are drinking less, go out with nondrinking students, and so on) and then build your options from there. We find that it helps to write these ideas down. During this process, don't discount anything. If it pops into your head, write it down. Think in bold terms—you and some friends could organize your own nondrinking party night and grow it into a campus-wide event. (School administrators would love you!) Begin to structure your alternatives and define and separate them as distinct choices. You can add related subcategories, but keep the main options as individual ones. Thus, you will have option A, but you may also have options A-1, A-2, and A-3. At this point, you may want to ask for advice from others who have already tried out some of your options. Then go through your alternatives and single out the ones that seem most feasible for your situation and implement them.

> **Note to Parents**
> *Drinking and driving is one of the most dangerous aspects of drinking at college. If your children have cars at school, you should talk to them—but not lecture them—about their responsibilities.*

## Booze, Cars, and Consequences

If you do go out and drink, one of the most important decisions you can make is to be sure you have a designated driver or another safe way back home before you step foot out the door. This is a given if you're going to abide by the prudent person rule—absolutely do not get behind the wheel if you've been drinking, and never get in the car with a drunk driver. Even if people tell you they're "totally fine" and can drive, don't believe them and certainly don't let them drive you! If you decide to drive after imbibing alcohol, and a police officer pulls you over and suspects you've been drinking, it's lights out for you. A DUI (Driving Under the Influence) citation has long-lasting and hard-hitting repercussions that can affect you for years to come. Your license will be suspended, you'll be fined and possibly even jailed, you'll have a serious offense staining your record, and some schools find that cause for probation, suspension, or expulsion. In addition, you're likely to have to explain your police record to future employers and whenever you're looking to get any type of certification, including being admitted to the bar as a lawyer or being licensed to be a doctor. Imagine having to justify that to a judge who is considering whether to admit you as a lawyer to the state bar!

On a harsher note, consider the consequences you will face if you injure or kill someone while driving intoxicated. The legal issues are bad enough, but consider the guilt that will haunt you for the rest of your life. And, if you get in the car with a drunk driver, you may never have the chance to learn from that mistake because you could die as a result.

So, designated drivers are a *must*, and even better, you should seek out parties within walking distance. And if you're ever in a bind, take the bus or call a cab. It's a good idea to have at least one cab company's phone number programmed into your cell phone and always carry enough cash for cab fare as not all cab companies accept credit cards. Don't be stupid. Many options don't involve life-threatening situations. Since you're smart enough to get into college, be smart enough to stay safe—and alive!

## To Sum Up

In the end, decisions about drinking and drugs are extremely individual. While many students are willing to deal with many of the consequences of drinking, such as making fools out of themselves, spending the entire night in the bathroom throwing up, having a hangover, and the like, it's much less common for students to consider the more significant potential consequences of their actions. The biggest issues with drinking and drugs are the unintended consequences: death, injury, and academic problems. Using drugs or alcohol is a decision that you have to make yourself, preferably in the light of day. Deciding to go out to a party, to drink, or to get into the car with someone who has been drinking are all decisions you should make when you're lucid, not when you're tired after a long day of studying or after you've already started drinking. Be proactive early on during your college life and make prudent person decisions about drinking and drugs. College is just as much about having fun as it is about learning, but you want to make sure you're there the next day and the next semester, too.

# Chapter 16

## Accessorize Your Academic Life

### Decisions about Extracurricular Activities

Jacqueline's freshman year of college started off with her entire class of 700 wide-eyed, scared but hopeful kids and their flustered parents scurrying all over campus like lab rats set free for the first time. Early in the morning, an organizer gathered everyone into one room to explain the day's activities. She projected a campus map onto a large screen for everyone to see. Then she started pointing wildly at various spots on the map. "Go here to have your ID picture taken and then go here to get the actual card. After that, you need to go to this building to pick up the key to your dorm, but before you can actually start moving in, you first have to go to the other side of campus to the campus safety office, ask for Earl, and sign off that you've received your key. Then you can move in. After that, you should probably go to the dining hall to choose a meal plan that fits your eating habits. We have 12 options. Then . . ." and on she went for nearly 10 minutes. Once she concluded, the students and parents (who were more confused than ever) took off, crazily attempting to complete the

> **Note to Parents**
> *Extracurricular activities serve an extremely important role in your children's college experience. You should encourage them to become involved in ones that will help them gain leadership and real-world experience.*

maze of tasks before they had to meet at 4:00 p.m. for the dean's welcome to the new students.

By the time 4:00 p.m. came, all 700 students plus their parents were collapsed in the seats in the auditorium, probably not comprehending very much of the important information being thrown at them in the dean's welcome. They all were too busy catching their breath and mentally pondering the remaining tasks on their to-do lists. About 10 minutes into the dean's speech, Jacqueline's mom suddenly turned to her and said, in a whispered shout, "A shower curtain!" A few parents in the same row looked toward the two of them, laughing knowingly and sympathetically, as their brains were probably sorting through a similar checklist.

While the dean's welcome is a vague memory for Jacqueline, mostly scattered with thoughts of shower curtains, quarters for the laundry room, and flip-flops for the shower, one point he made stuck in her mind. He said, "College is supposed to be a well-rounded experience. We believe that as much learning and growing takes place outside the classroom as in." And no, he wasn't talking about learning how to perfectly balance a keg stand or learning how many drinks it takes before you pass out. He was explaining that extracurricular activities are a vital part of the college experience. And while academics should always come first, creating a one-dimensional schedule—based on study, eat, study, sleep, study—will not help you grow and learn as much as you could if you led a more well-rounded, balanced life.

# Finding That Critical Balance

Many students feel overwhelmed with all of the options for involvement when they first visit for the accepted candidates' day or go to a club fair during orientation. After all, with only 24 hours in the day, how do you fit everything in? One student we know tried to do it all—took a full course load with a double major, played on an intramural soccer team complete with a travel schedule to other neighboring schools, wrote for the student newspaper, served as president of the Outdoors Club and the Latino Student Association, worked at the campus library, and actively participated in a multitude of other clubs that all had their own time demands.

This time of overinvolvement starts out with the best of intentions and before you know it, you find yourself doing your classwork between midnight and 3:00 a.m., being sleep deprived and unable to do anything well, and you end up getting sick. This particular student came down with a bad case of mononucleosis right before finals and ended up having to get extensions for all of his classes.

When you find yourself starting to add more to your plate than you can handle, take a moment and step back. Ask yourself, "What would the prudent person do?" Can you step down as president from one club? Cut back on your hours at the library? Schedule study time on the weekend to get ahead for the week? The busy student who got sick clearly didn't set his boundaries correctly. Remember you are human. Pace yourself. And don't be afraid to say to yourself, "Yes, I would love to be involved in that activity but I just don't think I can fit it in this semester. Maybe next year."

The key is to achieve the right balance. Not participating in any activities is at one extreme, and if you make this your choice, you will miss out on the broader college experience. Signing up during orientation for a myriad of club and activity participation, especially prior to knowing your academic load, is the other extreme.

> **Top 10 Reasons for Extracurricular Activities**
> 1. Delve more into your studies
> 2. Prepare yourself for your professional career
> 3. Learn a new skill
> 4. Improve an existing skill
> 5. Become more well-rounded
> 6. Get more involved socially
> 7. Volunteer to make a difference locally or globally
> 8. Do something with your friends
> 9. Learn more about yourself
> 10. Have fun!

## Pare Down the Multitude of Choices

Once you settle in a little, we're certain that you'll begin to peruse your college Web site, researching the various activities, organizations, and extracurricular opportunities they offer. That can be pretty overwhelming! Nearly all schools offer a mind-boggling array of clubs, groups, organizations, societies, teams, and so on, that are open for you to join. The range is practically endless. You can likely pick from honor societies and clubs; student government; intramural sports teams; student media that include newspaper, radio, and television; religious, environmental, human rights, or other issue organizations; and theatre clubs or rock bands. Where do you begin? You probably see quite a few that interest you or seem like fun, but how many activities should you take on and how should you prioritize those that you're considering? Let's look at a few students to gain some perspective from their experiences.

Scott was in this overwhelming position just last year. In the third week of his freshman year, all of the organizations and clubs got together and held an activities fair outside the student union. After class, Scott decided to stop by and check out the various booths to see if anything caught his eye. By the time he walked away, just an hour later, he had joined four different organizations and signed up to volunteer at a local school tutoring junior high school students in math. And these were piled on top of his having been hired one week earlier to write for the campus newspaper. That totaled six extracurricular activities now filling Scott's already hectic schedule. But being an optimist as most freshmen are, he was confident that he could juggle all of these activities. The fact that Scott was only three weeks into classes may have had something to do with his false sense of unlimited free time. He had maintained a very busy and full schedule during high school, so why wouldn't he be able to do the same now? How much harder could college classes be than the AP courses he'd taken in high school?

*Determining how much time you can spend outside of class should help you prioritize the activities you become involved in.*

As it turned out, Scott packed his schedule to the point that all of his commitments soon began to suffer. His academics were the first to slip, as so much of his time was consumed with the meetings, get-togethers, events, tutoring, and deadlines required by his extracurricular activities. In an attempt to raise his grades, Scott decided to sleep a little less. You can imagine what this led to. Before he knew it, he was a zombie with poor grades and numerous people and organizations peeved with him for missing meetings, deadlines, and events that he'd planned. Scott realized that the trick is quality not quantity. He thinned his schedule down to two extracurricular activities and kept his academics at the top of his priority list. He also maintained a minimum of six hours of sleep every night, with very few exceptions. After making these changes, he realized that he enjoyed a much more productive and less stressful second semester.

Obviously, Scott is an extreme case, but he should serve as a cautionary tale of what can happen if you become overzealous and feel that you can do it all. Extracurricular activities are as important in college as they were in high school—perhaps even more so. If you're looking ahead to graduate school, law school, or medical school, for example, it's important to demonstrate that you are well-rounded and can handle the pressures of multiple activities and deadlines that aren't all academic. Graduate schools want to see that you're successful in class while juggling activities out of class. Therefore, choosing your extracurricular activities accordingly is important. And, remember, college lasts four years, so you don't need to pile every additional activity into your first year.

Another student, Julie, had planned since the seventh grade to go to medical school and become a doctor. So when she started college, she began fashioning her activities toward this goal. She joined a sorority to show that she's personable, enjoys people and socializing, and maintains a well-balanced life, but also because she simply wanted to join one. Through her sorority, she participated in many volunteer programs since all members were required to complete at least 30 hours of community service each semester. For her second extracurricular activity, she decided to be a scribe at the local hospital. A scribe is an individual who writes down everything doctors say while with a patient. She reasoned that this activity showed medical schools that she had an active interest in learning all she could not only inside but also outside of the classroom. Her role as a scribe also demonstrated that she had hands-on, real-life experience in a medical setting. After four years of participating in these activities and earning excellent grades, she scored high on her MCAT (Medical College Admission Test). Julie went on to attend her first-choice medical school. She is now starting her residency as an emergency room physician. She believes her well-planned approach toward her participation in related extracurricular activities coupled with her excellent academic performance elevated her as a medical school candidate.

> ### Note to Parents
> *When you're asking your children about school, be sure to ask about their extracurricular activities as well. These can be some of the most important and exciting parts of their entire time at college.*

## Practice This Selection Process

Choosing the best extracurricular activities for you is important, as is choosing the right number of these activities. Overextending yourself like Scott did will typically distract you from your academics. Not being involved enough may diminish your potential college enjoyment as well as eliminate important ways to support your career aspirations. The following process provides a basic approach to help you select the best number and type of extracurricular activities for you.

Start by taking a quick look at the activities that are available to you. You can do this by looking over the Web site provided by the student activities center (or the appropriate similar resource at your school) or by going to an activity fair. At this point, you should begin to put together a list of those activities that have sparked your interest. Write them down. You probably will list more than you can be involved in, but don't remove any at this point unless you're certain you wouldn't want to do them.

Next, begin to evaluate those options, some of which will be more important to you than others. While doing your evaluation, consider these factors:

- Your likely level of enjoyment of the activities and related responsibilities
- The goals you want to get out of your time with this organization or group

❶ Your beliefs as to the likelihood that the activity will assist you with your professional goals

❶ Your time commitment if you join

An easy evaluation method is to list each of these factors on a simple table. See Figure 16-1 for our sample, which was completed by Henry, a student from a liberal arts school in Pennsylvania. As Henry did, you can place all of the activities you are considering into rows on the left of the sheet and then determine your enjoyment level, the goals you hope to achieve with each of them, whether you think they will help you with your career, and the anticipated time commitment.

**FIGURE 16-1  Evaluating Potential Extracurricular Activities**

| Activity | Level of Enjoyment | Goals | Help with Career | Time Commitment |
|---|---|---|---|---|
| Ski team | Very high | Enjoyment | No | High |
| Amnesty International | Medium | Helping others | No | Low |
| Chemistry club | Medium | Learning chemistry skills | Yes | Low |
| Campus newspaper | High | Learning writing skills | Yes | High |
| Student government | Medium | Involved with campus governance | Yes | High |
| Honor society | Medium | Assisting with career | Yes | Medium |
| Yearbook | Medium | Learning editorial skills | Yes | Medium |
| Comedy club | High | Enjoyment | No | Low |
| Model United Nations | High | Learning international knowledge | No | High |
| College Democrats | High | Promoting beliefs | No | Medium |

While Henry really loved to ski and assigned it the highest level of enjoyment, he knew it would entail a big time commitment, especially since it would take two hours to drive to the nearest mountain. The ski team required him to ski four days per month, which would take a big chunk of his valuable time. On the other hand, although working on the yearbook was something he believed he would enjoy less than skiing, it would take a significantly smaller amount of time and would also provide him with skills that would be applicable to his future career.

Once he completed the worksheet for all of his possible activities, Henry sorted and prioritized his list. He ended up deciding to participate as a sports writer for the campus newspaper, as one of the class officers for the student government, and as a member in the college Amnesty International group. A few months later, he still thought he made a relatively good decision, but as he had learned a bit more about campus groups in that time period, he decided to stop going to the Amnesty International meetings and became involved in the Model United Nations program instead.

After you have some sense of how well each of the potential activities is going to meet your needs, you can begin to go through them and select the ones that you think are best for you. One piece of advice: begin by taking small steps. Instead of thinking that you'll have no problem being involved in 12 activities and rushing into joining all of them and taking on big responsibilities in each one, join one or two to begin with, spend some time adjusting to these commitments, and only then decide to take on more activities if you think you're able to do so without jeopardizing your academics.

## Hedging Your Bets

Selecting activities involves comparing multiple factors. Learn to hedge your bet in your decision making. With each activity, you stand to gain or lose something, or perhaps you're unsure what the gains and losses are. If this is the case, hedge your bet. This involves a cost-benefit analysis to determine which option offers the highest positive returns or the lowest negative returns. And, in case your best estimate fails you, know that you can formulate a backup plan and still come out ahead. So, hedge your bet and join up!

Once you join groups and take on the responsibilities associated with them, you'll discover an ancillary benefit. You'll find that your involvement requires you to make many other decisions. If you're planning a major event, you're going to have to make good decisions about the logistics of the event. If you're the treasurer of a group, you're going to have to make good financial decisions. If you're in charge of bringing speakers to the school, you're going to have to make decisions about what speakers to bring based upon the advice of others, the cost of the speakers, and the benefit they will provide to the students who will attend.

In the process of writing this book, we consulted current students and recent graduates, professors, and administrators from a variety of schools. When we asked them about the decisions they make or see the students making, several of them have marveled at the overall good decisions made by the leaders of student organizations.

For example, one administrator stressed how members of the student government showed very good leadership skills and decision-making skills when it came to some of the most challenging decisions they faced. And while you won't always make the best decisions in these roles, it's important to remember that your involvement in these activities is also a good way for you to improve how you approach and make decisions—a skill that will be very important in your future career and life.

We all make mistakes sometimes, so if you find that you've bitten off more than you can chew, don't worry about it—do something about it! You need to make a decision about what to do; you also need to make a decision about the best way to do it. You can turn right around and take yourself out of an activity—but try to do it without disrupting the group with which you've been working. For example, if you write for the student newspaper, and you've decided that you can no longer write your weekly sports column, try not to tell your editor you're quitting an hour before your deadline. Offer to give the paper a week or two to find someone else. Likewise, if you're in charge of the casino-night fundraiser for your class, and you decide you can't do it, don't resign the day before the event. Find someone to replace you and train that person before you leave. You'll find that if you do this, not only will you earn the respect of others, you will also know that you didn't leave anybody high and dry because of your bad decision to take on too many activities.

## To Sum Up

In order to get the maximum benefit and the best experiences from your time in college, methodically weave extracurricular activities into your academic life. Activities should not surpass your coursework on your priority list, but rather they should complement your studies in a way that will prove both enjoyable and useful. Seriously and realistically consider how much free time you have first, decide what you want to gain from your activities, and only then choose accordingly. You should enjoy these activities and your peers within them, but they should also serve some purpose—be it networking, social, or career-driven purposes. And remember, cultivating a rich social life in college is also extremely important, and it's a form of networking, so don't feel that a social activity is a waste of time that should be spent studying. Just go into the decision knowing what you want to gain from these activities and let that guide you. Always remember that college has more to offer than merely classes and that you can learn as much about life and yourself outside the classroom as you can in it. By choosing the activities that provide you with a good balance of enjoyment, use of your limited time, and professional skills, you will get everything you're hoping for—and more—out of your extracurricular activities.

# Chapter 17

# Toga, Toga, Toga

## How to Decide If "Going Greek" Is for You

Jamie and her sister Amie are twins who attended the same college. Jamie immediately joined a sorority; it was one of the primary reasons for attending that college. Amie, on the other hand considered joining the sorority but in the end she decided it wasn't for her. Even though they were twins, the girls had always been very different. Jamie always knew what she wanted and made quick decisions—sometimes too impulsively. Amie was more thoughtful, and took time—sometimes too much—to make decisions. In this case, their decisions worked for both of them. Each was pleased with her decision regarding a sorority.

You may know a little or a lot about the Greek system. Maybe your family is steeped in Tri Delt and SAE legacies, or maybe you have absolutely no idea what we're talking about. Perhaps you're looking to attend a school that doesn't even offer a Greek system, in which case you can move right on to the next chapter. And maybe you don't even know what Greek refers to. Whatever your position on this subject, we will answer a few questions and help you on the path toward your decision about whether to go Greek or not.

Let's start by explaining what we mean by Greek. Many colleges have fraternity (for men) and sorority

> **Note to Parents**
>
> *Don't push your children into or away from joining a fraternity or sorority. Just because it was or wasn't right for you when you were in college doesn't mean they'll have the same experience.*

(for women) houses on, or even off, campus that are named for two or three letters of the Greek alphabet. So, SAE stands for Sigma Alpha Epsilon. Tri Delt is short for Delta Delta Delta. But on the house, the name is written using the actual Greek letters. Most fraternities and sororities are social in nature, but many are also dedicated to various disciplines, such as medicine, law, engineering, and so on.

Nationwide, only between 5 percent and 10 percent of students belong to fraternities and sororities, depending upon whether you include only social fraternities and sororities or if you also include academic ones. While that may seem like a fairly small number of students, at some schools the numbers are significantly higher— with many even reaching over 50 percent. At some schools, therefore, the Greek system might be antiquated and irrelevant (or even nonexistent), while at other schools, as the saying goes, you're either Greek or you're a freak.

## Party or Philanthropy—Greek Choices

To be completely honest, Greek culture tends to overwhelmingly be a party culture. Many *Animal House*-type parties take place at fraternity houses, and you will find sororities full of girls who spend more money on clothes and shoes than they do on tuition. However, this is not always the case. Many sororities and fraternities also contribute countless hours to community service and raise massive amounts of money for charity. Usually, each fraternity and sorority has a single charity it supports, and the members spend much of the year fundraising for this cause. Other Greek activities besides parties and fundraising include tutoring elementary school students, conducting neighborhood cleanups, sponsoring blood drives, participating in intramural sports, volunteering at shelters, organizing clothing collections, and many other types of volunteer activities. As mentioned, certain fraternities and sororities focus on specific academics, and although they are usually still social in nature, the members are all interested in the same academic issues.

Fun is a component of college Greek life, but academics and volunteerism can be as well.

## First Decision—Affiliate or Not

You need to make a number of decisions when you're on the fence about whether or not to join a fraternity or sorority. The first of these is whether you're going to take this step and become Greek. As with any activity in college, you can list many pros and cons to Greek life, and when making this decision, you need to weigh the benefits of joining a fraternity or sorority against the drawbacks based upon your priorities.

The presence of fraternities and sororities on campus can greatly affect your social life in college depending on how you feel about them. Attending a Greek-heavy school but not participating in fraternities or sororities can create a feeling of isolation. So, if you have a great scholarship to a school riddled with Greek letters and students in matching shirts, but you want nothing to do with it, figure out which other organizations and activities on campus suit you. After all, not everybody is interested in joining the Greek system, and many other students feel just as you do. So if you end up deciding that it's not for you, don't worry about it. You've made the best decision based upon the pros and cons that you

> **Note to Parents**
> *Joining a fraternity or sorority won't necessarily mean that your children will be sacrificing academics for a better social life. Many fraternities and sororities value and promote academics highly, as well as volunteerism and leadership.*

examined. Then you can seek out alternative forms of socializing and still have an absolutely amazing experience in college. We included an example that describes some of the pros and cons involved, although your list might include many others, not just those we list here. See Figure 17-1 for this list.

**FIGURE 17-1  Pros and Cons of Joining a Fraternity or a Sorority**

| Pros | Cons |
|---|---|
| Automatic social group | Could pose a big distraction from my academics |
| Formation of tight bonds and a sense of brotherhood or sisterhood | Can be expensive in terms of membership dues and other costs |
| Provides instant involvement in campus activities | Initiation can be timeconsuming and humiliating, as well as potentially dangerous |
| Provides valuable leadership skills | It may not be the right social group for me |
| Provides plenty of activities to be involved in, including volunteer activities | My social life and activities could be limited to those approved by the fraternity or sorority |
| Assists with postgraduation by providing connections with other alumni and through networking | I could be required to attend all events put on by the fraternity or sorority and get into trouble if I don't participate |
| Provides the opportunity to create lifelong friends and cultivate connections | I could experience stigma associated with being involved with something considered by many to be shallow and superficial |
| It can look good on my resume | Can be seen as paying to have friends |
| Other Pro: | Other Con: |

As you weigh the pros and cons, we suggest assigning the largest amount of weight to determining how joining a fraternity or sorority is going to affect your academics. You may find many benefits from your participation in Greek life, including leadership skills, great friends, and a lot of fun. And many sororities and fraternities pride themselves on their members' academic performance—in fact, this can be quite competitive between houses. Mandatory study hours in special study rooms at the Greek houses may also be part of the Greek life at your school.

# Second Decision—Time for Housework

Let's assume you've weighed your pros and cons and decided that going Greek is right for you. The second major decision that you have to make—and the one that is going to define your experience with your fraternity or sorority—is deciding which one to join. If you choose wisely, you will end up having a great experience, gaining valuable leadership skills, and making lifetime friends. If you choose poorly, you will end up spending time with other students who you don't like, you could be miserable due to the mandatory Greek activities, you could jeopardize your academic career, and you could even end up being thrown out of the Greek system entirely. (Sounds just like a Greek tragedy, doesn't it!) The good news is that, especially at schools that have a large Greek presence, the diversity of options will enable you to find the best fit for you. Make sure you don't simply join the first one you come across or the one that your freshman roommate joined or the one that your brother or sister at a different school joined. Make the decision for yourself or else you'll regret it in the long run. (In case you do regret your decision, you can resign from the sorority or fraternity, though you may end up forfeiting dues and fees. Find out how much these penalties are before joining.)

The process of joining (referred to as *pledging*) varies from school to school, and from one fraternity or sorority to another. At some schools, *rush*, which is a multi-activity recruitment process, takes place either during the spring or fall semester, depending upon school policies. Rush gives you a chance to get to know the members of sororities and fraternities and figure out which one you might like to belong to. The various organizations will hold parties and mixers for prospective members. This is a good way to feel out the different houses and start thinking about which groups, if any, you may want to consider joining. You also may find members in your classes or other extracurricular activities who can tell you more about what they like and dislike about the fraternity or sorority they're involved in. If you think you may be interested in going through rush, try to get to know these people and use what you learn from them to inform your process of elimination. This knowledge will make the formal rush process much easier for you, and it will decrease your chances of winding up in a fraternity or sorority that isn't right for you.

Fall rush typically begins the week before school starts or even during the first week of classes. This timing makes it more difficult to make a fully educated decision. At these schools you have to decide whether you're going to go through rush and sign up to participate before stepping foot

> Making a good decision about which fraternity or sorority to join is extremely important—it will define what type of experience you're going to have.

on campus. Secondly, you have much less time on campus for exposure to the Greek life before you must decide which houses would match your personality. Just remember, if you decide not to go through rush, you can always do it the following year, after you've had time to familiarize yourself with the various houses and the Greek culture in general. This may be a good option for you if you're uncertain about it. It's certainly better than making a poor decision and then regretting it later.

## A Walk Through Sorority Rush

As an example, let's walk you through the typical sorority rush. Fraternity rush will be different, and each sorority and fraternity will have their own unique processes, but this will serve as a useful example. The first round of rush is generally an open house in which participating female students visit every sorority on campus. The remaining rounds are by invitation only—the sororities invite back those women who piqued their interest during the open houses. You may get invitations from several houses, but you get to choose the houses to which you want to continue rushing. Throughout rush, this mutual selection process continues over and over. Sororities consider rush a very competitive process and may put on skits and hold other activities to sway your affiliation their way. Sororities extend invitations to increasingly smaller numbers, and students accept or decline the invitations. The catch, and for some women it's a heartbreak, is that participation in rush does not guarantee an invitation to join a sorority. By the same token, if you are invited to join a sorority, you are not obligated to join. Each sorority typically has a minimum GPA requirement for joining and remaining a member. In fact, at some schools, the all-sorority GPA is higher than the all-women undergrads' GPA.

Several of the students who we worked with have joined sororities and fraternities. Most of them tell us that they had a great time and made friends they still have to this day. This is not to say, however, that every person or every fraternity or sorority is the same. We've also heard stories of fraternity or sorority members feeling the pressure to "keep up" and partying their way to academic suspension. So, do some research and make sure you're staying true to yourself and to your actual goals. Don't sacrifice who you are and what you're trying to accomplish academically at college just so you can help plan the best party of the year.

One student, Jenny, joined a sorority and absolutely loved it. She made wonderful friends, thrived in the sisterhood atmosphere, had a great social life, and finished school in four years, as she had planned, with a stellar GPA. She basically managed to do it all. However, her sorority also held academics very high on the priority list, which many others don't. This particular sorority had maintained the record of highest GPA in the school's Greek Council for 35 semesters, and if a sister didn't maintain a certain level of academic success, she was suspended from all sorority functions until she brought up her grades. The leadership of the sorority knew that academics had to come first.

## Making Adjustments

Another student, Margaret, had a completely different experience. She joined a sorority merely because she attended a Greek-heavy school and knew that it was something most students did. She joined a house that did not fit her personality, but was afraid if she quit, she'd end up with no friends and no social life. Within a year, she'd had enough. After missing one of the weekly meetings due to an illness in the family, she was fined $100. Despite the fact that she'd followed protocol and submitted a formal request to miss the meeting, citing the urgent nature of the situation, and the request had been approved, the conduct board of her sorority decided to fine her on the grounds that she was a subpar sister due to her lack of enthusiasm. Even though Margaret represented her sorority on the school-wide Greek Council, she was considered uninvolved and apathetic by her sorority's leadership. After a back-and-forth ordeal, she formally quit the sorority at the request of the conduct board and the president. In the end, although she believed quitting the sorority was the best option, she wished that she had made the right decision in the first place by either not joining one or choosing a different one to join.

*Note to Parents*

*As long as your children make an informed decision about whether to join a fraternity or sorority, you owe it to them to support their decision to the end.*

A third student, Robert, decided he wanted absolutely nothing to do with fraternities. When he first got to school, he had heard horror stories about fraternities and decided they were childish and designed for jocks who only came to school to party. While he liked to party when it was appropriate, he was very serious about his academics. Greek life was only moderately important at his school, which was one of the factors that drove him to select the school in the first place. During his freshman and sophomore years, he was quite happy with his decision. He noticed what he thought of as silly behavior by the Greeks on campus—particularly during rush—and was glad not to be a part of it. But in his junior year, he started to become friends with some classmates who had leadership positions in a number of different fraternities, and he slowly realized that he probably would have actually enjoyed being involved in a fraternity. He came to believe that he had simply been closed minded and hadn't properly thought through the benefits membership in a fraternity could provide. Nonetheless, he spent time with his new friends in their fraternities when he wanted to, even though he was barred from some of the activities and missed out on the leadership experience gained through Greek membership. He wished that he had thought it through a little better, wondering if he would have had a different—and possibly better—overall college experience had he decided to join a fraternity.

## To Sum Up

The Greek experience isn't for everyone. In fact, the overwhelming majority of college students don't participate in fraternities or sororities. For some of those who do, it's a wonderful experience, while others wish they had not elected to go Greek. So before rushing into a decision one way or the other, educate yourself as much as you can and stay true to what you want to get out of college.

# Chapter 18

## Location, Location, Location

### On or Off—Make Housing Work for You

**M**arta was a junior at a large university, well on her way to a biology degree with honors. One of her friends convinced her to move off campus for her senior year with two other girls. To Marta it sounded like a good experience and a refuge from the academic demands. She could actually get away from the campus for the nights and weekends and almost lead a normal life. But it didn't work out. The other two girls partied too much, and Marta didn't have a place to escape where she could study quietly. The campus was 10 miles away, requiring commuting time she didn't plan on, and she ended up staying on campus almost all day because she had so much lab work to do. She couldn't go back to her room as she was used to doing, so she had to camp out in the library or the student center.

Financially, it was an even bigger mistake. It cost her more to live off campus, and she had to argue with her roommates constantly over their share of the expenses and who should pay for the food. Once they even had their electricity shut off because the girl who was supposed to pay the bill used the money for a party instead. Marta realized she made a bad decision to move

> **Note to Parents**
> *Your children's housing situation can affect every aspect of their college life: their study habits, their friends, their sleeping habits, and the amount they will party.*

off campus. Normally a thoughtful person, this time she had agreed without taking the time to make a good decision.

Housing may seem like a somewhat less important decision in comparison to the numerous other life-changing decisions you have to make during your tenure at school. However, it's actually much more important than you may think and can impact every aspect of your college life. Essentially, you have two choices: you can live either on campus or off. This may seem like a cut-and-dried decision, and in the grand scheme of your life, it may be. But it's important that you not rush into either of these options; rather, you should consider them carefully based upon the goals you want to achieve during a particular semester and how your living situation will affect your ability to realize those goals.

At some schools, you may have little leeway when it comes to making this decision. Increasingly, many schools—smaller schools in particular—are requiring students to live on campus for longer periods of time. The rules can range from requiring you to live on campus for your freshman year, which is not atypical, to requiring on-campus living requirements even through your senior year, although this is less common. If your school has requirements that apply to you, the on- or off-campus decision has already been made for you. Other schools, however, don't share this philosophy of requiring you to stay on campus as long as they possibly can. In fact, many schools are eager to get their students off campus because of campus housing shortages. Dorms are expensive to maintain and even more expensive to build, and as the enrollment of nearly every school in the country rises, so does the demand for housing. If that's the case at your school, then you may have to make this decision sooner than you may realize.

> Choose your housing options well because they will define how much and when you will be able to study.

## Who, What, Where, When, Why, How . . . Wow!

In addition to the decision about being on campus or off campus, you have to make other decisions about your housing situation. Who are you going to live with? Whether you're on campus or off campus, you will most likely not live by yourself. That means you will have at least one roommate. Are you going to choose a roommate who parties all of the time? Or how about one who smokes in the room? Or one who has overnight guests? While we deal with how to handle your roommates in other chapters in this book, it's still important to make conscientious decisions about who to live with in coordination with your decisions about whether to live off campus in any of a number of housing options or on campus in a dorm room or on-campus apartment.

# A Note for Freshmen

Your first year of college is a fairly crucial time in your academic career. For most people, this is when they begin forming friendships, meeting new people, and developing their circle of friends. It is usually far easier to do this when living in the dorm environment. Off-campus living can cause some degree of isolation, but maybe that's what you're looking for. The vast majority of schools don't allow you to live anywhere but in the dorms when you're a freshman, so this likely won't be a decision that you have to make immediately. Some schools, however, have off-campus housing options available to their students. Some schools buy apartments or even houses and then turn them into off-campus student housing. But these options are usually not open to freshman, so be sure to check school policy before getting your hopes up.

As a new student, it's important to decide what you want to gain from your freshman year when it comes to your housing situation. Seriously consider the convenience of having other freshmen, who are experiencing the same changes and growing pains as you, right down the hall or just a short walk away. Also think about the resources available on campus: the library, computer labs, cafeteria, and even your professors. While you're familiarizing yourself with campus and college, in general, wouldn't it be helpful to you to be in close proximity to everything the campus offers? So, as you're weighing your options, keep in mind the pros and cons of each situation. We can't list them for you, as they are a matter of personal preference, but it's an important step to take in making your decision.

Here's how one student and her parents approached housing (and Greek life). Janel was accepted at a university in her home town. Her dad had also attended the same school years ago, the first in his family to graduate from college. To afford to do so, he had lived at home, and now he thought that if living at home was good enough for him, it was good enough for his daughter. He did admit, though, that he felt he missed out on a larger social life by living at home for all four years. Janel's mother envisioned a completely different scenario. Janel's mom (a third-generation sorority member) had lived in the dorm her freshman year, pledged a sorority, and moved into the sorority house her sophomore year. That's what she wanted for her daughter.

As an only child, Janel wanted to experience dorm life and viewed it as a once-in-a-lifetime college opportunity. You're only a freshman once, she reasoned. Janel preferred a particular dorm because it was reputed to be the most fun dorm on campus. Janel's mother liked the same dorm for her daughter, but for an entirely different reason: it had its own cafeteria. That meant Janel would not have to walk from her dorm to another one on cold winter mornings just to have some breakfast—which everyone acknowledged Janel was very unlikely to do! Janel ended up in the fun dorm and still considers it the best year of her college experience. She did join a so-rority and moved into the elegant sorority house for her sophomore and junior years. She rented a house near campus her senior year with a combination of girlfriends from the sorority and the dorm. To this day, she has no regrets about any of her housing decisions.

Be aware that dorm configuration may hold a few sur-prises in store, too, as another student, Vanessa, and her parents discovered on her first day as a freshman. The col-lege has a tradition of male upperclassmen helping to un-load and carry boxes of incoming female freshmen up to the rooms, so Vanessa's parents didn't think anything of the high number of young men swarming around their daugh-ter's dorm. As Vanessa and her parents reached the top of the stairs to their daughter's third-floor room, Vanessa's mom noticed male names on the rooms to the right. She checked the information packet for her daughter's room number again and, sure enough, it was on the third floor. Then Vanessa's mom no-ticed all the female names to the left of the stairs. She gasped, "Oh, my goodness, this is a coed floor!" Needless to say, it was a shock to both of Vanessa's parents that men would be on the same floor as the women. They thought that in a coed dorm the men were at least on their own floor and the women on theirs. While her parents were shocked, Vanessa was delighted. She had a fabulous freshman year!

> Your roommates can become some of your best friends—or they can ruin your academic career.

## As for the Rest of You

If you've already survived a year of college, or two or three, you may feel pretty smug that you're no longer a freshman—and rightfully so. For those of you who were forced into on-campus living for at least a year, and now have the opportunity to get out of it, you're feeling pretty cool since you have the option to get a place of your own. You have the freedom to control your own living situation, not having to abide by the strict rules of the dorms when it comes to the quiet hours, the suitemates, the shared bathrooms, and the shared community areas. While living in your own apart-ment can free you from these restrictions, it still carries its own distractions.

You probably shouldn't make your decision strictly based on what your friends are doing. You probably want to live with your friends, and that should factor into your decision to the appropriate extent, but don't just follow what they're doing without an-alyzing what's actually right for you. Everyone has different needs and different ideas of what they want to accomplish. This is not to say that off-campus living will lead to your demise. In fact, it can lead to much better academic performance and a much higher quality social life. But it can also lead to the opposite, depending upon what the situation is and what type of person you are. The choice of a roommate is important whether you live together on or off campus. In both cases, compatibility is key.

## Don't Get Distracted

Living with your friends is an important idea to consider, but it should be followed by, "Are my friends a source of distraction? Would they negatively or positively affect my academic life?" Some students who are juniors or seniors may have already been living with a friend on campus and should be able to answer that question easily. As we all know, our friends can greatly impact our lives. If they like to party a lot, chances are, you'll be right there with them, staying out until four in the morning. If your friends are extremely bookish, then you're apt to spend more time studying and hanging out with them in the library. This isn't to say that some people aren't different from their friends, but it's safe to say that the people you call your friends are probably called that because they're pretty similar to you. They share your interests, your academic and social needs, and perhaps your expectations and life goals are the same. Your friends will definitely influence your decisions. So calculate that into the equation as you consider what your friends are doing about housing and if you should go along with them.

Next, what environment do you think would be most conducive to academic success and to your social life at the same time? Do you find that the dorm poses a distraction because it's too noisy for you to study there? Does living in such close quarters hinder your study habits? Or, on the other hand, do you love being so close to the library that you can easily walk there to find a quiet place to study? While you may feel that the dorms are too noisy and pose too many distractions for you, it's important to remember that off-campus life can be just as chaotic, if not more so. When you're off campus, for example, you're living with other students who may have drastically different schedules than yours. Just because they like to study a lot doesn't mean that they won't be drinking or watching television when you're trying to study or vice versa. Some living environments off campus seem to be a perpetual open house, with friends dropping in nonstop. Off-campus housing may also afford fewer restrictions than dorms—in fact, your roommate might decide to purchase a dog or some other pet, which can be an asset or an annoyance, depending upon who ends up being responsible for its care. As you might guess, it's not always the owner!

One student, Andrew, decided to move into a house with five of his buddies during his senior year. He thought that this was a great idea. They were all on a budget, and splitting rent six ways made the house affordable for everyone. He also wanted to get away from campus because he found too many methods of procrastination there, and he really wanted to concentrate on school during his last year. On campus, he found that he was too tempted to wander around visiting people, go up to the student center to play Ping-Pong or hang out, or even go up to the library just to see if there were any cute girls there. He believed removing these temptations would allow him to give school his full attention—or at least more attention.

But he soon found out that he was completely wrong. In his new situation, he never had to wander around to find people because five other people lived with him. Somebody was always around. Andrew also didn't have to leave his apartment to find a Ping-Pong table because he and his roommates decided to put one in their backyard. Essentially, they had turned their house into "procrastination haven." It was noisier than the dorms, plus no residence assistant was available to keep the peace and maintain order. As if the cards weren't already stacked against him at this point, he found that he was so far from campus that he consistently missed his classes or showed up late for them. Needless to say, Andrew's senior year was not his strongest, and though he had a lot of fun, he paid a high price for that fun academically.

Living in an apartment can free you of many restrictions and distractions, but apartment life may carry its own distractions.

## Paying the Bills

Another important component to off-campus living that you must consider is how much it will cost. All too frequently, students vastly underestimate the cost of living off campus. If you are receiving scholarships that help cover your housing expenses, then you should know that you may very possibly cease to receive these funds once you move off campus. Also, you must begin to pay for your own electricity, gas, water, trash removal, renter's insurance, and any other services you desire. That high-speed Internet you've grown to rely on will now be accompanied by a bill. The same goes for cable television and meals. And when you sign the lease (which is a legally binding document), you will need a security deposit and, most likely, the first month's rent prepaid.

Now, maybe you've done the math, and it would be more cost effective for you to pay the rent, utilities, and other expenses that come with living on your own. If that's the case, mark that down as a pro on your living choice pros and cons list for moving off campus. But in many cases, this will not be so. Also, you should anticipate issues that may arise in sharing expenses. Sometimes one roommate can't come up with his share of the expenses and the others have to cover for him.

Darren had this problem when he moved off campus with three friends. One of his roommates kept spending all of his money on beer, so he didn't have enough to pay his share of the rent and utilities. Darren constantly had to come up with the additional money because he was the most responsible member of the group, which forced him to sacrifice going out himself. He eventually resented this and had a difficult relationship with his other roommates. In any roommate situation, the responsibility for collecting the money and paying the bills needs to be clearly defined and agreed on. One person we know who lived off campus had his Internet connection shut off because nobody got around to paying the bill.

The point is not that moving off campus is a bad choice. In fact, it could be the best decision you can make. But you need to know that it's a big decision and comes with a whole new set of risks and responsibilities.

# Overlooking Finances Is Costly

When choosing an off-campus apartment or house as compared with on-campus options, the stakes get a little higher. Not only do you need to seriously consider your compatibility in terms of sleeping schedule, partying habits, studying habits, cleanliness level, and so on, but you also have to consider how financially competent your potential roommates are. Rent is due whether your roommates put up their share or not, and if they aren't able to pay, then the burden falls on you. The same is true for all other bills. Nothing is more jarring than sitting down for breakfast at 9:00 a.m., ready to start the day, and you suddenly hear a strange click. Then, darkness. Utility companies aren't fond of providing services to people for free. But maybe you like taking cold showers and doing your reading by candlelight. If not, then you'd better make sure you have roommates who are responsible and can hold up their end of the bargain. If you are considering moving off campus by yourself, then similar considerations need to be made. Are you able to afford this? Are you ready to break out the checkbook or use online payment options to pay your bills responsibly? Are you good at housekeeping? If you don't like to cook, are adequate restaurants located nearby?

You should consider the positives and the negatives of your choice by creating a simple pros and cons list. We've gone ahead and provided the basics of a pros and cons list for this decision in a Decide Better! worksheet, shown in Figure 18-1. You can add more pros and cons to the list in the open spaces, but this will provide you with a basic set of positives and negatives that you should consider.

Another excellent approach to decision making that can help in this area is an exercise that we like to call See If It Fits. This technique allows you to try on different

**FIGURE 18-1 Worksheet: Should I Live Off Campus?**

| Pros | Cons |
|---|---|
| 1. I will have more freedom to come and go as I please and to do what I want, when I want. | 1. I will have to put up with the habits of my roommates, rather than being able to have a single room in a dorm. |
| 2. My apartment could be less busy and less noisy than a dorm, which has people coming and going constantly. | 2. I will have to deal with hooking up my own cable, phone, and Internet access. |
| 3. I won't have to share a bathroom with strangers. | 3. I will be farther away from the library and from campus in general. |
| 4. I will be able to cook my own meals. | 4. I will have to cook my own meals. |
| 5. It may be cheaper to get an apartment than living on campus in the dorm. | 5. It may be more expensive than living on campus when I add rent, food, transportation, and the cost of utilities. |
| 6. I can choose the people I share my living space with. | 6. I will have to buy more furniture, including a bed, a desk, and a dresser. |
| 7. I will have a rental history, which will make it easier to get another apartment after college. | 7. I will have to deal with paying rent every month, a security deposit, and a lease. |
| Other Pro: | Other Con: |

options by imagining them. You imagine your living situation choices and then examine your feelings about each imagined option. See yourself with your roommates hanging out in the living room, talking, and having fun. Imagine parties and the fun of your friends coming over. Then imagine your room in relation to the noise level if you're trying to study or complete a paper at the last minute while a party is going on. Ponder in your mind how you'd all share one bathroom with morning classes starting at the same time for each of you. Try out the commute a few times to see what it's like. Envision an argument over paying the bills or your anger at someone who ate the leftovers you'd planned for your dinner. Try out as many scenarios as you can depict. The See If It Fits technique generally requires some time to simulate your various options, so allow sufficient time for this exercise. Take the time for a fitting and see if the circumstance truly fits.

# To Sum Up

Regardless of whether you're a freshman or a senior, you should consider numerous aspects when trying to decide where to live. Decide what you want to get out of your living situation and with whom. Use Decide Better! pros and cons lists and the See If It Fits techniques to figure out which option is most conducive to your needs and desires. For freshmen, we strongly advise choosing on-campus accommodations. This way you will be surrounded by people who are in the same situation as you are in and, together, you can fully familiarize yourselves with the campus and all it has to offer. You may find that this inherent camaraderie provides a wonderful introduction to college life. Regardless, we know this is a personal decision, so be honest with yourself regarding what's best for you and then go from there. Happy dorm or house hunting!

# Section IV.

## Relationship Decisions

Some of the most important decisions that you will make during your college years involve other people—your relationship decisions. Living in a confined space with other people with whom you have had little previous familiarity, and under difficult and stressful academic and social circumstances, may make these decisions challenging. In addition to roommate decisions you will also likely make very important decisions about your romantic life—decisions that may have huge ramifications for your future.

The first chapter of this section, chapter 19, focuses on roommate decisions. When you move to college your freshman year, you probably will know little about your new roommate. You may have e-mailed back and forth a few times, mostly coordinating what you'd bring, your music preferences, and other likes and dislikes. It's less likely that you've actually spoken with each other on the phone or in person. The new experience of moving in with someone you've never met can be nerve-wracking, but it's one of the most important and common experiences in college. You could become lifelong friends or immediate enemies. Chapter 19 guides you through this major adjustment process and offers decision-making advice to help you and your roommate come to an understanding about common decisions. How late will you stay up? Will you have a

Balancing your relationships successfully—whether they are with your friends, roommates, boyfriends or girlfriends, or your parents—will determine much of your enjoyment level in college.

study room or a party room? Will you allow overnight guests? Will you allow smoking or drinking in the room? How will you accommodate each other's schedules? How much will you play video games or watch television? All of these are decisions that you need to work out with your roommate, preferably earlier rather than later. In addition, those of you who have survived your freshman year then have another challenge—how to select your roommate or roommates for your sophomore, junior, and senior years. Should you room with your best friends? Or by yourself? Or with someone who you think will help you academically? This decision is crucial for how well you do in your classes, for how well you fit in with your friends, and for how you balance your academic and personal lives.

> ### Note to Parents
> *Your relationship with your kids is going to change—you hope for the better. They will have new friends, new boyfriends or girlfriends, new roommates, and new associations that will change their lives. But you should still be some of the central people in their lives.*

Chapter 20 pertains to the decisions you're going to have to make regarding dating, romantic relationships, and sex. Let's face it—dating and sex are difficult topics to talk about or read about, but avoiding making personal decisions about your behavior has its perils. Prior to college, your relationships may have been restricted based on the rules set by your parents. But now that you're in college, these rules aren't only relaxed, they're completely nonexistent. You now have the freedom to do what you want to. But, just as with drinking or drugs, you now need to make a conscious decision about sex. Deciding whether to have sex should be a decision made in the light of day. Moreover, you also need to make decisions about the extent to which you're going to let your new romantic relationships take over your life. Dating and love can take up a lot of time and energy, but having a good balance with the academic and social goals of college can be one of the critical factors to both your success and level of enjoyment in college.

The final chapter in this section, chapter 21, addresses your changing relationship with your parents. They've been there for you through the good times and bad, and you can be sure that they'll be there for you throughout college. But, as soon as you leave the structure, rules, and restrictions of their house, your relationship with them is going to change drastically. Only you can determine whether that change is for the better or for the worse. It's important to understand that your parents have put a lot into who you are—they've imparted their values, their experiences, their mistakes, and their love. They've given up a lot for you, and they will continue to do so. But at this point you need to show them that you're going to continue to seek their help, their love, and their admiration, as well as assure them that you're going to keep communicating with them. By talking to them before you leave for college, you can agree about your mutual expectations for your ongoing relationship, not just while you're at college, but over the course of the rest of your life.

# Chapter 19

# The Odd Couple

## Learning to Live with a Roommate, Whether Friend or Foe!

**P**aula always liked her environment to be neat and clean, but unfortunately she was paired with a roommate, Stephanie, who seemed to be the exact opposite. The first few weeks were miserable for both of them, and each wanted to change to a different room. But they called a truce for a while, and eventually worked out a reasonable way to live together and went on to become best friends.

Whether you were an only child or came from a family with many siblings, your living situation drastically changes when you get to college. You may have had your own bedroom that you could decorate, arrange, and clean when you wanted to, or maybe you shared a room with a pesky younger brother or sister. Perhaps you shared a bathroom with your siblings and your parents, or maybe you were lucky enough to have your own.

Regardless of what your rooming situation was at home while growing up, you will have quite a bit of

### Note to Parents

*While you may have been successful in directing your children's lives up until this point, you need to let them be who they are. One place to start is to let them complete their freshman roommate questionnaire themselves—without your reading it afterward.*

learning to do when you get to college and move into your 10 ft × 12 ft dorm room, only half—or worse, only a third—of which is yours. Dorm life and living with a roommate are often the biggest adjustments for incoming freshmen. This is especially true for the vast majority of students who either opt for or are required to choose the "potluck" roommate selection—the daring choice to let the school select your roommate for you. Moving into cramped quarters with a complete stranger and then attempting to create a homelike atmosphere in which both people can live comfortably and peacefully is a daunting and scary experience. But there are steps you can take to minimize potential conflicts.

The stories in this chapter are not designed to scare you. In fact, some of them should inspire you. It's important for you to understand that the roommate relationship and the decisions you make are intricate parts of the college experience—for better or worse. You could end up with a freshman-year roommate who becomes your lifelong friend or your enemy for four years. More likely, you will simply survive together through good experiences and bad experiences.

Whether you like it or not, that dorm room is your home for the next nine months, and finding and maintaining a tolerable level of relative peace with your roommate will make your lives much easier. While many of the tips and decisions in this chapter are most relevant for freshman year, when you likely will have very little roommate selection input beyond your completion of the freshman-year roommate questionnaire, many of the topics covered will also be useful as you continue to deal with roommates during your subsequent years in college. Making the decision about your roommates during these years is also important, and choosing the right people for you will lead to a better overall living environment and a successful academic and social life throughout college. After all, isn't that what college is all about?

# Preparation for the Match Game

Let's begin chronologically, in your freshman year when the majority of roommate disruption and drama occur. You may find yourself in the most precarious of roommate situations this first year because you will have little control over who is assigned as your roommate. Colleges send out a roommate questionnaire with their enrollment forms to solicit your input, and that is about all you can do if you are electing to room with someone you don't know already. You're going to be spending a lot of time with this person, and it's natural to feel both excited and apprehensive that someone you don't know is making the decision on who this person will be. (In fact, many schools have current students assign roommates for incoming freshmen,

**Quick Tips to Survive Living with Your Roommate:**

- Coordinate what you and your roommate will bring with you ahead of time
- Complete the freshman roommate questionnaire correctly and honestly
- Don't expect that you're going to be best friends with your roommate
- Establish house rules that you will both abide by and then don't break them

which can be either great or terrible, depending on how this student envisions who you are based on your questionnaire responses.)

The questionnaire will include a list of topics that will be used to match you with your future roommate. Look at the questionnaire seriously because it will help you get matched with someone who is at least moderately similar to you. If you really don't care who you are matched with, then you won't need to worry much about how you fill out the form. The wide variety of questions is designed to reveal more about you and your interests. These are some questions that are typically asked on the questionnaire:

- What are your sleeping habits (early to bed, early to rise; late to bed, late to rise; number of hours of sleep you like or need every night)?

- How would you describe your level of cleanliness (i.e., cleanliness and order are important, moderately important, not important)?

- What type of music do you listen to (heavy metal, rap, country, hip hop, classic rock, etc.)?

- When you study, do you listen to the radio or watch television?

- What temperature do you prefer to keep your bedroom (cold, average, hot)?

- Are you open to rooming with an international student?

- Are you open to rooming with a member of a different ethnic group or sexual orientation?

- How high would you rate the importance of social life, academics, friends, athletics, and extracurricular activities?

- Would you prefer to room with a night person or a morning person?

- Do you envision your room as more of a place of privacy or a place for friends to hang out?

- How would you feel about your roommate borrowing items from you, including clothes, food, and toiletries?

These are less common questions on the roommate questionnaire, but ones that would enable you to get right to the heart of the matter:

- What are your expectations for school?
- How do you like to relax after a stressful day?
- What is your favorite food?
- What are your interests?
- Do you smoke? Do you drink? (Some students lie about smoking or drinking on their forms because they fear their parents will read them.)

# Friend Mates—Wow or Woe

For those of you who are attending the same school as a friend and have decided to live together, don't think you're off the hook. Those setups can be some of the most tumultuous and dramatic of all of the roommate situations because a pre-existing emotional investment may complicate living together. This may come as a shock, but read our real-life example to back up this claim.

Kim and Sara met during their ninth grade year and immediately hit it off, mostly because they were in a few of the same clubs and had some of the same friends. They became very close friends in high school, and by the time they were applying to college and making decisions regarding which schools to go to, they had known each other very well for nearly four years. This substantial amount of time seems like enough time to really know one another, warts and all. So after applying to similar colleges and being accepted to many of the same ones, Kim and Sara decided to enroll in the same school and to live together.

This seemed like a logical decision. They could help each other ease into college, make new friends together, and support each other through the first potentially lonely weeks when everybody else was bumbling around like lost and scared puppies. During that time, they'd have each other to lean on, keep each other company, and help each other acclimate. Or, so they thought. The first few weeks together seemed mutually beneficial because they didn't have any awkward stage in college with no friends and nobody to hang out with other than an unfamiliar roommate. Kim and Sara did realize after a while, though, that by relying so

Moving into cramped quarters with a complete stranger and attempting to create a home-like atmosphere can be a daunting and scary experience.

much on each other, they missed out on many of the social activities the school had specifically designed for incoming freshmen to meet other people.

Then within the first two months, Kim found a serious boyfriend who pretty much moved into the girls' room—much to Sara's dismay, especially considering the boyfriend had his own dorm room. At that same point, Sara had made a couple of good friends who weren't friends with Kim, which upset Kim quite a bit and caused some jealousy issues. But little did Kim know, Sara was jealous of Kim's boyfriend taking up all of Kim's time—and Sara's room. After only a few months, the two had essentially stopped communicating completely. The only time they would talk was to yell or gripe at one another for some petty reason or another. Needless to say, the situation was tense.

By the end of the first semester even the fighting had ceased. If both girls were in the room, it was silent unless the radio or television was on. Despite living only a few streets apart from one another back home, they didn't see each other once during the winter break. It wasn't until Kim came to pick Sara up for the drive back to school that they laid eyes on each other and spoke. Surprisingly, they managed to have a fun-filled five-hour drive and seemed to resolve many of their issues. For the first time in months, they communicated and voiced their concerns and complaints. For the first two days back at school, they were more or less alone. Kim's boyfriend hadn't returned, nor had Sara's friends. They spent the whole time together just like old times.

Those two great days quickly ended when the boyfriend and their friends returned. Resentment, jealousy, and hurt feelings came rushing back in full force. By the middle of their second semester, they were actively lashing out at one another—unplugging alarm clocks to cause the other to sleep through class, "accidentally" throwing away each other's mail, and even disposing of one another's possessions if they crossed the imaginary my-side, your-side line they'd created through the center of their room. The situation was worse than ever. At the end of the year, neither of them could get out of the dorm room fast enough. After taking the summer off and not talking to each other at all, they reconnected the next year and managed to save their friendship. We hear far too many stories that are similar to this one, though, where the people involved were unable to get their friendship back. It's a shame to lose a long-term—and potentially lifelong—friendship because of the stresses of living together.

If you're attending the same school as a friend, then you have a big decision to make regarding your living situation. Most people, including experts, will tell you that agreeing to be a freshman roommate with a friend is a bad idea. Rather than making such a black-and-white statement, it's probably better to just let you know that it is a decision to take very seriously. If relations between you and your roommate get rocky, but you're not close friends, it probably won't affect you as much in the long run as it would if the roommate is also a close friend. If living with a friend is an option, you need to carefully consider each of your personalities and how they will mesh in close, stressful conditions.

## Personalities and Decisions

The first year of college presents more stress and learning experiences than you've probably faced up to this point. Expect that being away from home, adjusting to collegiate-level academics, and being thrown into unfamiliar surroundings with unfamiliar people entails a learning curve. Since your roommate is going through the same growing pains, the emotional component is compounded. So, when deciding whether to room with a friend or with a complete stranger, examine how you and your friend each deal with certain situations and figure out if you, as a pair, will complement or clash with each other.

> Your freshman year roommate could become your best friend—or your enemy. But either way, you have to make it work, and you'll both survive.

While you may have some experience dealing with different personality styles, living with a roommate will force you to deal with the frustration of making decisions with someone who approaches them differently than you do. We discussed personality differences and the way people approach decisions in our first book, *Decide Better! for a Better Life*, and these characteristics apply strongly to learning how to live with roommates. The Myers-Briggs Type Indicator (MBTI) is a useful method for examining personality-based differences in how people make decisions. The MBTI defines four dimensions of personality characteristics and two opposite personality types for each characteristic.

The first characteristic separates Extroverts (E) from Introverts (I). Extroverts prefer to reach decisions interactively, that is, by talking them through with others. They believe in consensus through discussion and assume that all involved will express their opinions. When people do not express opinions, the Extrovert interprets their silence as consent. But that's not always the case.

Introverts (I) don't make their decisions through interaction with others, but through private reflection. Here's an example of how the decision paths of an Extrovert and an Introvert roommate differ. The Extrovert roommate says, "It might be interesting to have a party this weekend," by which she only means that she's thinking out loud about that option and is soliciting her roommate's opinion. But the introvert roommate interprets this as a unilateral decision to have a party and then gets upset because "she didn't even discuss it with me first."

Introverts have such a strong preference for making decisions in private that they may even prefer a written proposal to a verbal argument. As you can see, major obstacles can impede Introvert and Extrovert roommates from making a joint decision that satisfies them both.

The second Myers-Briggs characteristic relates to the information different people need to make a decision. Sensors (S) prefer to make decisions by looking at detailed facts and are very reluctant to reach a conclusion until they have all the facts they think they need. Sensors, in other words, are analytical and wary of analytical error.

In contrast, Intuitives (N) typically want to consider alternatives at a less-detailed level so they can make decisions within the context of the broader picture. If roommates, S and N, are trying to decide on getting a refrigerator for their room, S begins by gathering details on various models, including costs and dimensions. N gets resentful of being forced to review all the details, and pushes back. "We haven't even discussed if it makes sense, and you're already picking one out." To this, S will respond, "How can we decide if we are going to get one without knowing any facts?" And so the fun begins.

The third major division in the Myers-Briggs Type Indicator is between Thinkers (T) and Feelers (F). Thinkers don't mind making the difficult decisions themselves and can't understand why anyone gets upset about issues that aren't relevant to the decision. They tackle decisions in a detached fashion and tend to be objective and logical. Rarely do they get emotionally involved in a decision. They tend to assume that every problem has a correct answer, and it's their business to figure out what that answer is.

In contrast, Feelers believe that a good decision must take into account the feelings of others. They are driven by interpersonal involvement and tend to approach decisions subjectively, trying to incorporate all the expressed points of view into a decision that will prove to be acceptable to everyone.

For example, F may say, "Mary wants to stay with us for a while because her roommate has her boyfriend staying there, and I told her it was okay." T then may respond, "But there isn't enough room, and we have exams coming up. It doesn't make sense."

The final personality characteristic influences how easy or difficult people find decision making to be. Judgers (J) are decisive, deliberate, and reach decisions without much stress. They like everything to be organized and controlled, and they readily make the decisions necessary to achieve and maintain control. At their extreme, Judgers will sometimes make uninformed and even indefensible decisions, just to have them off their agendas. Furthermore, they may find it very difficult to change a decision once they've made it, even an obviously bad one.

Perceivers (P), on the other hand, don't want to be forced to make a decision. They like to keep their options open. Making decisions causes them anxiety. They prefer to take a wait-and-see attitude, deferring decisions until they've gathered more information. At their extreme, Perceivers are virtually incapable of making decisions and make every decision more complicated than it needs to be. When a J and a P face a joint decision, it's often an exercise in mutual exasperation. Suppose that roommates J and P are considering redecorating their room. J is ready to make a decision after discussing it briefly and wants to get it done. P reacts negatively to this, to say the least. "How can you make such a rash decision? We've haven't even talked about all the alternatives." J will respond, "We don't need to consider every possibility." Even if J gets his way for now, the battle may not be over. Tomorrow or the next day, P may insist that they reconsider their choices. So on and on it goes. J can't tolerate indecision. P dreads making a mistake.

# From Conflict to Friendship

We've spoken with many students who have griped about their freshman year roommates. Some of them have ended up becoming lifelong friends with these people who were complete strangers to them the day before college started. But that doesn't mean they didn't experience conflict at the time. Living in such close quarters, it's only natural for friction to occur. Maybe one of you is coming home too late and waking the other up. The other one has friends in the room when you want to study. Or you both want to listen to different kinds of music when you're studying. Over time, even the little issues can lead to tension and problems. It's key to understand that disagreements are going to happen regardless of whom you live with, but you can't let those conflicts get the better of you and negatively affect your academic and social life.

> The nature of the close living situation with your roommate is that friction is going to arise. If you work to understand the differences in decision-making styles, you'll maintain your dignity and respect.

On the other hand, you cannot allow yourself to justify confrontation and conflict. You and your roommate should not make a habit of blowing up at each other anytime something goes wrong in your lives. Occasional friction and annoyance are understandable. Yelling and outright fighting are unacceptable. You need to decide to get along the best you can in order to achieve a roommate relationship that is livable.

One student, Jessica, had to live on campus while taking summer classes. Unfortunately, none of her friends were staying for the summer so she was paired with a complete stranger—just like she had been her freshman year! She couldn't believe that she'd have to go through that again. And once they met and started getting acquainted, they both quickly realized that they were as different as night and day in nearly every way—from the hours they kept and the music they liked, to their majors and food preferences. They didn't agree on one subject except for their desire to have a peaceful and happy summer.

For the next nine weeks, they utilized respect and communication to cultivate a healthy roommate relationship and a serene living situation. By the time the summer was over, it dawned on each of them that they had surpassed the roommate stage and had actually become friends. They each started to like the other's taste in music and fashion and even opened each others' minds on the subjects of politics, religion, and culture. They were still as different as could be, but they had learned from each other and grown. They also experienced the benefits of good communication and realized that they had both done much better in this roommate situation than they had when they were freshmen. They had approached their summer situation more maturely by learning to understand each other's needs and expectations and by maintaining a respect for their differences.

# Make Some Common Decisions

You and your roommate will make many decisions together. You can make them individually within the heat of the moment, or you can make them in advance by logically talking them through. We suggest the latter. Take some time when you start your new relationship to navigate some common decisions.

We provide a worksheet to get you started (Figure 19-1) on page 220. You can choose to actually fill it in and compare your decisions with your roommate or just discuss it casually. (The worksheet has spaces for an answer from roommate A and roommate B.) If you fill it in, you can use it as a future reference of your agreement. Most likely you will just use it to get started on a fruitful discussion of your common decisions. Add to it other decisions that you think are important. You may need to compromise to reach concurrence, but this is part of the process of getting along. What this worksheet should help you do is to begin to understand the issues that may arise and to head them off before they strain your relationship with your roommate or roommates. Some of these topics may be more important to you than others, and you may want to bring up the less important ones in a more informal way with your roommate. Even if you don't agree on something, you will begin to understand what's important to each of you, and thus you can avoid triggering conflict unnecessarily. And it's better to do this at the beginning of your cohabitation instead of confronting each other in anger later on.

Either of you may change your decision over time as circumstances change. You should agree to have an open discussion of these common decisions when necessary but to use the previous decision as the starting point. Discuss what has changed and why the decision should be changed. While compromise is standard procedure for many roommate scenarios, if this seems impossible, seek a mediator or resident assistant for help. If the situation is intolerable, you may simply need to work with the residence staff and change rooms.

## To Sum Up

Not every roommate relationship is going to end in either hatred or friendship. Some people simply coexist and then part ways at the end of the year. What you're aiming for is to avoid excessive doses of confrontation and to learn how to manage the conflict that does arise. Going into this new situation, remember that this dorm room is as much your roommate's as it is yours. Decide to get along, realize you will need to compromise, and learn to respect one another's wishes.

**FIGURE 19-1  Worksheet: Roommate Common Decisions**

| Questions | Responses |
|---|---|
| 1. Do you want to have defined quiet hours for study? | A: _____<br>B: _____ |
| 2. Do you want a specific "lights out" time? | A: _____<br>B: _____ |
| 3. Do you want to allow overnight guests? | A: _____<br>B: _____ |
| 4. Do you agree to smoking, drinking, or drugs in the room? | A: _____<br>B: _____ |
| 5. Do you want to establish guidelines for the room? | A: _____<br>B: _____ |
| 6. What items do you want to share (e.g. TV, stereo, refrigerator, etc.)? | A: _____<br>B: _____ |
| 7. Other decision 1 | A: _____<br>B: _____ |
| 8. Other decision 2 | A: _____<br>B: _____ |
| 9. Other decision 3 | A: _____<br>B: _____ |

# Chapter 20

# The Dating Game
## Romance and Sex in the College Setting

Everything was going great for Maria at college. She got good grades and was very popular. One night she went to a huge party and had too much to drink. She met a great looking guy, and they went back to his room. She didn't recall much about that night, but she obviously had sex because shortly after that night, she was pregnant. She dropped out of school the next year to have the baby, but she still hopes to complete college eventually. While she certainly loves her child, Maria wishes that she had made a more careful, sober decision that night.

We're going to go out on a limb here and assume that your parents, while you were living under their roof, never gave you free rein when it came to dating. Your significant other was probably never allowed to spend the night in your room, let alone in your bed. You most likely had a curfew, and if you two were going to watch a movie or listen to music, you did it in the family room or in your room with the door left wide open. Perhaps you were raised in a more

*Note to Parents*

*Here's the hard fact—it is highly likely that your children will be sexually active in college, whether you like it or not. The real challenge for you as a parent is to be sure they're responsible. Ignoring the idea of them having sex will not prevent them from getting a sexually transmitted disease or becoming pregnant or getting someone else pregnant.*

laissez-faire environment, but these boundaries usually ring true for the vast majority of high school students.

These rules and restrictions helped to limit your romantic activities and allowed your parents to maintain some control over your love life. But at college, these restrictions and bans are nearly nonexistent. Some schools regulate when and if boys are allowed in girls' dorms and vice versa, but most colleges give their students unlimited access to one another. Some schools have single-sex dorms with curfews intact for members of the opposite sex, but within a week of living there, most people have figured out how to bend or even break these rules.

Unless you decide to attend a fairly strict college, the world is your oyster as far as romance—and sex—goes. This thought probably keeps your parents up at night, but it's probably one of the more alluring aspects of college for you, the student. So how should you, the newly free freshman, go about making decisions regarding relationships and sex?

While relationship boundaries may seem like an irrelevant subject or something that you can't plan ahead for—thinking it's a bridge that you'll cross when you come to it—it's actually very important. And the mentality that you'll figure it out when you get there is exactly what you should avoid. You can't plan who you're going to have a crush on, who you're going to date, who you may casually meet and have sex with, and who you're going to fall in love with. But you can rationally predict that some events like these are going to happen. After all, you're a teenager with this new freedom, and you want to take advantage of that.

# Make a Sober Decision

As with partying and drinking, dating and, more specifically, sex, are issues that should be pondered during the sobering light of day. Don't wait to make decisions about whether you're going to have sex with someone until after you've been drinking and hormones and beer goggles are clouding your judgment and some random person is pulling you toward a dorm room. Studies have shown that as many as 70 percent of all students state that they've engaged in sexual activity primarily as a result of being under the influence of alcohol or drugs. Is that a statistic you're going to add to?

The lifting of restrictions on dating and sex can be alluring in college, but that doesn't lift the restrictions you should place on yourself to be a responsible adult.

# Are Relationships for You Right Now?

Relationships themselves should be taken very seriously, as they can have major repercussions. You may, for example, find your true love at college. In fact, many people do fall in love in college and end up marrying that person. Many, many others do not. But most will find someone they are attracted to and end up in some type of relationship together. While love and dating and sex are a part of college life, remember that relationships can disrupt your academics as much as—if not more than—drinking too much or being involved in too many extracurricular activities.

Moreover, you can move too quickly and, by doing so, ruin something that could be special. Think of it this way: On the one hand, you have this new, wonderful person in your life. You want to spend all of your time together and, for the first time in your life, you can do just that! But is that the wisest step? Starting a new relationship is extremely exciting and can severely impair your judgment, but it's important to try to combat this and approach this addition to your life seriously. A relationship can impact your life—both socially and academically—in profound ways, both negative and positive. If you spend too much time with your new significant other, you may not only impair your academics (and the rest of your social life), but you could even damage your relationship with this person you've come to love and admire. In other words, you may want to consider taking it slower, rather than rushing into having your new boyfriend or girlfriend move into your dorm room. You could end up upsetting your roommate, falling behind in your classes, and then breaking up with this person. College relationships can be very complex and have many unintended consequences.

> Don't make a decision about having sex with someone when you've been drinking and hormones and beer goggles are clouding your judgment and some random person is pulling you toward a dorm room.

You should make specific decisions about your college relationships. Do you want to have a single serious relationship throughout your college years, or do you want to get to know more people before considering a serious relationship? Do you want to commit the time and energy to a serious relationship at this point in your life or take it more slowly? How will you know if someone is really special? What criteria must be met before you will engage in sex with someone? How long do you need to know that person? What emotional level in a relationship do you need to reach before engaging in sex? What types of sex will you engage in (what are your limits)? Will you risk unprotected sex?

A relationship decision involves calculating the risks and rewards. You may not make the best decisions early in the process, but that's part of your learning curve. Try doing a "decision autopsy" after these early decisions—a postmortem examination, so to speak. Identify what was right and what was wrong and apply these lessons in your future relationship options. Below are some questions that you can use as part of this process:

- Was this a good or a bad decision? Most likely you will be more eager to learn from your bad decisions because you will be motivated to correct them.

- What would have been a better decision? With hindsight, you will probably have an opinion of what you should have decided.

- Why would this have been a better decision? This will lead you to understand what you should have considered or tried to find out before making the decision.

- Did you know about this other option at the time of your decision? Maybe you could have considered it but didn't, or maybe it was a complete unknown.

- What should you have done differently? The essence of the decision autopsy is identifying what you can do differently the next time around.

- How can you use this experience to make a better decision next time?

# No Time to Gamble

Sex can be a really uncomfortable subject to broach for many people. However, as you head off to college and acquire all the freedoms and possibilities that come with college life, this subject will present itself whether you're comfortable with it or not. We don't presume that we have the faintest idea what your stance is on sex. Maybe you've decided to wait until marriage or until you're in a long-term, committed relationship. Or maybe you're waiting for the first opportunity to jump into the promiscuity pool. So rather than giving advice that may or may not apply to you, here are some tips regarding decisions about sex to let you make up your own mind.

Whether you think so or not, sex is a big deal, and it can lead to life-changing consequences. You are no doubt well aware of these consequences from your sex education class in junior high school. Disease and pregnancy, of course, are just a couple of the effects sex can have on a person's life—not to mention the emotional and psychological aspects it entails. In fact, a recent study by Columbia University found that 20 to 25 percent of all college students have had or do currently have a sexually transmitted disease. That's roughly one in every four students and most likely includes many people you know.

Having sex is a lot like partying in the sense that it may not seem like a big deal at the time, but the repercussions span the spectrum from an embarrassing "what was I thinking" moment to something that can alter your life forever, such as a disease or a pregnancy. So, with that in mind, it's important to make decisions about sex while you are sober and thinking clearly. You should be strong in your convictions— whether you've decided to wait or decided to give it a try with whatever safety precautions you decide to take.

When you start dating someone, it's important that you make decisions regarding how long you'll wait until hopping into bed with that person. Maybe you're willing to sleep with someone on the first date. Or maybe you've decided to set a five-date rule before even considering taking that step. You can make these decisions with that person or on your own. Regardless of your beliefs, informing your dating partner of your stance on the subject ahead of time is helpful. That way, you won't have to deal with unwanted advances late at night after dinner and drinking.

With the freedom in college, sex is an issue that will present itself in a blossoming relationship much more quickly than it did when you were in high school. Much of that is due to the fact that you have more opportunities to engage in sexual intercourse and fewer restrictions on your behavior. Be ready and know how you feel about the matter. Stick to your guns and be prepared for potential pressure from your partner. Know what you'll say to defend your point and how you'll combat persuasion. Just because you're dating someone doesn't mean that you owe that person sexual favors. And if you're on the other side—where you're ready to take the next step, but your partner isn't—be respectful, understanding, and don't use pressure or persuasion tactics to try to get what you want.

If you're facing decision pressure, following these steps may help you decide your response:

- Acknowledge the pressure.
- Assess the underlying motives of the person pressuring you.
- Is the pressure really for your benefit or is the person who is applying the pressure doing so for self-serving reasons?
- If the reason is for that person's benefit, is there a legitimate reason for the pressure?

- ❗ If you remove the pressure, what is the real decision and how do you feel about it based on the facts alone?

- ❗ Reintroduce the pressure and decide whether to agree to it or resist it.

If your views on sex differ from those of your partner, then you need to sit down with the other person and make decisions about where to go from there. Is the conflict a deal breaker? Is it important enough to end the relationship? Or can one of you—preferably the person who's ready for this step—be patient and understanding enough to give in to what the other person wants? Sex is a two-way street, and it should not even be considered unless both parties feel they're ready for this step. It must be a mutual decision between two people who are willing to be respectful, understanding, and compassionate toward one another. If you're the "ready-and-willing" partner, the elements of respect, understanding, and compassion especially apply to you.

Of course, in college that's not always the case. More often than not, it's about two people in the same place at the same time throwing their hands up in the air and saying, "Hey, do you want to hook up?"

> Just because you now have the opportunity to have sex without restrictions doesn't mean you have to take advantage of that opportunity.

It's important to remember that deciding to engage in sex, like many other similar decisions, can have unintended consequences. College students don't generally intend to get pregnant when they have sex, but tens of thousands of them do every year. They don't intend to get a sexually transmitted disease, but tens of thousands of them are infected each year.

# Love's in the Air

What about the fun aspects of love, dating, and relationships in the boundary-free college world? You will be meeting lots of new people throughout your entire four years in college. At some point during that time, you're probably going to find someone you're attracted to. You'll start dating the person and see where it goes, right? But you may want to consider some potential consequences before diving headfirst into the type of relationship where you are attached at the hip, can't live without each other, and have no time for anything or anyone else.

Time management is crucial. (See chapter 8 on The Balancing Act of managing your time.) Most likely, when you were in high school, your parents laid down the law regarding how much time you could spend with your significant other. They probably regulated the "family:school:significant other" ratio pretty strenuously. They made sure your priorities were straight, and if they sensed your school work was slipping, they most likely cut down the time you could spend with that special someone. Now, however, you are the sole keeper of your time and no one is standing over your shoulder and keeping you on track. This freedom becomes especially dangerous when it's coupled with blossoming romance because you most likely want to spend every waking minute with your new love. This combination can seriously hinder your academic life if you're not careful and responsible. Time spent with your boyfriend or girlfriend (or that person you hope will fill that role soon), also needs to be included in your breakdown of time allocated for each subset of activities in college. If you decide just to spend time with them whenever you want or whenever they want, you're likely to be headed for lower grades and possibly other academic—and social—problems.

## Making Time for Each Other

You can avoid this problem by making smart and mature decision. You and your new beau or beauty need to decide on a mutually beneficial schedule. Don't forget about your friends and extracurricular activities either. This schedule needs to include all of your priorities, but it can't be unrealistic. This schedule, or allotted times for responsibilities, needs to be something you both can stick to, with some flexibility for specific circumstances, of course. Maybe you decide to spend time studying at the library together. That way, you're with each other, but you're also productive. You can also combine priorities by bringing your significant other along when you hang out with your friends. Maybe you don't want to do this every time you spend time with friends, but occasionally this mix of social priorities might be efficient. This will also help integrate your significant other into your life. Many young couples have a tendency to lock themselves away in isolation and to see no one except each other. Very often this can be a bad decision—especially if it continues over a long period of time—because it can lead to relationship burnout. If that person is the only human you see outside of class, eventually he or she will drive you crazy.

> If you decide to spend time with your significant other whenever you want, you're likely to be headed for lower grades and possibly other academic—and social—problems.

Take James, for instance. He was driven, smart, active on campus, and had a great many friends. During the end of his sophomore year he met a girl, Erin, through a fraternity brother, and he was immediately love struck. James and Erin began spending lots of time together, getting to know each other and gazing adoringly into each other's eyes. It was great! All of his friends loved seeing him so happy and in love. But after a while, they started missing James. They rarely saw him, and when they did, Erin was always with him, and they'd spend their time off in a corner whispering sweet nothings into each other's ears.

This went on for nearly six months. It caused major problems between James and his roommate, between James and his fraternity brothers, between James and his flag football team, and even between James and his professors. He went from giving 150 percent on everything to barely showing up for class, fraternity events, and meetings. Everyone understood his actions for the first month or two, but after a while, it got old. His friends, fraternity brothers, and teammates got weary of seeing James and Erin joined at the hip. Then, it happened. One morning, James came storming into his dorm room—where he had rarely been in nearly two months—and informed his roommate that his relationship with Erin was over. They'd had a huge fight, and she called it quits. Because they'd lived in an unrealistic, fairy-tale land for six months, they seemed unable to deal with real-world problems. The first time they faced conflict, the relationship crumbled. In a way, the breakup was a blessing. James got his normal life back, and when he started dating Jennifer early in his junior year, he knew which pitfalls to avoid. This was a classic case of learning from your mistakes—something we all do.

> *Note to Parents*
>
> *If you've gone ahead and flipped through this chapter, remember that your children are now responsible adults, so don't pressure them to abstain from sex—it may actually push them into promiscuous activities. Trust them and talk to them about being responsible.*

## To Sum Up

Decisions are extremely important when it comes to new love and sex. If you decide to spend the night with each other in the dorm room, for example, then you need to check with respective roommates first. Don't become so self-absorbed that you forget about others around you who are affected by your actions when you are "blinded by love." Part of growing up and getting the most you can from college is learning responsibility.

Love is complicated, but it's also a wonderful and exciting part of life that everyone should experience. Whether it's casual fun or a long-term, marriage-bound relationship, love can mix your life up if you're not careful. Everything has consequences, so it is important to approach relationships, dating, and sex with a good, rational head on your shoulders.

# Chapter 21

## The Parent Trap

### How to Mutually Manage the Changing Parent-Child Relationship

Patrick attended a college that was about a three-hour drive from home. He was close to his parents and was an only child. His parents missed him and, at first, he missed them too. They came to visit him almost every other weekend. While that was fine for the first few weeks, it quickly became a problem. Patrick needed to study more and wanted to spend more time with his friends than his parents. He had to tell them not to visit him as often. It took a little while but they eventually reached a common understanding on the parent-child relationship.

Your parents are the people who've been by your side since the day you were born. They've showered you with unconditional love, support, and life lessons. They're also the folks who come down on you when you step out of line or fall beneath your potential. They utter the words, "I brought you into this world." Oh, dear old parents. You can't live with them, but you can't live without them. They've probably seen you through the process of applying to schools, driven with you to campus visits, and waited for the day that your fate was

> **Note to Parents**
> *Just because your children are going off to college doesn't mean that they're leaving your life forever. It's their chance to gain some independence and your chance to see them take on the responsibilities of being adults.*

*Note to Parents*

*You and your children will have the most rewarding relationship with each other throughout their college years if you agree on some guidelines ahead of time.*

decided. They cheered along as you ripped into your thick envelopes and ached for you when those telltale thin letters arrived in the mail. You've been through it all together, and now you're about to embark on another adventure. But this time, they won't be accompanying you. For the first time in your life, you won't be living under their roof with their guidance and rules. This is a huge transition for all parties involved and is best approached with compassion, understanding, and respect. This new situation will affect each of you very differently, and while it may evoke excitement and a sense of freedom in the college-bound student, it may be causing sadness, concern, and a deep sense of loss in the soon-to-be empty nesters.

The key here is to practice that old adage "walk a mile in someone else's shoes." You each must try to put yourself in the other's position and then act as you would want to be treated. Don't merely do what suits you. Let's analyze how this changing relationship will affect you both, students and parents, and how this new relationship will define much of your future lifelong relationship.

You may be thinking that nothing will really change when you go to college—your parents will always be your parents. But you will redefine how you view them, how often you're in contact with them, and how big of a part of your life they will be. If you only take one idea from this chapter, it should be this: student and parents will have the most rewarding relationship with each other throughout college if they agree on some guidelines ahead of time. Making decisions about what you expect from each other during this important time in your life will help to ensure that you actually achieve these expectations and get the most out of your first lengthy time apart.

## For the Student

For 18 years, your parents have looked after you. They've seen you through the good times and the bad. They've kissed boo-boos, stayed up all hours helping you with projects, and been there whenever you needed them. Now, they're sending you off to tackle the world on your own. If you have a project, they can't be there to help. If you hurt yourself, they can do little to make you feel better. And if you have a problem, the most they can provide is reassurance over the telephone or through e-mail that you'll be fine. They can't hug you and let you know everything will be okay.

All of these realizations will come to your parents as your high school days come to an end and you begin to prepare for college. These realizations will possibly cause them to cling to you for dear life, burst into tears for no apparent reason, and even begin touting the academic prestige and benefits of your local community college in the hope that you'll change your mind at the last minute and stay closer to them. Try to be patient and understanding. Remember that it's always more difficult to be the one left behind than to be the one doing the leaving. While you go bounding off on this new adventure, they will return to life almost as usual, but minus a significant piece of their life—you! After dropping you off and helping you settle in, they'll head back to their house, but there will be a huge void—an emptiness.

> Remember that it's always more difficult to be the one being left behind than it is to be the one doing the leaving.

Having said that, you have no reason to feel guilty about heading off to college. This is your time to shine and to take control of your life. You're embarking on a thrilling journey of learning and self-discovery, so while empathy and understanding are essential, don't let these feelings transform into guilt or regret. For the summer before you leave, decide to spend certain times with your family. Wisely plan your final fleeting days at home. You undoubtedly will want to spend all your time with your friends, as you're leaving them too. But make an effort to spend quality time with your parents and siblings, as well. Plan your days with both your family and yourself in mind, and try to strike a balance. The time-management decisions you make during this period can help make the transition easier and smoother for you and your folks. A smooth transition may possibly prevent the clinginess, uncontrollable crying, and the community college public relations campaign.

Once you're at college, your ongoing relationship with your parents has an impact on your behavior, at least according to a major recent study. A National Survey of Student Engagement (NSSE) completed in the fall of 2007 indicated that staying in touch with parents lessened students' risky behavior. Specifically, the 86 percent of first-year students who maintained frequent contact with their mothers were likely to keep drinking under control. (The definition of "frequent" was not stated.) The 71 percent who stayed connected to their fathers, the study claimed, were not as prone to risky sexual activities.

The *Wall Street Journal*, also reporting on the NSSE, noted that "75 percent of college freshmen and seniors said they almost always took their parents' advice." A *USA Today* article on the NSSE reported that students who had "high levels of contact with their parents or guardian, and whose parents frequently intervened on their behalf were more satisfied with their education and reported deeper learning activities than students with less-involved parents." (The entire study can be found on the NSSE Web site at http://www.nsse.iub.edu.)

Thus, you shouldn't feel that you're the only student still staying in touch with your parents. The majority of other students are as well—and research shows this connection is to your benefit.

# For the Parents

It's time to let your little ones fly alone. You've spent nearly two decades instilling values, morals, and lessons into your offspring, hoping that someday they would become productive and upstanding adults. Today is that day. If your children are heading off to school fairly far from home, reassure yourselves that you've probably also provided a strong sense of security and independence. After all, they obviously have the courage to venture into college and all it entails, leaving behind anything familiar for the promise of higher education.

This is a testament to you as parents. You've helped them gain the wings and confidence to progress to the next step, and they probably couldn't have done it without you. But with this independence, security, and confidence comes the bitter fact that they're leaving you.

Let us first say, it will be okay. Remember when they were going through their particularly difficult, bratty phases? Maybe they were around the ages between two and three or 14 and 16, and you used to daydream about the day they would move out. You used to imagine your house rid of piles of laundry, toys scattered all about, sullen teenagers locked in their rooms listening to horrid music and hoards of kids—not your own—constantly coming and going and eating all your food. You always thought about the peace and quiet and calming serenity of a childless home. Just you and your spouse, with no worries, concerns, or soccer team carpools. Well, guess what? That time has arrived!

Maybe it arrived a little more quickly than you expected, or maybe you were finally starting to like your kids again and now they're leaving. It's a tough transition but not an impossible one. Before they fly away for good, plan a nice summer with them. The summer is a great chance for some quality family time. However, be warned: your children are going to want to spend a lot of time with their friends. After all, they're saying their goodbyes to them as well. Don't put guilt or pressure on your kids to spend every waking minute with you. This will just make them want to move out of the house that much faster. Together, decide on a schedule that works for all. The key here is communication. Then, when they leave, remember that they are on a journey and you have a role in that journey. It hasn't ended the second they walk out of the door. You will always play a major part in their lives. They probably aren't going to want to talk to you every day, write letters two times a week, and fly home every weekend. Be realistic. Try to remember when you were that age and act accordingly. This is the time for them to spread their wings, and this can't happen if you're constantly trying to keep them under your thumb!

> By deciding together what reasonable expectations will enable you to both maintain a good relationship and to provide for a certain level of freedom, you will both be happy.

One of the most common times that problems arise between parents and their college student children is when the students arrive back at home after their freshman year. While many students take classes or are otherwise involved in some activity during the summer, the vast majority of them return home, and this can cause difficulties for both sides almost immediately. After children have experienced freedom and have managed their own lives—doing whatever they want, whenever they want, with whomever they want—living under their parents' rules again may not suit them well. In order to prevent major problems from becoming an impediment to a successful and well-rounded long-term relationship, parents should sit down with their children and discuss the rules and expectations on both sides before the summer starts. This can head off any of these major problems from arising.

## Parent-Student Decisions

Students and parents, you must each communicate what you want out of the summer before college and then the school year itself. You must come to some common understanding of what you expect from each other throughout these college years. Listen to each other and be reasonable. Understand each other's point of view. Compassion is important, as is respect for each other's positions and feelings. Discuss expectations in terms of trips home for holidays and the frequency of contact. Not having a clear understanding of what each of you wants will likely lead to someone—or everyone—being upset. Deciding on reasonable expectations together will enable you to maintain a good relationship and still provide a certain level of freedom. This is not the time for anxious parents to turn into hovering, overprotective parents!

Parents and students need to make decisions collectively. The worksheet in this chapter (Figure 21-1) will help you talk through these decisions. You may want to look at it individually or together. You may also want to add other decisions specific to your situation. The idea is for each of you to answer these on your own and then compare answers and finally come up with some type of workable compromise. This point in your relationship can be very exciting and dynamic. In many cases, this transition begins the transformation of your relationship from parent/child to parent/adult. But don't expect this to happen overnight. When children leave the house, they take the first step toward adulthood, their parents begin seeing them as adults, and eventually, the new adults begin seeing their parents as individual people—not just as Mom or Dad. It's certainly not a quick process, but it is a process and it starts now.

Parents are perhaps the most essential players in their children's college experiences. (As noted earlier, research supports our belief.) Parents can continue to offer life experience, advice, and support, but they should understand that this is also the time your children are most likely to try to push you away. If this happens, try not to force your advice on your children. Allow them to need and miss you. Give them the chance to come to you. As long as the lines of communication are kept wide open and each party treats the other with respect and understanding, this transition may end up being much easier than you all think it will be.

Our advice to the students is to try and avoid this tendency to push your parents away. Your independence will not be threatened if, at some point, you find that you need or miss your parents. It's only natural. After all, your entire reality has just changed, and you may not be fully happy with your new reality at first. The secret to maturity and adulthood is learning to ask for help when you need it. Your parents will always have your best interests at heart and can be a valuable resource as you stumble your way through life.

## To Sum Up

The hardest time will be the first few months in college when the new adjustments in your lives haven't set in yet, and the new balance is still being ironed out. But you will find that balance, especially if you continue to work at it hard enough. Whether it's as simple as a weekly phone call, an e-mail update about how the dog is, or news about a particular project you're working on, even the smallest contact can be crucial to maintaining an appropriate balance of communication and can set the stage for your lifelong relationship. Take the time before you start college to work through these mutual decisions with your parents.

> *Note to Parents*
>
> *This is the time for your children to spread their wings, and this can't happen if you're constantly trying to keep them under your thumb.*

**FIGURE 21-1 Worksheet: Student-Parent Shared Decisions**

| | |
|---|---|
| 1. How many times per week do you expect to communicate by phone? | Student: _____<br>Parents: _____ |
| 2. How many times per week do you expect to communicate by email? | Student: _____<br>Parents: _____ |
| 3. How often will the parents visit? | Student: _____<br>Parents: _____ |
| 4. Will the student return home for the summer? | Student: _____<br>Parents: _____ |
| 5. Which holidays and breaks will the student return home for? | Student: _____<br>Parents: _____ |
| 6. Will the student be expected to work? | Student: _____<br>Parents: _____ |
| 7. Other decision 1 | Student: _____<br>Parents: _____ |
| 8. Other decision 2 | Student: _____<br>Parents: _____ |
| 9. Other decision 3 | Student: _____<br>Parents: _____ |

# Section V.

## Financial Decisions

ollege is expensive. Not only are tuition expenses high, but everything else related to spending four years in class full-time can add up: travel expenses to and from school; housing expenses, whether on campus or off campus; food expenses; everyday expenses. However you look at it, your time in college is not going to be cheap. Of course it's worth it, but in the long run you will be much better off if you approach these expenses in a responsible manner by making the best decisions possible when it comes to the financial aspects of college. These decisions are the focus of this section.

The first chapter of this section, chapter 22, focuses on the decisions that you will have to make regarding education-related expenses, including tuition and fees, room and board, books and supplies, personal expenses, and travel expenses. These costs, which can be as high as $150,000 or more over a four-year period, may seem like more than you can handle. But if you approach the decision about how to pay for these expenses in a responsible and structured manner, you will be able to pay for them in a way that is best suited for your family and will keep the long-term amount you pay to a minimum. Colleges—and the federal government—have their own view of how you should pay for college, and they base their offers of scholarships and financial aid on these formulae and tell you how much you need to pay. You, on the other hand, will have your own view of how to come up with the "magic number" of what you need to pay for each year of college. We provide you with a method that you can follow with your parents to come to the best decision about how much you each will pay up front each year and how much will be taken out in loans, as well as who will be responsible for paying these loans back. By taking a structured approach to your education expenses, you will be better off in the long run.

The second chapter of this section, chapter 23, addresses the importance of making intentional and responsible decisions about your personal finances. College is a time when students experience their first financial freedoms, being responsible for their own expenses and deciding what they're going to spend their money on. While this freedom provides much experience that will stay with you throughout your life, if you are not responsible with the money you have, you will regret it. Making good decisions related to your spending by deciding ahead of time to create a budget—and to stick to it—will be a decision you can be thrilled about. One of the major problems that students face in regard to money in college is credit cards. If you get your first credit card after you start college, as most students do, deciding how you will use it will determine if you graduate in a relatively good financial situation or in a terrible financial situation. In chapter 23, we discuss ways for you to make responsible decisions about using a credit card and how to ensure that you don't end up in debt up to your eyeballs at graduation.

# Chapter 22

# Robbing the Piggy Bank 101
## Decisions About Paying for College

**B**rad just finished his senior year in high school and was looking forward to attending a college in his state's university system. It was an excellent system—considered to be one of the best in the country—and he was extremely excited to start a higher academic level of study. Then he received the bill from the university for the upcoming semester, which was a shock. As soon as he received it, he showed it to his father. They were both surprised. They had both completely neglected to think about how they were going to pay for college, assuming that since it was a state university, it would be reasonably priced. While it certainly was less than private school tuition, the cost of tuition and room and board was $6,500 for the first semester alone. They had a general idea of the costs when Brad applied, but when they received the bill, they were confronted with the reality of deciding how to pay for it.

Having assumed that they wouldn't need to take out loans, Brad hadn't applied for any of the student loan programs available from the federal government, the state government, or the college itself. Now he and his parents were stuck. How were they going to come

> ### Note to Parents
> *Take a minute to just breathe. College is expensive but you will be able to get through this. We give you a template to work through the decisions you need to make.*

239

up with $6,500 within the next six weeks? After much stress and countless hours searching to see if it was too late to get financial aid—it was—Brad finally asked his grandparents for assistance with his first semester. They agreed to give him the money for this semester but under one condition: that he learn from this lesson and not neglect to make a conscious decision about how he was going to pay for the rest of his academic career. He agreed to use an appropriate combination of grants, scholarships, loans, and personal money in the future. Lesson learned.

# Making a Conscious Decision

College is expensive, but through a comprehensive package of scholarships, grants, loans, and other options, you will get through it.

Four years of college can cost $150,000 or more. But believe it or not, you can afford it. Costs—including tuition and fees, room and board, books and supplies, personal expenses, and travel expenses—vary at each institution. You need to figure out how you're going to pay for them based on the school you're planning to attend. Many options are available to help you avoid paying the entire amount outright. These options include grants, scholarships, work-study programs, both subsidized and unsubsidized student loans, and private loans. You can use a number of resources to determine which of these programs will work for you, but this chapter will help you navigate through all of the major decisions you're going to have to make to pay for college. If you make responsible decisions about handling these costs, you will be much better off in the long run.

If your parents are going to underwrite your college expenses, that's great. You won't have to worry as much about paying for college. But very few people have this option available to them. Even if you do have this option, they would no doubt appreciate it if you took advantage of some options available for you to reduce the costs of attendance, many of which will be discussed in this chapter.

For everyone else, you need to understand the variety of options available and make responsible decisions that will help you afford college and not drown in debt. Responsible decisions will ensure that you will be able to manage your college expenses in the best way possible. You and your parents will need to make a series of decisions together throughout the process, such as the following:

- How much is the student going to pay and how much are the parents going to pay?
- How much will be used from money that has been saved?

❶ How much will be taken out in loans, how much will the loans eventually cost, and who will be responsible for paying back the loans?

❶ How much will come from the parents annual earnings? From the students?

The goal of this chapter is to help you to approach these decisions calmly and rationally, giving you confidence that you have made the best possible decisions. It will also help you make the trade-offs between paying now and what you will eventually pay later when you repay any loans. Finally, this chapter provides a framework for the students and parents to use together to agree on how much each is paying.

The way you make your decision on how to pay is different than how the college makes its decision on how much financial aid to offer you. In fact, it's the inverse decision process. We will summarize a typical college process and then provide you with a proven effective process that you should follow to decide how to pay for college. We will then provide some alternatives, including some creative ones, on how to come up with the money you need. But first, read on for information about how much college actually costs.

# It Costs What?

So, how much will you, in reality, be expected to pay? As mentioned, the total cost of attending college includes tuition and fees, room and board, books and supplies, personal expenses, and travel expenses. The most expensive of these is usually tuition, followed by room and board. To look at the overall costs, as estimated by the College Board, you're looking at somewhere in the range of $13,126 per year for a two-year public college; $17,336 per year for a public, four-year college if you qualify for in-state tuition; $27,791 for the same university if you don't qualify for in-state tuition; and $35,374 per year for a private, four-year university.

**FIGURE 22-1 One Year Cost of Attending College**

| Type of School | Tuition & Fees | Room & Board | Books & Supplies | Transportation | Personal Expenses | Total Expenses |
|---|---|---|---|---|---|---|
| Public two year | $ 2,361 | $6,875 | $921 | $1,270 | $1,699 | **$13,126** |
| Public four year (in state) | $ 6,185 | $7,404 | $988 | $ 911 | $1,848 | **$17,336** |
| Public four year (out-of-state) | $16,640 | $7,404 | $988 | $ 911 | $1,848 | **$27,791** |
| Private four year | $23,712 | $8,595 | $988 | $ 768 | $1,311 | **$35,374** |

*Source: College Board—Trends in College Pricing 2007 (http://www.collegeboard.com)

As you can see from Figure 22-1, these totals include all of the expected costs of attendance. Moreover, the costs for tuition and fees as well as room and board are expected to increase approximately 5.5 percent per year. According to the College Board, from the 2006–2007 academic year to the 2007–2008 academic year, costs have increased 5.9 percent for public, four-year universities for in-state students; 5.4 percent for public, four-year universities for out-of-state students; and 5.9 percent for private, four-year universities. (No data were available for public, two-year colleges.) So, if you're wondering about how much it will cost for four years at today's rates, assuming a 5.5 percent increase per year for tuition and room and board, but no increase in the other expenses, Figure 22-2 should show a pretty good approximation for a student who begins college in 2009 and graduates in 2013.

**Figure 22-2  Estimated Four Year Costs of Attending College**

| Type of School/Student | 2009–2010 | 2010–2011 | 2011–2012 | 2012–2013 | Total Expenses |
|---|---|---|---|---|---|
| Public two-year | $14,170 | $14,735 | N/A | N/A | $ 28,905 |
| Public four-year (in state) | $18,872 | $19,704 | $20,581 | $21,507 | $ 80,664 |
| Public four-year (out-of-state) | $30,509 | $31,980 | $33,533 | $35,172 | $131,194 |
| Private four-year | $39,026 | $41,003 | $43,090 | $45,291 | $168,410 |

*Source: College Board—Trends in College Pricing 2007 (http://www.collegeboard.com)

# The College's Decision Process

In their decision process on how much assistance they intend to provide, both the schools and the government start with an estimate of how much money your family should be able to contribute toward the cost of college. In other words, you are expected to use your resources first. The formula used by lending agencies is based on four components: available income of the parents; available assets of the parents; available income of the student; and available assets of the student.

The schools and the government use a complex formula to determine what they call the Expected Family Contribution (EFC), but it may be useful for you to take the time to understand it. They compute your parent's available income from income tax filings with a number of adjustments, including how much they expect your parents need to live on (called income protection). They expect that a big portion of what remains will be used to pay for your college education. They then look at the amount of savings your parents have, allow some asset protection that is generally based on the age of your parents, and they then expect that the remainder will be used to pay your college expenses, generally at some conversion rate such as 12 percent a year.

They also assume that your own income and assets will be used to pay your expenses, only at a higher rate than your parents. Typically 50 percent of your after-tax earnings and 20 percent per year of your savings are calculated in their formula.

> **Example of Your Expected Family Contribution (EFC)**
>
> - Percent of your parents' available income
> - Percent of your parents' available assets
> - Percent of *your* available income
> - Percent of *your* available assets

As you might expect, this estimate calculated by colleges to make a decision on how much to use to pay for college leads to all kinds of issues. If you or your parents work hard right before going to college to make and save extra money, you may get less financial aid than if you wait until you are at college. Taking a year or two off to work and save money may actually penalize you by diminishing the amount of aid you could get. But in general, the approach the schools and government take does tend to provide more aid to those who need it and less to those who don't. You might hear stories of parents who try to move assets or manipulate income in preparation for this estimate, so they get more financial aid. This isn't the purpose of this chapter; we only want to give you an insight into how the colleges determine their financial-aid packages.

In general, students who have fewer financial resources pay less for college than those who have more. A typical college provides an average discount on tuition of about 30 percent, and those who need it get an even bigger discount, while those who can afford to pay full price will not get a discount. In some colleges, this means that those students who pay full price actually pay more than cost—a controversial topic within colleges and with parents. Sometimes this encourages those who can pay the full amount to attend lower-cost state universities. One parent, for example, told his son that if he attended a lower-price state university, he would buy him a new car. He saved a lot of money that way.

This is the college's view: based upon how much the school wants you to go there and your financial situation, the school will tell you that you need to pay the total amount of the tuition and fees, minus the amount it offers you in scholarships and grants. In the school's effort to help you pay this, it will offer you some level of student loans, and you will be responsible for the remainder. This works out to be: Tuition – Scholarships – Student Loans = Your Cost.

# Your Decision Process

The way colleges view their decisions on how much to give you in aid is not the way you should view how you are going to pay for it. In fact it's the inverse view. They make assumptions about how you will pay for college when they decide how much aid you deserve. You now need to take the bottom line amount you have been given and decide how you are going to pay for that amount of the cost.

How? We're glad you asked. Unfortunately, this isn't the type of decision for which a simple formula determines the solution. We wish it were that easy, but it's not. This is actually a very complicated decision that requires putting together a very specific plan. The decision is, how are you going to piece together a plan to pay for college that maximizes your ability to reach the magic number of the total dollar cost, while minimizing the total amount you have to pay in the long run? Far too many people approach this decision by simply winging it. Let us give you a little advice: Winging it won't work to your advantage. You will be much better off if you approach this decision with much deliberation. Paying less money is better than paying more, so how can you make your decisions about paying for college so that you pay less?

To help you understand how the process of making this important decision works, let's look at the Jones family, whose son Eric was about to leave that fall for a private liberal arts school. The school was not cheap—it was going to cost $39,000 for the first year, including tuition and fees, room and board, books and supplies, personal expenses, and travel to and from school. Additionally, Eric's parents estimated that the costs would increase 5 percent per year, which is just a little under the average of 5.5 percent per year. In an effort to get a full understanding of the total cost, Eric's parents forecasted all four years of college. (Too many people don't approach this as an intentional decision but rather try to figure this out as they go. Planning out all four years, as the Joneses did, is a much better approach.) As you can see from Figure 22-3, the total cost is approximately $168,095—quite a bit of money. Once they figured this out, Eric's parents decided to sit down with Eric and plan how they were going to pay for college not only for his first year but for his entire four years, which prompted Eric's father to comment: "You'd better not take more than four years to graduate!"

With Eric's final financial aid offer from the school in hand, which included an excellent $15,000 in scholarships per year, the three of them sat down and discussed options for paying for college. They decided that they would roughly split the cost of college, with the parents agreeing to pay a little more than half if needed. The parents would pay more of their portion up front, while Eric would pay off many of his student loans after college. They agreed, however, that for any loans above and beyond the subsidized and unsubsidized loans, they would split the payments with him. Now they had a framework within which to begin planning.

**FIGURE 22-3  Paying for College**

| | Annual Cost | | | | | Eventual Cost Parent | Eventual Cost Student |
|---|---|---|---|---|---|---|---|
| | Year 1 | Year 2 | Year 3 | Year 4 | Total | | |
| Gross Cost | $39,000 | $40,950 | $42,998 | $45,147 | $168,095 | | |
| Scholarships & Grants | $15,000 | $15,000 | $15,000 | $15,000 | $ 60,000 | | |
| Net Cost | $24,000 | $25,950 | $27,998 | $30,147 | $108,095 | | |
| **Payment Method:** | | | | | | | |
| Subsidized loans | $ 3,500 | $ 4,500 | $ 5,500 | $ 5,500 | $ 19,000 | | $26,430 |
| Unsubsidized loans | $ 2,000 | $ 2,000 | $ 2,000 | $ 2,000 | $ 8,000 | | $12,466 |
| Private loans | $ 5,000 | $ 5,200 | $ 5,500 | $ 6,650 | $ 22,350 | $22,266 | $22,266 |
| **From Current Assets:** | | | | | | | |
| Parents | $10,000 | $10,000 | $10,000 | $10,000 | $ 40,000 | $40,000 | |
| Student | $ 2,500 | $ 0 | $ 0 | $ 0 | $ 2,500 | | $ 2,500 |
| **From Annual Income:** | | | | | | | |
| Parents | $ 1,000 | $ 3,000 | $ 3,000 | $ 3,000 | $ 10,000 | $10,000 | |
| Student | | $ 1,250 | $ 2,000 | $ 3,000 | $ 6,250 | | $ 6,250 |
| Total | $24,000 | $25,950 | $28,000 | $30,150 | $108,100 | $72,266 | $69,912 |

The three of them put together the table in Figure 22-3. As you can see, they listed the gross cost for each of the four years, subtracting from that the amount of his scholarship, which left them with the net cost of college for each year. Then they determined how much money they could get in subsidized and unsubsidized loans. The current figures from the federal government enabled them to borrow $3,500 in subsidized loans for the first year, $4,500 for the second year, and $5,500 for each of the third and fourth years. In addition, they were able to borrow $2,000 per year in unsubsidized loans. This amounted to the maximum loan amounts the federal government permitted them to borrow. The standard interest rates quoted by the government for these loans were 6.5 percent for subsidized loans and 8.5 percent for unsubsidized loans, giving Eric a total repayment of $26,430 for the subsidized loans over 10 years and $12,466 for the unsubsidized loans over 10 years. (Of course, these costs would be less if he decided to pay them off early.)

Before moving on to private loan amounts, however—since these loans were going to be the most expensive with the highest rate—they decided to focus first on how much money they could afford to put in to begin with. His parents decided that they would be willing to contribute $10,000 of their assets toward Eric's education every year, which they would obtain primarily by selling off some of their investment stocks and some stock options Eric's father had from his company. This totaled $40,000. They also agreed that Eric would contribute $2,500 toward his education out of his savings account, which had grown to roughly $5,000 from his employment during the last three summers. He agreed that putting this entire amount in for the first year was the best option. His parents decided that they would be willing to contribute $1,000 of their income for the first year of his college, and $3,000 for each additional year, money which they would find from cutting back on their expenses, including taking a less expensive vacation for each year that Eric was in college. They also discussed having Eric make money by working during the summers or by taking a part-time job during the school year to pay a small percentage of the costs for his second year ($1,250), his third year ($2,000), and his fourth year ($3,000). He was more than happy to do this and could figure out exactly what combination of work he would need to do over these coming years to accomplish that.

Finally, they decided to cover the additional gap by taking out private education loans, which they estimated at an interest rate of roughly 15 percent per year. The amount they determined they would need to borrow from private lenders was $5,000 for his first year, $5,200 for his second year, $5,500 for his third year, and $6,650 for his final year, bringing the total loan amount to $22,350. When they factored in the interest rate, payable over 10 years, it meant that Eric and his parents would each have to pay $22,266, since they had agreed to split the costs.

In total, they were able to figure out a way to meet the financial expenses of college by using a plan that combined federal government loans, private loans, and contributions from the assets and income of both the student and the parents—a model that works for the vast majority of students. While you will have your own breakdown that will combine some or all of these payment methods, using this process will ensure that you are able to find a way to pay for college that will minimize the amount you have to pay in the long run. In our example, Eric ended up with an estimated total eventual cost of $69,912, most of which would be paid over the 10 years after college, and his parents had an estimated total eventual cost of $72,266, which would be split in various ways between immediate payments, payments over the four college years, and payments over 10 years. It was a formula that worked for them, and they were glad they went through the process together to make these decisions, rather than simply try to wing it over each of the four years.

# Funding Options

There are a lot of financial concepts to get your head around if you're going to fully understand the alternative ways of paying for college. Here is an overview of the options.

## Grants and Scholarships

A major component of your funding should (hopefully) come in the form of grants and scholarships. These are the best kinds of money because you don't have to pay them back. Grants and scholarships are offered through a variety of sources, including your school. When you receive your offer letters from each school you've been accepted to, they may include an offer to provide you with some type of grant or scholarship, depending upon many factors. Schools have a variety of grants and scholarships available for students who have different backgrounds, come from different areas or from different types of high schools, and who are planning on studying various subjects. You need to be aware of what's available from your college and be sure to inquire about these prior to submitting your application. If you express interest in a particular grant or scholarship, they'll probably consider you for it when they otherwise may not have.

But don't stop there. Outside of your college, tens of thousands of grants and scholarships are available to students from all financial backgrounds, with all levels of GPAs, with interests in all types of academics, sports, or other activities, and with all sorts of future career plans. Your local bookstore should have an entire section full of guides for obtaining grants and scholarships, so we won't go into them in depth here, save to say that the effort is well worth it in the end. For some grants and scholarships, spending a lot of time on them is useful. At some point, however, it can become a numbers game. The more grants and scholarships you apply for, the more likely you will be to get one.

In addition to using the scholarship and grant guides and speaking with your new college, you should ask your high school college counselors if they're aware of any that you could qualify for. You should also work with your parents to identify the greatest number of grants or scholarships for which you have the best chances of acceptance. Remember, they know you well and should be a good resource to help you determine your likelihood of getting these. It's also quite likely to be in their best interests to have you receive as much support from grants and scholarships as possible. Many—but not all—grants and scholarships can be applied to the estimated family contribution, thus reducing the overall amount of money that the government requires you and your parents to pay up front for your education.

## Subsidized and Unsubsidized Student Loans

Another way to pay for your college education—one that the majority of students must pursue—is through loans. Unless you've got a free ride through grants or scholarships, or your parents are going to pay for the entire cost of your college tuition, then you're going to have to take out some student loans. Two types of loans are designated *student loans*. The first are called *subsidized* loans because the federal government subsidizes them on your behalf. This essentially means that you won't have to begin paying interest on these loans until after you graduate because the government is backing this money, and it also usually means that the interest rate is lower.

An *unsubsidized* loan, on the other hand, is not backed by the government. These loans are very similar to private loans, in that the interest begins to accrue the moment the money is issued, just like any other personal loan. Moreover, if you don't begin making payments on the loan as soon as it's sent to your college, the interest is going to be added to the principal and you will owe even more money. In addition, the interest rate is higher than that of a subsidized loan. Simply put, subsidized loans are better for you in the long run than unsubsidized loans. Put more accurately, however, you will not have the option of choosing subsidized over unsubsidized. The amount of money that you can borrow that is subsidized is determined for you by the federal government based upon your need. If you can establish that you are unable to pay for college without these loans, you will qualify for a higher amount of subsidized loans. The less need you prove, the more unsubsidized loans you will need to take out.

The way these loans generally work is that if you file the Free Application for Federal Student Aid (FAFSA) form by the deadlines, the government will consider how much in each type of student loans it is going to be able to provide to you. The deadlines for submitting

**Subsidized Loans:**

These loans are backed by the federal government so you don't have to pay interest until you begin to repay it after graduation. They will also have lower interest rates.

**Unsubsidized Loans:**

These loans are not backed by the government, so interest will begin to be accrued from the moment the loan is issued. They will also have higher interest rates.

these forms vary by state and some are as early as February for the following fall semester, so be careful not to miss the deadline. Information about how to file the FAFSA can be found online at http://www.fafsa.ed.gov.

The federal government also sets out maximum amounts for how much a student can borrow, both subsidized and unsubsidized, which changes depending upon what year in college you are borrowing for. Currently, the maximum combined amounts that you can borrow, as you can see in Figure 22-4, are $5,500 for your freshman year, $6,500 for your sophomore year, and $7,500 for each of your junior and senior years. This figure includes a maximum level of subsidized loans of $3,500 for your freshman year, $4,500 for your sophomore year, and $5,500 for each of your junior and senior years, as well as an additional $2,000 per year of unsubsidized loans. If you are not qualified for the maximum amount of subsidized loans, you are allowed to increase your unsubsidized loans up to the total combined amount allotted for a given year. This means that if you are only approved for $2,500 in subsidized loans for your freshman year, for example, you're going to be able to take out $3,000 in unsubsidized loans instead of $2,000. (We've also included the going interest rate for each of these and the total payback amount you will pay based upon these rates.)

**FIGURE 22-4   Current Subsidized and Unsubsidized Loan Limits**

| Type of Loan | First Year | Second Year | Third Year | Fourth Year | Total | Interest Rate | Total Payback |
|---|---|---|---|---|---|---|---|
| Subsidized | $3,500 | $4,500 | $5,500 | $5,500 | $19,000 | 6.50% | $26,430 |
| Unsubsidized | $2,000 | $2,000 | $2,000 | $2,000 | $ 8,000 | 8.50% | $12,466 |
| Total | $5,500 | $6,500 | $7,500 | $7,500 | $27,000 |  | $38,895 |

## Other Loans

Of course you can consider an unlimited number of loan types to help you pay for school. Some of these may be good options—for example, you may get a better rate taking out a loan yourself than you can through the unsubsidized loan programs you find through the school or the government. On the other hand, many of these loans are not the type that you want to pursue. Asking your parents to take out a second mortgage on their house, for example, may be one of the more drastic options to consider. But if you—and they—aren't being approved for other loan options or if the rate is much better, then it may be an option to consider. But perhaps it should be one of the last options, along with personal credit lines and credit cards, which can often prove to be some of the worst ways to pay for school.

One person we know simply didn't do his research before making his decision about how to pay for college during his first year. While he had some support in the form of a grant from the college, and his parents had given him a portion of the remainder due, they expected him to contribute the rest by taking out loans to cover the difference. They believed that it would instill a sense of responsibility in him if he took ownership of his own education and thought that he should be able to navigate the loan process to learn how to take control over his financial life. Unfortunately, they probably took too much of a backseat in the process, and didn't adequately monitor his progress or his decisions. After only briefly looking into the various loan options, he ended up deciding to simply pay for his portion of the costs on his credit cards—which had an average annual percentage rate (APR) of 24.99 percent. He reasoned that he would pay them as the school year progressed by working part-time as a waiter. By the time he had finished his second semester, however, the credit card bills were exorbitant, and he was in a very bad financial situation overall. Needless to say, he had to confront his parents at the end of that year and ask them for help not only to take over the loan process for his second year, but to help him sort out his new, messy financial situation.

This won't happen to you if you take control over your school loan process. Do your research, make responsible financial decisions, and you'll be thankful you did.

## Work Study

Another way that schools (and the federal government) will help you pay for the costs associated with college is the *work-study* program. These programs will provide you with a part-time job while you're in school that will help to defray the costs of attending. The money either goes directly toward reducing the price of tuition or goes to you to help cover your expenses. Many schools will offer these programs to the students with the highest need and will offer them to students by working through the list from the highest level of need to the lowest level. But, don't forget that these programs are often like revolving doors—just because you aren't offered a position during your first semester doesn't mean that you won't be offered something in any subsequent semester. In fact, many students will find another job or another type of work study that they prefer to the one they have, so be sure to follow up during your first semester and indicate your desire to have one of these positions. The federal work-study program is backed by the government and is available at over 3,500 colleges nationwide.

## Get Creative—Work at School

Aside from a work-study position, a host of other options are available for working while attending school. Here's one example. Carol was really struggling financially after her first year in college, since the majority of the money she had went to her tuition, fees, room and board, and books and other supplies. These expenses left her with almost no extra money, not to mention considerable debt. In order to improve her financial picture during her sophomore year, she decided to make a plan. She took a position as a resident assistant (RA), who lives in a dorm as a type of supervisor, or guidance counselor, for the incoming freshmen students. While being an RA had many responsibilities, it also came with a lot of rewards, specifically providing Carol's entire room and board to her at no cost. While this may or may not have given her specific experience that would help her in her long-term career, it did allow her the opportunity to become more engaged in the activities on campus while reducing the funds she needed to pay for her education. She ended up loving the position and even took a leadership role as the head RA for a dorm during her junior year as well.

Another example involves Carl, a student from a liberal arts school who majored in political science. He was very involved in activities throughout many areas in college and wanted to defray even a small portion of his costs for his junior and senior years. One day he mentioned to one of his professors his interest in working as a departmental research assistant for the spring of his junior year. The professor happened to be looking for someone to fill in for his current student research assistant who was going to be studying abroad for that semester. After only a short discussion, Carl was offered the position and his pay was deducted from his overall tuition bill. He loved his new role, and he not only made money toward his tuition but also gained valuable experience in his area of study.

## Get a Regular Job

One of the less-recommended ways to pay for a portion of your college expenses is to take a regular job. While it can certainly help you with expenses, having a job outside of college is a really time-consuming proposition—one that can significantly reduce the time and energy you have left to spend studying. Moreover, unlike a work-study program, an employer outside of college isn't very concerned about your responsibilities as a student. While a job at the library—or even the dining hall—may afford you some schedule flexibility during exam week, your boss at the local coffee shop likely won't look too kindly on your extensive cramming while customers stand impatiently in line waiting for their morning coffee. You could be fired for such unreliability, and if you're counting on that income for the next month's tuition payment, you'll be scrounging around trying to find it elsewhere.

If you absolutely have to get an outside job, you should maximize your options. Taking a job with a lesser time commitment (so that you have sufficient time to study) is obviously better than one requiring more hours. Also, a job that has specific time commitments is better than one with fluctuating time commitments that aren't based on an academic schedule—or worse, that are based on an academic schedule but require working more hours during the busiest academic time frames. (A job such as this could include being a waiter or a waitress or a bartender.) A job that allows you to do some reading, for example, during slow work periods, has its advantages as well. (A job like this could include any type of position that requires you to be available in case something comes up, such as a part-time medical job or a part-time receptionist.)

## Other Government Programs

A number of other federal and state governmental programs are also designed to help you pay for college, usually based upon your level of need. The Federal Pell Grant is an automatic grant you may qualify for if you are deemed to need it, and it never needs to be repaid. You can qualify for anywhere from $400 to $4,310 per year. Additional money from a program called the Federal Supplemental Educational Opportunity Grant (FSEOG) is available to students who receive the Pell Grant but need additional funds. These grants can range from $100 to $4,000 per year and also do not need to be repaid. Another type of grant, known as the Academic Competitiveness Grant, is also available based upon both need and merit to those students in their first or second year who receive the Pell Grant and who qualify for it based on a higher GPA. These grants are available in amounts ranging up to $750 for first-year students and up to $1,300 for second-year students. For third- and fourth-year students who receive the Pell Grant, have a high GPA, and major in various sciences, math, engineering, or certain foreign languages, an additional grant of up to $4,000 per year is available. Known as the National Science and Mathematics Access to Retain Talent Grant (National SMART Grant), this one, too, does not have to be repaid. State governments also offer their own similar programs that you should look into—especially since many of them do not need to be repaid.

## Military or Community Service

Public service can provide you with a few other options to helping you pay for college, particularly if you're feeling strapped for money or want to take a less-traditional route. One of the most common strategies for paying for college is the Montgomery GI Bill, which will pay for as much as $1,321 per month as of the 2008–2009 school year if you've served in the military. That works out to a fairly sizeable percentage of your tuition and expenses, depending upon which school you select. Of course, this option generally requires that you take two or three years off from school after high school before starting college, so your college graduation will be delayed. Becoming involved in the Reserved Officer Training Corps (ROTC) at college will also help to cover tuition expenses, but this option requires you to provide military service after college.

Another related option is to participate in a community service program such as those offered by AmeriCorps. These programs require you to commit to serve for one to two years in a largely volunteer capacity (your expenses are usually covered) assisting with a wide variety of community-oriented needs, including teaching students in inner-cities and providing other services. In exchange for fulfilling this commitment, the program will provide you with a subsidy, usually up to about $5,000, to use for education. These options may delay your expected graduation date, but they will provide you with financial assistance and reduce your long-term financial outlays for education. (If you're considering taking a year or more off, please read chapter 5 that focuses on gap year options.)

## Financial Aid Packages and Financial Aid Officers

Shortly after you receive the big and small envelopes containing your acceptances and your rejections from college, a series of other envelopes will begin to arrive. These will constitute your *aid packages*. Each of the schools that you've been accepted to will send you their *offer* that will include a combination of grants and scholarships, work-study offers, and subsidized and unsubsidized loan amounts, as well as defining the amount that they're expecting your family to contribute to your education.

In comparing your overall aid packages, you are also comparing schools. We strongly believe that it's of paramount importance that you choose the school that is the best fit for you, not the school that offers you the most money. After all, if you end up dropping out or changing schools, you're more likely to have increased your costs above and beyond what they would have been had you gone straight to the school that was the best fit initially. (If you're still considering which school to select, please be sure to review chapter 4.)

Keep in mind when you're comparing aid packages that financial aid officers use many different strategies and formulae to come up with the offer they create for

Financial aid officers have wide latitude to change the packages they've awarded you, so be sure to use your best negotiation skills to get more money.

you and the way they present that offer to you. The better you understand what they're talking about, the better off you will be. Financial aid officers make you think that their hands are tied regarding the offer they make to you and that you need to make a decision whether to take their offer or go to a different school. The truth is that they've got some leeway in making these offers, and they can—and quite often do—make concessions if you simply ask them to.

The offer you receive will reflect a number of different factors, including your financial need, as previously discussed, as well as how badly they want you. This is the entire basis behind schools that offer full scholarships to star athletes. If you have a skill that they think will be a good addition to the academic, social, or other component of their college, their desire for that quality may be reflected in the amount of money they offer you. In fact, you may recall from chapter 3 that many schools are using software applications to help them create a comprehensive plan to determine which students to accept and which ones to offer specific amounts of money to. After they input all of the data about all of their applicants, the system calculates how much money it will take to get a specific student to accept an offer of admissions. In other words, the processes for creating financial aid packages are very refined.

But that doesn't mean that you can't negotiate. If you need more money, be sure that you, the student, take the lead in any negotiations with the financial aid officer. The officers are much more likely to consider changes to your package if you express your sense of responsibility for taking ownership over your own education. Remember that financial aid officers also know that they will be asked by many students to increase their aid awards. In some cases, the first offer that financial aid officers make to you will be in expectation that you're going to come back to them to negotiate. They may even build that consideration into their first offer. Don't accept that offer without trying to negotiate something better.

It is also important to remember that these financial aid packages are fixed for only one year. You will have to go through this same process every year, so it's best to inquire right from the beginning if the school intends to offer you a similar package for the next year and every subsequent year. (Also, they will usually only offer you this type of financial aid for four years of school, so if you get behind in earned credits and need to take a fifth year, you may be at risk of losing your financial aid.) You don't want to have to take out unplanned, high-interest student loans in order to finish school.

# Reducing the Cost of College

One father of triplets was very concerned about how he was going to pay for college for his three daughters. As they approached the end of their time in high school, it was clear they were all going to attend the same expensive university, a truly wonderful school, but also an expensive school. Prior to his daughters beginning their freshman year, he realized that family members of college employees were eligible to attend the school for free. Armed with that knowledge, he promptly quit his job and was hired by the college. Even though his salary was lower in this new job, with free tuition, it was absolutely worth it to him.

While we can't all pay for college by having our parents work at the college, determining how you're going to pay for college is only part of the strategy. Another component that can help you equally well is to reduce the overall cost of college. But how can you do this when the prices are fixed by your school? There are a number of steps you can take to substantially or minimally reduce the overall costs.

## In-State Tuition

One of the best—and easiest—ways to reduce your cost of college is to attend a state university in your own state. Virtually every state school offers significant discounts on the overall cost of tuition to in-state residents. Looking at the costs in Figure 22-1, the total cost of tuition and fees is 62.8 percent less if you're an in-state student rather than an out-of-state student. That's a huge difference. Proving residency can sometimes be challenging, as the residency requirements for state universities are specifically designed so that people don't abuse the system, claiming they're residents just to attend the university at a discounted rate. Since every state maintains its own residency requirements, if this is an option you're considering, you need to find out how the state school you're looking at establishes its residency requirements.

Of course, if you don't live in a state with a very good state university system, or if you simply don't want to attend any school within that system, your options to reduce tuition costs this way are significantly reduced. However, many states also have reciprocity agreements with other states—most commonly with the states on their immediate borders. Before you dismiss the idea of being able to save yourself money by attending a state school in the state that you want to but that isn't where you live, be sure to look into the reciprocity agreements to see if you qualify. Moreover, don't forget that attending a state university as an out-of-state student is still about 30 percent cheaper than attending a private college. So even if you don't qualify, you may be better off financially if you go to a state school than a private school.

## AP Courses and CLEP

Another method for reducing the total amount of money you will spend for college is to simply reduce the number of credits that you have to pay for. Two ways you can do this are through advanced placement (AP) courses and through the College-Level Examination Program (CLEP). As you're probably aware, while you're still in high school you can take courses designated as advanced placement courses which essentially count as college-level courses. Currently 37 courses in 22 disciplines are offered as AP courses. These classes are generally much more difficult than their high school equivalents, and they require you to receive a high grade for them to count toward your college requirements. Scored on a 1.0 to 5.0 basis, some colleges will require you to earn a 3.0 to receive credit for an AP course, while others may require a 4.0. Additionally, AP courses typically last a full year, but only offset a single semester course—generally three credit hours. Still, the prospect of taking a course in high school that counts not only toward high school graduation requirements but also affords college credits is a great option. Unfortunately, if you're reading this book, you're more likely to be beyond the time when you can sign up for an AP course. But if you're currently enrolled in one, this may be the stimulus you need to do well and be sure that you get those extra credits!

CLEP is another option for reducing the number of credits you will have to take as a college student. This consists of a range of exams that you can take that will prove to your college that you've already completed the requirements for understanding the basics of a particular course of study. For example, the CLEP offers exams in general studies, including English, Social Science, and other general courses, as well as more specific exams such as Physics, Chemistry, Foreign Languages, and others. There are currently 2,900 colleges that will offer you actual credits for CLEP exams that you pass. In addition to the general courses, 34 subject-specific courses are currently available for you to take. While the tests generally cost about $75 each, they can save you thousands of tuition dollars in the long run. (You may want to consider whether you think you're going to pass before spending this money, but with so many exams offered, you could already have the knowledge to pass one or more particular exams and get the corresponding credits.)

## Summer School

Another method for reducing the number of credits you have to pay for is to take courses during the summertime at a different college that is less expensive and where you can gain credits that will transfer into your school. Of course, you need to use your summertime very wisely, and this may or may not be the best use of this time, but it can reduce the overall cost of attending your college. Moreover, if you take enough courses, you may actually reduce the time it takes you to graduate. If you do decide to take this route, just be certain that the credits will indeed transfer before you commit to and pay for these classes. You want to avoid running up additional costs without getting those credits applied to your graduation requirements. If this is something you may be considering, you should also consult chapter 11 which discusses how to make good decisions for your summers.

Reducing the costs of college is even better than finding more funding options since it means you need to find less money.

## Reduce Your Lesser Expenses

Finally, you can reduce the total amount you spend on school by simply reducing some of your nontuition expenses. One simple example of this could be your books. Most college bookstores offer used books to students, and these are generally a great idea for saving money. You can usually save about half of the money you would spend on new books by buying them used. If you can't find them used at your bookstore, other options now exist for finding them for less money than you would pay for new books. For example, you can buy them online from a variety of sources, such as Amazon.com, eBay.com, or Half.com.

You can also reduce your living and travel expenses. If on-campus housing is proving to be an expensive option, perhaps you need to consider moving off campus and sharing an apartment or a house with a larger number of students. While this may be a good option for many reasons—including financial reasons—be careful to evaluate all of the positives and negatives of this option before making that decision. (You can look at chapter 18 on selecting housing options for assistance with this decision.)

You can also reduce travel costs by coming up with creative measures. If you drive between school and home during vacations, consider carpooling and splitting the costs of gas and tolls. If you take the train, consider taking the bus or buying your tickets far enough in advance so that the costs are lower. If you fly, costs can often be significantly reduced if you travel on a less-popular day, so shop around considering different days as options and buy your tickets accordingly. Finally, you can reduce many of your other expenses by creating a budget for personal expenses—and sticking to it. This is covered more in chapter 23.

# To Sum Up

College is expensive—but it's worth it. Your challenge is to make the most responsible decisions on how to pay for it. This chapter contrasts how colleges make their decisions on how much aid to provide you against how you make your decisions to pay for college. You and your parents must consider many options for how your college education will be paid for, and we give you a proven worksheet to help make those decisions. The chapter also highlights alternative ways to pay for your college expenses. You can work closely with your parents to be certain that this personalized approach meets your needs and fits your budget. It will be extremely worthwhile in the long run if you make these crucial decisions responsibly—and early enough in your college planning so that you have the most options available to you.

*Note to Parents*

*You can work closely with your children to ensure that they make the most responsible financial decisions for paying for college, including the best combination of upfront payments, scholarships and grants, and student loans.*

For an electronic version of the decision worksheet used in this chapter go to: http://www.DecideBetter.com/college.html.

# Chapter 23

# Preapproved

## How to Make Responsible Decisions about Personal Expenses, without All the Credit Cards

A s soon as Vince arrived on his college campus, he received a "gift"—his first credit card. And he got a college T-shirt with it. For him the credit card was like getting an iPod, a new computer, and new skis! He also used it to pay for travel and to buy Christmas presents for his family. When his credit card maximum limit was reached, he found a solution—he got another credit card. He managed his expenses this way throughout college. After all, when he graduated, he would have enough money to pay off the cards—or so he thought. When he graduated he got a job that paid him $24,000 a year, yet he had $17,000 of credit card debt on his four cards and more than $3,000 of annual interest payments. His financial life was miserable. All of his extra money went to pay the interest on his credit cards. Vince regretted his decision—or rather his lack of a thoughtful decision—to use credit cards in college.

*Note to Parents*

*College is a great time for your children to learn about personal finances. But it's also a time when they can make huge mistakes, especially when credit cards are involved. Work with them to help instill a sense of financial responsibility that will stay with them forever.*

# The College Credit Card Scheme (or Scam?)

College credit cards are a scheme, and you are the victim. College students are a very attractive market for credit card companies. Most students don't have any financial affiliations, so they are open to being sold to practically any bidder, and credit card companies hope these students will become long-term customers. College students don't need to have a job or income because it's assumed they will have both when they graduate. Most students are novices with credit, so many will fall for schemes offering low initial interest rates that escalate. And students are easily identified; in fact, colleges help to sell credit cards to students.

Many college students graduate owing more than $10,000 in credit card debt, a burden that accompanies them for a long time. A typical credit card solicitation to a college student promotes an interest rate of only 4.9 percent APR. But the fine print may state that the rate increases to 18.5 percent after six months, and costs can go much higher when late fees are added. College students are bombarded with credit card solicitations—dozens every semester.

Another important aspect of the scheme is this: the colleges—usually their alumnae associations—get paid to sell credit cards to their students. The college alumnae group can receive hundreds of thousands or millions every year to help sell credit cards to students. A 30,000 student university alumnae association, for example, receives roughly $1 million a year to market credit cards to students. For many alumnae associations, credit card kickbacks provide a major portion of their funding. The alumnae associations provide credit card companies with student names, addresses, phone numbers, and e-mail addresses in return for long-term contracted payments. The typical deal for the associations is that they receive 0.5 percent of the total dollar amount of student purchases on the credit cards issued and three to six dollars per year for every active student credit card. They want you to spend and borrow.

# The Real Cost

We know it sounds familiar and like something that's directed at all of the other college students, not you, but this message is for everyone: Don't overdo it with credit cards. We all have expenses and need to make a conscious decision whether we're going to live within our income sources (that is, we don't spend more than we have) or whether we're going to flout common sense and use our credit cards for purchases we can't otherwise afford or don't really need. While this is a life lesson in general, it's also a lesson for how to manage your personal expenses while in college. This is the time when many credit card companies initially target you for their product: *you've been preapproved*! But you need to know the real cost of credit before you decide to use credit cards.

Jenny, a fifth-grade teacher we know in New Hampshire, tells this story every year when she teaches about financial responsibility. As she walks into the room, she asks her students if they like her sweater. Of course, some inevitably tell her they do. Then she tells them that they should like it because it cost her $650. The students are all amazed: "You paid $650 for *that* sweater?" "Yes," Jenny replies. "I bought it when I was in college on my credit card for $50 and now it has cost me $650 in interest because I've never paid it off." The message is usually well-taken by her students.

Stories like this abound, although most people don't like to talk about them and, more tragically, many people who have had these experiences don't learn from them. It's highly likely that the first time that you will assume responsibility for your own personal finances is when you are in college. And that's a big step toward adulthood. Now that you're an adult, you're going to need to learn how to manage your spending as it relates to your income. Simply put, you *can't* spend more than you have. Put more accurately, you *shouldn't* spend more than the combination of what you have and what you expect to have in the short run. Why? Because if you do, you will run into problems in the long run.

# Personal Finance Basics—Sticking to a Budget

Once you get to college, you will most likely be solely responsible for deciding how to spend your money. Nobody is going to tell you not to buy those clothes you really want or to spend a lot of money going to visit friends on the weekend. But if you decide to spend that money, you're probably going to have to make some sort of trade-off. Let's assume that you have $1,000 to spend during a semester on all of your personal expenses. (This number will vary for individual students, depending upon how much money they've saved and how much support they're receiving from their parents and their student loans.) If you buy a sweater for $50, you obviously only have $950 remaining. That's simple math. But if you go through your semester buying what you want when you want, you will probably run out of money quickly.

A better approach is to make the decision up front to establish a budget—and stick to it. You should decide to prioritize your spending by determining the expenditures that are important to you and those that aren't as important. Nobody can simply go out and buy everything they want all the time, including college students.

In short, if you're going to make responsible decisions about your financial situation that will leave you in a good place, you need to balance your budget. Looking at Figure 23-1, you can see that while $1,000 is a lot of money to be able to spend in college, it won't go very far if you don't plan your expenses carefully and appropriately. For example, with $1,000 for your fall semester (after paying for tuition and fees, room and board, books and supplies, and travel expenses), you essentially have $250 per month (September, October, November, and December). In the sample budget we've provided, you can have pizza (or some other food from outside the dining hall) once per week ($50 per month); you can buy one or two items of clothing; you can go out with your friends every weekend (spending only $25 each time); and you can buy $100 worth of housekeeping items for your dorm room or apartment. In addition, you will have $25 per month left over for any miscellaneous items. Of course, if you don't want pizza or don't want to buy anything else for your dorm room, you can choose to spend that money another way.

**FIGURE 23-1   Sample Personal Budget for One Semester***

| Items | Sept. | Oct. | Nov. | Dec. | Total |
|---|---|---|---|---|---|
| Clothes | $50 | $50 | $50 | $50 | $200 |
| Food | $50 | $50 | $50 | $50 | $200 |
| Personal activities | $100 | $100 | $100 | $100 | $400 |
| Items for dorm or apartment | $100 | $0 | $0 | $0 | $100 |
| Other | $25 | $25 | $25 | $25 | $100 |
| Total | $325 | $225 | $225 | $225 | $1,000 |

*Does not include: tuition and fees, room and board, books and supplies, or travel.

However, you want to avoid spontaneous, irresponsible financial decisions. Financial responsibility begins with intentional decisions about spending. Are you going to create a budget for yourself and, if so, are you going to stick to it? Using a method similar to the sample in Figure 23-1 is a good place to start.

You also need to determine, as part of your budgeting decision, whether you're going to spend all of your money or save at least some of it. Once again, base this decision on your specific situation. Saving money is a great way for you to have some cushion following graduation, to help you become involved in a specific activity, or to pay for travel during your summers. Moreover, if you've got student loans—particularly of the unsubsidized type—you may want to consider starting to pay them off. You may remember from the previous chapter that if you have unsubsidized loans, the interest begins compounding immediately, so if you don't pay off that interest starting when the loans are issued, the interest will be added into your principal. Even paying only your interest will save you a lot of money in the long run.

# It's Your Credit, Not Theirs

Credit cards are an interesting innovation of the twentieth century. They allow you to make purchases without having to carry around a lot of cash or to take the time to write checks. They also allow you to buy online—virtually every online merchant requires you to pay by credit card or debit card rather than using your actual bank account. Credit cards are an amazing and revolutionary invention, and they do provide certain advantages.

There are many good reasons for you to get a credit card while you're in college. First and foremost, they can streamline the purchase process. Whether purchasing online, at the bookstore, or buying clothes, something for your dorm room, or food, paying with credit cards makes purchasing a whole lot easier.

A second important reason for you to consider getting a credit card is to build up your credit score. You may be familiar with the phrase "you can't get credit unless you already have credit." This is just as true today as it was 50 years ago. If your credit score is too low, you will not be approved for a car loan or a mortgage. You won't even be approved for a credit card. But as a college student, you're in a unique situation. No other segment of the population is offered a credit card with no job—only college students. Why? Because the credit card companies have done the math and know you're a likely profitable target. While you may not have a job now, the card companies know that you probably can pay at least the minimum payment on your card through the end of college and, after that, you will most likely have a job. You need to know that once you get a job, you can get credit cards with a better interest rate and then close your account on your old card. But in the meantime, the banking company will make billions of dollars off of you and the other students who have agreed to accept their preapproved credit card offers. Don't forget, though, that it's your credit you're playing with, not the banks'. They don't care if you make irresponsible decisions, as long as they get your money.

Building up your credit score is crucial to your financial future. A low credit score will prevent you from getting a loan to buy a car. It will prevent you from getting a loan to buy a house. It could prevent you from getting a cell phone without paying a deposit or getting cable or Internet service at your apartment. It could even prevent you from getting an apartment without having your parents cosign. On the other hand, a high credit score can help you avoid these unfortunate consequences, and it will ensure you get the best rates when you do negotiate loans.

A survey of college students conducted by the Institute for Higher Education Policy looked at credit card ownership and use by college students, and the results are worth a quick mention here. Of all college students—including freshmen—only 36 percent reported not having a credit card; 50 percent reported having one, two, or three credit cards; and 14 percent reported having four or more credit cards.

When asked to rate whether specific reasons for using credit cards were important in their decisions about when to use them, the students in this study responded as follows:

- 52 percent thought it was important to build up a credit history.
- 45 percent thought it was important to have the credit card for emergency use.
- 32 percent thought credit cards were useful because they are more convenient to use than cash.
- 31 percent thought credit cards were useful because they stretch the students' buying power.
- 18 percent thought it was useful to be able to buy something now and pay later.
- 14 percent stated they use their credit cards because they receive some type of gift or bonus.

Students charge a wide variety of expenses to their credit cards. For all students with credit cards, when asked about their purchases in the last year, 77 percent reported that they have used their cards for routine, personal expenses; 67 percent used them for occasional and emergency expenses; 57 percent bought books and supplies with them; 12 percent paid for tuition and fees; and 7 percent used credit cards for room and board. While credit cards have many good uses, you definitely need to create a strategy for paying for your education-related expenses using some combination of methods that does not include credit cards. (Please see chapter 22 for decisions about paying for college.)

**What Are You Going to Use Your Credit Card For?**

- Emergencies?
- Routine personal expenses?
- Occasional items?
- Tuition or other education expenses?

Fortunately, the majority of college students who use credit cards do so responsibly, but that doesn't mean there aren't millions of students who use them irresponsibly. The study found that 59 percent of students pay the entire balance off every month, while 33 percent pay something more than the minimum amount due, and 8 percent routinely pay only the minimum. Out of the estimated 11 million college students, therefore, that means that roughly 880,000 students only pay the minimum due. Moreover, that means that 3.63

million students pay something more than the minimum amount due but less than the entire amount they owe on their average monthly bill. Those numbers add up to a lot of people who are poised for unnecessary debt when they graduate from college. (Data obtained from *Credit Risk or Credit Worthy? College Students and Credit Cards.* June 1998. The entire study can be viewed on the Web site of the Institute for Higher Education Policy at http://www.ihep.org.)

# Making Decisions in Advance

Credit cards can be dangerous. Credit cards are not free money—they are simply a way for you to borrow money to buy something. But you need to pay it back. So, just as you wouldn't borrow $100 from friends if you had no intention of paying them back, you can't borrow that money from the bank and not pay it back. Moreover, the annual percentage interest rate (APR) for this borrowing activity can be extremely high. Many cards charge you 19.99 percent or even more—some charge 24.99 percent, 29.99 percent or even 34.99 percent! That means that a charge of $100 might actually cost you closer to $140 if you take a year to pay it off.

If you look at Figure 23-2, you can see the breakdown of how much some common items may cost you in the long run, based upon an APR of 24.99 percent, which is pretty modest for the cards that are given to college students. A $3 slice of pizza, if you don't pay it off for 10 years, will cost you close to $30! That had better be the best slice of pizza you've ever had. Moreover, a simple $25 bookcase for your dorm room, over 10 years, will come to well over $200. That $50 sweater that we mentioned earlier in the chapter? It will cost close to $500 at this interest rate. The worst, of course, is your tuition and fees. If you pay only $1,000 worth of your tuition on your credit card, it will cost you almost $10,000 in 10 years.

**FIGURE 23-2   Estimated Cost of Using Your Credit Card (Based on 24.99% APR)**

| Item Purchased | Original Price | One Year | Two Years | Three Years | Four Years | Five Years | Ten Years |
|---|---|---|---|---|---|---|---|
| Slice of pizza | $3 | $3 | $4 | $5 | $7 | $9 | $27 |
| Bookcase | $25 | $31 | $39 | $48 | $61 | $76 | $232 |
| Sweater | $50 | $62 | $78 | $97 | $122 | $152 | $465 |
| Portion of tuition | $1,000 | $1,249 | $1,562 | $1,952 | $2,440 | $3,050 | $9,305 |

How do you prevent this from happening? It's actually quite simple. Decide in advance how you're going to use your credit card. You can use credit cards in three general ways:

1. *No Balance*—Use them for their convenience to buy those items you can afford to buy if you didn't use them.

2. *Small Balance*—Use them for expenses that you can't afford this month but will be able to afford next month when you will pay the balance in full.

3. *Big Balance*—Use them for items that you can't afford this month or next month.

If you decide you're only going to use credit cards because they're easy to use and you're going to pay them off in full every time you get the bills, you're going to be in the best financial shape. If you decide you're going to use your credit cards to simply "float" your purchases for a month but will pay them off in full after your next paycheck or after your next wire transfer from your parents, you will probably be in a safe position—assuming you do actually pay them off. The third route, using your credit cards to buy items that you want but really can't afford, could put you in a precarious financial situation. Being financially responsible requires you to make good financial decisions that won't jeopardize you in the long run.

## To Sum Up

You have several decisions to make that, when put together, will comprise your personal financial situation when you're in college:

- Will you create a budget for yourself—and stick to it?
- How will you prioritize your expenses?
- Will you save money while you're in college?
- Will you begin to pay down your student loans?
- Will you get one or more credit cards? If so, how many?
- What will you use your credit cards for? Emergencies only? Emergencies and occasional purchases? Everyday purchases?

- *Ø* Will you use your credit cards to pay for education-related expenses, including tuition and fees, room and board, and books and supplies?

- *Ø* Will you carry over a balance every month, or will you pay off the entire balance each month?

- *Ø* Will you pay just the minimum every month?

These may sound like small decisions, but your choices will make a huge difference in the long run. They will determine how your financial future will begin. They will affect your credit score coming out of college. They will set a track record of financial responsibility (or irresponsibility) that will be used as a basis for your future financial matters. So, are you going to pay $650 for a $50 sweater? Make that decision now, before it's too late.

# Section VI.

## Postgraduation Decisions

**W**e've detailed pretty much all of the decisions that you're going to face in college and how to get the most out of your time at college by making these decisions well, but here is just a little more information that will be useful for you.

Most importantly, chapter 24 explains why and how to make the most crucial decision for yourself about what you're going to do after you graduate from college. While nobody is expecting that you're going to have your entire career planned out before you even finish your undergraduate degree, you do need to think ahead and approach this decision in a structured way. Chapter 24 provides you with a method for doing this that will enable you to take both your short-term and long-term goals into account. By mapping your priorities and your options, you will ensure that you understand which options are best for you to consider at this point in your life.

You essentially have three options available to you after college: going to graduate school right away, taking some time off from academics and then going to graduate school, or not going to graduate school at all and entering the workforce right away. The sky is the limit in terms of your options for the next year, two years, or even five years. Like your decision on what to major in (chapter 10), this decision is similar to a game of chess. If you make a good move early on, for example a decision about what to do right out of college, you will be opening up certain career and life options, while closing others off. You want to avoid making a mistake early in the game and causing yourself to reverse a move you've already made.

It's okay if you don't know what you want to do for the rest of your life. If that's the case, then keep as many options open as possible, while reducing the number of options that you're closing off for yourself. In this case, one thing you can do is to hedge your bets and pursue multiple options concurrently. Additionally, as with many other decisions, timing means everything. That's why it's important to approach this decision as early as possible.

Decision making doesn't end when you graduate from college. In fact, it's really just getting started. Chapter 25 provides you with a review of the lessons that we've discussed throughout the book. Most of these lessons travel well into other contexts. While they may have been focused on the decisions you faced in college, you can use their overall broader lessons throughout the rest of your life. This chapter reviews these decision-making techniques and shows you other situations where you can implement these lessons to improve your decision making—from your relationships to your career or job to your financial decisions.

# Chapter 24

# Choose Your Own Adventure

## The Next Most Important Step: What to Do Next?

**A**s a senior in college, Jeanine was an exceptional student, earning straight As in most of her courses and double majoring in political science and philosophy. She was also very active in campus activities. She was captain of the basketball team, president of her sorority, and editor of the college newspaper—and was extremely busy as a result. She was friends with students, faculty members, and campus administrators. She was even asked to speak at her graduation ceremony, an honor given to the student with the best combination of high academics and campus community activities.

She was ready. She wrote her speech four weeks before the ceremony—so that she wouldn't be too stressed about it during finals—and had the college president and her faculty advisor review it with her. She practiced it over and over until she got it perfect. At the graduation, her delivery was amazing, and she received several standing ovations throughout the speech. She couldn't have been happier. But when the ceremony was over,

*Note to Parents*
*So much effort has gone into the college process that it's sometimes easy to overlook the importance of making good decisions about what to do next. Work with your children to ensure they make good decisions about their next steps.*

everyone came up to congratulate her, and they all asked, "What are your plans now?" She had to answer, "Ummm, I'm not sure." She had no idea what she was going to do. She had been so busy with schoolwork and extracurricular activities that she simply had overlooked thinking about her future.

Jeanine is not alone. Far too many students overlook planning for life after graduation. Many others simply fail to make the best decisions about their postgraduation life. Your first few years out of college are most likely going to serve as the foundation of your future career, but they also can provide you with time to get to know yourself and what you want out of your future. What do you want to accomplish by the time you're 30 years old? How about by the time you're 50? If you don't know the answer, don't worry too much. Most people don't know. But if you don't make decisions about what you want to accomplish by the time you're 30 until you're 29 years and 364 days old, you definitely won't achieve it.

# Narrowing Down Your Options

So, how do you go about making a decision for what to do right out of college? Well, we suggest the best way to do this is to use a structured approach:

- ❶ First, identify your long-term priorities, if you have them
- ❶ Second, identify your short-term priorities
- ❶ Third, identify your options
- ❶ Finally, make a decision

This is the decision process we will be laying out for you in this chapter. But first, to make this a little simpler, you can also look at it another way. In essence, you have three general options:

- ❶ Go straight to a graduate program
- ❶ Work for a few years and then go to a graduate program
- ❶ Go directly to a career job

The fallback to all three of these options is to just get any job. That may seem like an oversimplification, but it does serve well as a starting point for this decision-making discussion. If you decide to go straight into a graduate program, you will have to start working on those applications early in your senior year to ensure that you meet all deadlines. If you decide that you want to work first before going to a graduate program, you may want to consider job alternatives that will help you get into the best programs in your field of interest. Finally, if you are absolutely certain that you're not going to attend any type of graduate school, then you need to plan both your immediate and longer-term future accordingly.

Of course, you still have flexibility. If you think that you never want to go to graduate school, for example, you don't have to sign anything saying that you're never going to change your mind! The same is true with regard to deciding to work for a few years before going to graduate school. If you begin working and decide that you don't need or want to attend graduate school, you can always adjust your plans accordingly. If you decide that, even though you told yourself you would never go, you've made a mistake, you will always have the option of obtaining a graduate degree when you're ready. The point is that you are deciding what path to create, or what path to take on an adventure, if you will.

> You will always have a lot going on—especially during your senior year—but you have to start thinking early about your next steps if you're going to keep your options open.

Flexibility is the key. In the first few years after college, you're going to have some time to reflect upon the goals that you want to pursue in the longer term. If you don't know what you want to do the day after you graduate, don't panic. You don't need to have your life's plan in place immediately. But, just the same, make sure that you're not needlessly wasting your time.

# Keeping Your Options Open (Or, How to Win at Chess)

You likely want to remain flexible and open to new choices as your life unfolds. By following a process similar to that outlined for choosing your major in chapter 10, you can make this decision without closing yourself off from any future possibilities. Most people don't know exactly what they want to do for the rest of their careers on the day they graduate. And you shouldn't necessarily be expected to know either. (If you do know what you want to do for your career, you're probably ahead of the game.)

Planning your postgraduation future is just like playing chess: the move that you make upon graduating from college may open or close other options. Moreover, you may be able to undo that move with the next move or a few moves down the line. The only problem with undoing moves is that it requires you to spend the time to undo them—so you may be wasting precious limited moves.

**Possible Options for Your First Year Out of College:**

- Teach English in a foreign country
- Intern at a company or a non-profit organization
- Go to graduate school
- Get a job
- Travel or work random jobs in an exotic city
- Take some time for yourself to figure out what you want to do
- Move in with your parents and do nothing

Set your time horizon for planning your first years out of college by envisioning yourself five years down the road. Do you want to have a graduate degree? Do you want to have begun progress toward a mid-level position at a company or a nonprofit? Do you want to have started your own company? Do you want to just be finishing a graduate program after having worked for a few years? Do you want to have a good idea what career you're going to have? Do you want to be settled down with a family? Do you want to have paid off your student loans and be financially stable? These are valid questions to ask, and it's good to start mulling over these types of questions as you enter your senior year. It's important to set goals so that you can work along a successful time line. Setting goals also has other benefits. In *What They Don't Teach You at Harvard Business School: Notes from a Street-Smart Executive*, author Mark H. McCormack mentions a 1979 study that asked Harvard MBA students whether they had set written goals and plans for their accomplishments. Only 3 percent could answer affirmatively, while 84 percent were without goals and 13 percent had unwritten goals. In a follow-up interview 10 years later, the 13 percent with unwritten goals were earning twice as much as those without goals, and the 3 percent with specific written goals were averaging 10 times the income of the combined students in the other two groups.

## The Four-Step Process

The four-step approach we recommend for your postgraduation strategy is designed to help you make decisions by taking into account what is important to you. It is a very personal process. You need to fill in your own interests, needs, desires, and goals.

Let's look at an example. Jerry had just entered his senior year and wanted to consider his postgraduation plans early so that he didn't miss any opportunities. But he wasn't sure what he wanted to do and didn't know exactly how to go about deciding between options. He was a history major and thought that he might enjoy teaching, but being a lawyer was also appealing. He became flustered thinking that he needed to decide exactly what he wanted to do with the rest of his life. After consulting his professors, his parents, and others, he realized he had more leeway than he had previously thought. One of his professors suggested that Jerry should structure his decision process. So Jerry decided to use the four-step approach.

# Step 1: Identify Your Long-Term Goals

The first step in the process for making this important decision is to identify and prioritize your long-term goals. Many college students don't know what they want to achieve in the long term. If you already know exactly what you want personally and professionally, you're ahead of the curve. If you don't, don't fret.

But you should take some time during your senior year to consider some of the goals you want to achieve. These could be very general goals, both personally and professionally: you want to travel widely, you want to eventually teach college students, you want to have a family, or you want to make a lot of money. They could also be very specific: you want to compete in the Olympics for figure skating, you want to have an article published in the *New York Times*, you want to find a cure for cancer, or you want to be a commercial airline pilot. Some of these achievements could be ones you "might like to do," while you may categorize some as goals that you "would do if the opportunity presented itself," and some may be those that you "were born to do" or "want to do more than anything in the world."

Jerry decided to make a list of ideas, in three broad, overlapping categories:

- ❶ Personal accomplishments
- ❶ Professional development and accomplishments
- ❶ Career goals or objectives

**FIGURE 24-1 Goals to Accomplish in the Long Term**

| Personal Accomplishments | Professional Development and Accomplishments | Career Goals |
|---|---|---|
| Travel widely | Write a book | Be a professor |
| Marry and have children | Learn a new language | Be an attorney |
| Buy a house | Get a graduate degree | Make good money |
| Live in a foreign country for a period of time | Publish one or more articles in a major newspaper or magazine | Have a job that is interesting and enjoyable |
| Help people in need | Speak at events and conferences to teach skills to others | Be the best in the world in one area related to my job |
| Run a marathon | Constantly learn new skills | Start a company |

He found that this informal list (shown in Figure 24-1) helped him structure his thinking. Some of his goals were related to a possible future career. Some related to what he wanted to do or learn that could help him accomplish more both personally and professionally. And some of them he believed would be personal experiences that would help him have an enjoyable, fulfilling life. By writing these down, Jerry began to shape how he envisioned his life and future accomplishments.

## Step 2: Identify Your Short-Term Goals

The second step in this process is to consider your shorter-term goals. While you have identified the goals you think you may want to accomplish in your overall personal and professional life, you should also consider the more immediate term. This immediate term is a very general time frame, but we advise people to think in terms of two or three years for this step. (As mentioned previously, when planning your first few years out of college, it is important to look on the five-year horizon, but for the purposes of this specific step, two or three years works better.) These short-term goals are not the life goals that you identified in the previous step, but more modest, immediate goals. These goals could be related to your longer-term goals, or they could have nothing to do with them.

For example, Jerry wanted to take advantage of this time that was after college but before settling down to begin to accomplish some of the goals that he didn't think he would be able to do once he had a career and a family. These included traveling, possibly living in another country for a few months or longer, spending lots of time doing activities he enjoyed, and in general having experiences that he would remember for the rest of his life. At the same time, however, he wanted his work involvement to help him define and focus on his future career choices. Finally, he wanted to spend this time doing something that would

**FIGURE 24-2  Goals to Accomplish in the Short Term**

| Personal Accomplishments | Professional Development |
|---|---|
| Travel | Decide whether to pursue a graduate degree |
| Live in an exotic city (either in the United States or abroad) | Achieve some understanding of what to do for a career |
| Give back to the community in some meaningful way | Begin to develop professional experience to help with my career |
| Spend time with friends and family | Perform an entry level job or internship |
| Become involved in a local nonprofit organization | Begin to network with other young professionals |
| Create a blog about restaurants | Begin to develop skills to help with my career |

not only help him determine his career but would also be a step toward the end destination of a fulfilling and enjoyable career.

Jerry wrote out his list, which he categorized into two broad categories: personal accomplishments and professional development. His list can be seen in Figure 24-2.

Writing these goals down may help you determine whether they are realistic and how you should prioritize them—especially if you realize you will be unable to complete all of them within your time frame.

## Step 3: Identify and Evaluate Your Options

The third step in this process consists of two parts: first, identifying the options available to you, and second, evaluating each of these options in terms of which goals you will achieve with each option. The first part of this process is the creative part. If you could do anything in the world for the first few years after college, what would it be? The options are truly endless—how creative do you want to get?

Jerry put together a list that included his top 10 options (see Figure 24-3) and ranked them based upon an initial assessment of how interested he was in each one. Some of them were less realistic for him to achieve, but at this stage he was merely laying them out. He might not be accepted to a top-tier law school right out of college, for example, but that didn't mean he wouldn't try. He would be able to work at the hardware store in his hometown, however, since he had worked there for most of the summers since high school, and the owner said that Jerry could work there again after college.

The second part of this process is more difficult to achieve than the first. It requires evaluating your options not only for what they will enable you to accomplish both in the coming years and over the life of your career but also how they will enable you to link the achievement of your short-term and long-term goals. In other words, you will need to reevaluate and prioritize both sets of goals in your evaluation. In this step, you will also need to find some balance between achieving your personal goals and

**FIGURE 24-3  Postgraduation Options**

| Rank | Option |
|------|--------|
| 1 | Get a job in Paris |
| 2 | Go to a top-tier law school |
| 3 | Go to a top-tier PhD program |
| 4 | Work at a Fortune 500 company |
| 5 | Work as a paralegal |
| 6 | Teach English in China |
| 7 | Work for a nonprofit organization |
| 8 | Work at the hardware store |
| 9 | Join the military |
| 10 | Join the Peace Corps |

achieving your professional goals. Of course, you may be able to achieve them both with the same option, but not necessarily. This step sounds more complicated than it actually is, so let's look at how Jerry did it.

As you can see in Figure 24-4, Jerry listed his 10 options along the left of his worksheet and then placed many of the goals he identified along the top. He then evaluated whether his options achieved his goals. Once he had completed going through his list and identified whether each option would achieve each goal, he could look at the list and get a better understanding of how each option would play out in his future. Of course, he couldn't simply count the number of times he listed yes next to a given option and choose the one with the most since not all of the goals could be considered to have equal weight. But this evaluation still enabled him to visualize a rough idea of the desirability of his options. And now he had to make some decisions.

## Step 4: Make Your Decisions

If you've done the previous steps correctly, making your decision should be the easy part. Unfortunately, however, this is not one single decision, but rather a series of decisions, like the game of chess. When you decide what you're planning to do your first year out of college, you may be setting yourself up for your next decision about the following year. For example, if you decide that you want to go to an MBA program, you obviously are making your decision for the first two years out of school since these programs are two years long. But you're also setting a path for yourself to follow after earning your MBA. How? Because after obtaining your degree, you will then have different options available to you than you did when you began the program.

Jerry knew that he would need to pursue several of his options simultaneously, including possibly spending time up front on options that he didn't consider his first choice. He decided that he would keep as many options open as possible, so he applied to Doctorate (PhD) programs as well as Juris Doctorate (JD) programs, both in the top tier for their respective programs. He also decided he would pursue jobs at a Fortune 500 company and as a paralegal in New York City. While his first choice would be to work for a year in Paris, he knew this would be difficult but pursued the option anyway. He had some friends there and actively sought jobs there using the Internet. Finally, Jerry knew that many of the options on his list of possibilities were ones that would essentially be offered to him if he wanted to take them, most of which had no specific deadlines. These options—including teaching English in China, working at the hardware store, joining the military, and joining the Peace Corps—would serve as backups if he was unable to do one of his higher choices. In the end his decision was pretty easy—he was accepted to several of the top law

**FIGURE 24-4  How Do Activities Achieve Your Objectives?**

| Options: | Ability to Travel | Gain Skills | Make $$ | Learn a New Language | Get a Graduate Degree | Live in a New City | Give Back to the Community | Net-working | Develop Career Goals |
|---|---|---|---|---|---|---|---|---|---|
| Get a job in Paris | Yes | Maybe | Yes | Yes | No | Yes | No | No | No |
| Go to top-tier law school | No | Yes | No | No | Yes | Maybe | No | Yes | Yes |
| Go to top-tier PhD program | No | Yes | No | No | Yes | Maybe | No | Yes | Yes |
| Work at Fortune 500 company | Maybe | Yes | Yes | No | No | Yes | No | Yes | Yes |
| Work as a paralegal | No | Yes | Yes | No | No | Yes | No | Yes | Yes |
| Teach English in China | Yes | No | No | Yes | No | Yes | Yes | No | No |
| Work at a nonprofit | No | Yes | Yes | No | No | Maybe | Yes | Yes | Maybe |
| Work at the hardware store | No | No | Yes | No | No | No | No | No | No |
| Join the military | Yes | Maybe | Yes | No | No | Maybe | Yes | No | Maybe |
| Join the Peace Corps | Yes | Maybe | No | Yes | No | Yes | Yes | No | Maybe |

programs, but not to the top PhD programs. He also wasn't able to figure out a way to live in Paris for the year. So he evaluated the three JD programs and chose the one he thought would be the best fit for him.

# Timetable

Timing is everything and can often prove to be absolutely crucial to your success as you plan for your postcollege years. That's why you need to set up a timetable to pursue the options that you've laid out. For example, if you've decided to apply to a graduate program, you had better be prepared to meet the admission deadlines. Likewise, if you're hoping to get that great, but extremely competitive job, you had better be certain that your application is submitted well in advance of the deadline.

Not all of your options will require acting within the same time frames. One way you can track your activities and deadlines is to keep a notebook with a page for each of your options. On each page, you can write down each component of the process you need to go through to be sure you're on schedule. This could include taking any standardized tests for graduate programs, getting transcripts mailed to schools or potential employers, setting deadlines for asking professors to write you letters of recommendation, and setting any other important deadlines that you will have to meet in order to stay on track.

If graduate school is on your list, you may want to refer back to chapters 2, 3, and 4 and rewrite the worksheets with the new criteria that apply for your new program.

# Hedging Your Bets

While many decisions that you have to make in life require your complete dedication, the decision about what to do after college is, thankfully, one of those decisions that lends itself to hedging your bets. Here's an example. Charlie was an extremely bright student who was preparing to graduate with high honors from a large, public university. He had majored in computer science and minored in engineering and had done very well in both subjects. While he had some general career goals in mind (which is what initially prompted him to choose the major he did), he still wasn't exactly sure of the specific route to take to achieve these goals. He really wanted to be involved in consulting for computer software and hardware development, but he was torn about the best route to take to get to this goal. He knew he would probably need either a an MBA or a PhD, but he wasn't sure if he would be better off taking a few years to work beforehand.

Charlie decided that he would hedge his bets. Since he wanted to attend only a top-rated MBA or PhD program, he decided that he would apply only to the top programs. If he wasn't accepted, he would work for a few years to prepare himself for applying to these programs again by spending his time doing activities that would enhance his likelihood of acceptance. This way, a top program would be his first option, but if he wasn't accepted, he would go a different route and work to make himself more appealing before trying again.

Charlie ended up applying to Harvard, MIT (Massachusetts Institute of Technology), and Wharton business schools, as well as the University of Chicago, Yale, and

Princeton for PhD programs in computer science and engineering programs. Concurrently, he began to interview for jobs. In the end, he was accepted to Harvard and MIT business schools, the University of Chicago and Princeton for PhD programs, and was offered great entry-level jobs at three top-tier Fortune 500 companies. Charlie hadn't needed to hedge his bets, but he was still glad that he followed this approach rather than applying to lower-tier business schools and settling for getting his degree from one of them in the event that he was rejected by his top choices. He decided on Harvard Business School and was grateful he had followed this process.

> You don't need to know what you're going to do for the rest of your life to make a good decision about what you're going to do for the next year or two.

## To Sum Up

You don't need to know what you're going to do for the rest of your life to make a good decision about what you're going to do for the next year or two. You just need to consider what each of the possibilities is going to get you in the short term and where each will position you for the longer term. This should be a fun decision process for you. After all, it will shape what you do for the next few years. It will also determine what options to keep open and what options you will eliminate. Finally, it will enable you to explore activities and pursuits that may become less available to you as you get older and become more established. The sayings go "enjoy it while you're young" or "you're only young once." Believe those sayings but be responsible about your decisions for what to do next, and make your decisions only after fully evaluating all of your options.

## Chapter 25

# Conclusion: A Lifetime of Decisions

## How to Apply These Decision-Making Lessons Throughout Your Life

N ow that you've come this far (both in your college experience and reading this book), it's time to look at how you can apply the lessons that you've learned here throughout the rest of your life. That may sound like a challenge, so we've summarized the major lessons that we believe you should be able to use in your life easily and effectively.

> **Note to Parents**
> *This chapter is for you, too. This will help you make better decisions and have a better life.*

### A Good Game of Chess

Something that is stressed in two places in the book, chapter 10 and chapter 24, is how life can resemble a game of chess—the decisions that you make (like the moves that you make in chess) will open up certain options for you and close others. As we discussed in chapter 10, your decision about what to major in can truly have an impact on your career choices. While becoming an engineer is not ruled out if you major in art history, you would have to go back and take a lot of classes to be able to follow that path. A good "chess" move in the first place will help you open up options without closing off others.

Likewise, chapter 24 discussed decisions on your next moves after college. You can always change your career down the road, and while your first few years after college won't necessarily define the rest of your professional life, you should try to keep your options open and not close any off that you would possibly like to pursue.

Just as it is foolish to take back a move in chess because it was a bad move, so in life it is unwise to have to repeat yourself or undo something you've spent a lot of time and energy on. Obviously, it's better to do something right the first time. This chess lesson can apply to a number of decisions that you make throughout your life, but most importantly, will apply to your career and to your family life—as well as to the interplay of the two. We've already mentioned how early choices can affect your career. If you're a secretary, becoming a physicist will be difficult—not impossible, but very difficult. In your personal life, the game of chess could come up just as often. Once you have children, for example, you're going to be restricted in your career options (How easy will it be to pack everyone up and move to a new city or country for a job?) as well as your personal life (Can you decide to go backpacking in Europe for the summer?). If you decide to have children within the first few years out of college, you will be making a chess move—possibly the right one or possibly not—but one that you can't take back. The same applies if you wait a few years before having a family. The most rewarding life will be the one that is played wisely, like a good game of chess.

# Frog in Boiling Water

Another lesson in this book relates to inaction. When you fail to make a decision, often that decision is made for you. For example, in chapter 5 we wrote about the importance of making a decision ahead of time when considering whether to take a year off before college. If you leave this to the last minute and don't plan ahead adequately, your decision will be made for you because your options will be dramatically reduced the longer you procrastinate.

In addition, chapter 9 described the importance of making a decision when it comes to graduating from college in four years. Simply gliding along in college will not guarantee that you're going to finish in four years. On the other hand, if you make it a priority to decide ahead of time that you are not going to take any longer than

Now that you have learned these decision-making skills—either because you made good decisions or bad decisions—be sure to take these lessons with you. They can prove to be timeless and applicable everywhere.

four years to finish your degree, then you're going to be better off, and this commitment increases the chances that you actually do graduate in four years.

Chapter 9 also discussed a story that describes the lesson of the frog in boiling water. As the story goes, if you place a frog into a pot of boiling water, it will immediately jump out to save itself. But if you place that frog into a pot of room temperature water and slowly bring the water to a boil, the frog will sit there in the boiling water until it dies. This story provides us with a lesson about staying in steadily deteriorating situations and not proactively making intentional decisions to accomplish specific outcomes, such as graduating in four years.

In your life, you will continually encounter situations where inaction will determine the decision. For example, people often decide not to make a decision about their job or a relationship and continue to stay in a job they hate or continue to stay in an unhappy relationship. Examine your situation and make a conscious decision about your job; don't just take what comes along and stay in a job if you are not getting what you want out of it. Make a conscious decision about where you want to live; don't just end up someplace. You also may find yourself acting like a frog in boiling water with your health—as your health begins to slowly deteriorate, you fail to act to correct it.

Combating the frog-in-boiling-water syndrome is not always easy, but you can use these tricks to assess your situation correctly and avoid being stuck in a steadily deteriorating situation. Step back from time to time and take stock of areas in your life such as your health, your relationships, your job or career, your business, and your investments. You might take stock on New Year's Day, your birthday, or quarterly. Remind yourself that you're too smart to be complacent about an increasingly worrisome situation.

# Make Intentional Decisions

A decision-making lesson that is somewhat related to the frog-in-boiling-water lesson is roughly the opposite but equally important. Instead of failing to make a decision and letting that decision time frame pass you by, you make the decision without adequately thinking about it. As you may remember, particularly from the chapters on partying, relationships, and even on time management, it's best to make decisions ahead of time and intentionally. Spur of the moment, in the heat of passion, and rash decisions that are not properly thought through will be detrimental and lead to less-than-optimal results. This is especially true if you are tired, drunk, emotional, or under peer pressure or stress when you make these spontaneous decisions.

Looking back at some of the times this came up in the book, there are several places where we discussed this. This lesson applies to the decisions outlined in chapter 14 about partying, chapter 15 about drinking, and chapter 20 about relationships and sex. If you approach decisions about partying, drinking, and sex as intentional decisions, you will be making more responsible decisions. If, on the other hand, you don't make these decisions intentionally and instead make them "on the fly" as the situations occur, you're bound to make mistakes.

Develop the habit of making intentional decisions throughout your life. Purposefully decide on your relationship commitments; don't just go with the flow. Waiting to make decision until the last moment is simply irresponsible decision making—not to mention potentially dangerous. Throughout your life, you will be faced with last-minute and split-second decisions. But if you plan ahead for them, you will know what to do when faced with these situations. For example, if you have an important job interview, you may not know what questions you're going to be asked. But you do know that you may be faced with any of a number of potential questions, likely about your major in college, your work experience, and what you know about the particular company. If you don't prepare for the possibility of being asked these questions, you're unlikely to do as well as those applicants who did prepare.

## Structured Approach to Decision Making

Just as you should make your decisions intentionally, you should also make them by following a structured approach. Several chapters in this book provide you with structured decision techniques that, while they may appear to be very different from one chapter to another, can actually be applied to many of the decisions you will face in life. In addition to chapters 2 and 4, where we laid out a very detailed and structured approach to making the decision about which colleges to apply to and which college to ultimately attend, we also provided you with a structured approach for making a decision about planning your summers (chapter 11), whether to take a year off before college (chapter 5), whether to study abroad (chapter 12), and whether to transfer to another school (chapter 13).

Chapter 11 challenged you to examine all of the possibilities for what to do with your three valuable summers in college. By clearly identifying your goals and then matching them to your options, you will be certain to achieve everything you're hoping to with your summertime. In addition to making a responsible decision about the objectives that you want to accomplish with this time, as part of this decision process you also need to make sure you understand how the deadline processes work and how to accomplish the goals you've decided on.

Chapter 12 discussed the process of deciding whether to study abroad for a semester or possibly for an entire year. Again, to be certain you make the best decision, you need to follow a disciplined decision process that will help you decide what your priorities are in terms of what you want to achieve through a study abroad program and then match these goals with your various options. Likewise in chapter 13, if you're considering transferring to a different school, you need to approach this decision in a structured way that helps you analyze your reasons for wanting to transfer and the feasibility of doing so without disrupting any of your other goals in college.

You will face countless major and minor decisions that will significantly affect your life—what job you should take, where you should live, whether you should buy a house (and if yes, which one), where you should send your kids to school, where you should go on vacation, or which car you should buy. The list goes on and on, but let's take one example and apply it.

A few years out of college, Tom and Ling had the opportunity to buy their first house. It was a major decision for them, and they wanted to do it right. Tom suggested they use a structured decision approach (similar to the one described in chapter 4). They put together a similar decision worksheet, except that they used categories that were appropriate for the decision to buy a house, and they put the alternative houses across the top instead of colleges. The categories they used were: 1) the characteristics of the house, such as size, number of bedrooms, yard, etc.; 2) the location, including the distance they would need to commute, the neighborhood, convenience to shopping; 3) the cost, including purchase price, mortgage costs, taxes, and renovation costs; and 4) future flexibility, which included the ability to expand it for children, the ease of being able to sell it if they wanted to, and so on. Tom and Ling used this structured process to make a decision that they felt was absolutely the best one.

The types of decisions you will face will be varied, but you can rest assured that if you use a structured approach to these decisions, you will be certain that you made the best decision you could based upon the information you had available to you and how you interpreted the benefits and drawbacks of each option. Prioritizing your goals and matching them to your options will help you decide better every time.

# Unintended Consequences

Decision making always entails consequences. Planning ahead certainly helps to get a grasp of the intended consequences, and then you can decide accordingly. However, decisions may also lead to unintended, unpredicted consequences that even inordinate planning could not prevent.

We divide unintended consequences into two categories: those that you are reasonably able to predict, and those that you are not. If you ride in a car, and the driver has been drinking, and you get into an accident, while you certainly didn't intend for this to happen, you should have been able to foresee that was a possible consequence. Or, if you decide to skip class and fail your midterm exam, you should have seen that as a possibility. On the other hand, if you decide that you're going to go study at the library and you trip and fall on a crack in the sidewalk, then that would be considered an unintended consequence that you couldn't predict.

As mentioned in chapter 15, applying the prudent person rule aids in understanding unintended consequences. This rule states that if you could have rationally predicted that a particular consequence would result from a decision that you make, and then act in a way that takes this consequence into consideration, you have abided by the prudent person rule.

When it comes to unintended consequences in the decisions that you will face throughout your life, you should apply the prudent person criteria and consider the potential consequences and implications of your decisions. This process will carry over directly to your life after college. The unintended consequences of drinking, drugs, and relationships are the same after college. You will also face new decisions with unintended consequences you should anticipate. Deciding to smoke or drink in excess may have unintended consequences on your health. Deciding how hard to work may have unintended consequences on your job performance and on your family. Deciding where to live will have both intended consequences as well as unintended consequences.

Don't be careless by ignoring the possible unintended consequences of your decisions, but don't agonize over the consequences of your decisions that the prudent person could not have rationally predicted. Finding this balance will be critical to a life that is full of good experiences and the correct amount of prudence.

# Personal Financial Responsibility

Money is a fact of life. Some people have a lot of it. Some people only have a little. Everybody could use more of it. Regardless of your financial situation, you are never going to be able to simply go out and buy everything you want in life. Because of this fact, you have to be prepared to make good financial decisions. Chapter 23 discussed the importance of making a conscious decision about planning your finances when in college. If you only have $1,000 to spend in a given semester for purposes that aren't related to school, making a decision ahead of time on how to allocate that money will help you to be sure that you don't overspend or run out of money.

Likewise, when it comes to using your credit cards, you should consciously make a decision ahead of time as to how you're going to use them and for what purposes. Are you going to use them because they're easier than paying with cash and pay them off as soon as you get the bill? Are you going to use them to float your expenses until the next month, when you can pay off the bill? Or are you going to use them to buy items you actually can't afford, knowing that you really don't have any immediate way to pay them off? If you don't make this a conscious decision before you begin to use them, you may find yourself saddled with debt that will take you years of hard work and sacrifice to pay off.

Chapter 22 detailed how you can make responsible decisions when it comes to paying for college by understanding the process and making the best decisions about how to balance payments that you make up front with loans that you will repay after graduation. We also discussed decisions you can make that will help to reduce your overall costs of attending college—choices that will lead to you having more money in your pocket in the long run.

Now that you're leaving college, an important decision-making lesson that will have an enormous impact on your life is the one regarding making conscious decisions about your finances. If you buy everything you want, you're never going to be able to repay this debt load, and your credit score will pay the price. If that happens, you may be refused a home loan, a car loan, credit cards, jobs, phone lines, cell phones, cable service, and many other items that are normal and necessary for everyday life. But if you understand your financial situation and make purchasing and savings decisions according to what you can afford, you will avoid these pitfalls. This goes for credit cards as well. The lessons you learned in college about when and where to use credit cards are lessons that will stay with you forever. Ideally, you escaped college without too much debt on your cards, but if you didn't, how will you make spending decisions in the future to reduce your debt and not increase it? Establish a plan and maintain a disciplined approach to your finances and you will be well served.

Moreover, when it comes to major purchase and spending decisions, just as paying for college, deciding up front to plan out your best course of action for affording these costs will benefit you in the long run. If you plan how you're going to afford buying a house before you actually sign the contract, you're going to better understand your financial situation and make the best decision about how much to spend on that house. Financial decisions are often some of the most important and stressful decisions that you will make throughout your life. But if you make these decisions responsibly and according to the rules you set for yourself about purchases, you can balance not only your budget but your level of stress.

Maria and Stan applied these financial decision lessons after college. When they got engaged, Maria told Stan he had to make better financial decisions. He had run up a lot of credit card debt, buying whatever he wanted. Maria was adamant that they couldn't live that way, and Stan agreed. So they sat down and used a similar approach for how they would use their credit cards and how they would budget their spending.

## Time Management

College was most likely one of the busiest times you've had in your life. Studying, going to class, taking exams, hanging out with friends, traveling back and forth from home, being involved in extracurricular activities, writing papers, and, hopefully, spending a little time relaxing occupied your waking hours. You've learned to manage your time and have come to some sense of balance—or at least we hope you have—that enabled you to spend the right amount of time on your academics, your extracurricular activities, and your personal life. Now here's the bad news: It doesn't get any easier; it will be just as hard balancing your time after college.

Chapter 8 described decisions to find the proper balance that will enable you to achieve your extracurricular goals without harming your studies. Included in this process are tools to take with you: the need to actually plan your time by breaking out how much time you're going to spend on each of your activities and possibly even scheduling your time for each day of the week. You only have 168 hours in the week, so using them wisely is important. We also discussed the need to first set a baseline of the time you will need to set aside for achieving your academic needs, including going to class, doing your regular homework, and doing any special projects including papers and exams. Only after that should you plan your nonacademic time, including your extracurricular activities, your basic needs (for example, sleep and food), and your personal life.

Chapter 16 discussed extracurricular activities and how to go about prioritizing them. You can't do everything in life, so you need to take a careful look at the different options available to you and evaluate them along the same bases. For example, for each activity you should determine your goals, the level of enjoyment each will provide for you, the effect it will have on your career in the long-run, and the time commitment it would entail. Then assess them and choose the ones that will enable you to have the cross section of these various criteria that you determine best fits your needs.

These two chapters, in particular, should serve as a good starting point for balancing your time and your activities throughout the rest of your life. You still only have 168 hours in every week, and it is still a good choice to schedule them—even if it is a rough schedule—to maximize that small amount of time. Just as you decided how to spend your time in college, you likewise need to determine what you value now, what you want in the future, and how to effectively spend your time reaching your goals. What is important to you? Is it your job? Is it spending time with your family? Is it enjoying what life has to offer? Is it traveling? It is likely going to be some combination of these options, and you need to determine an appropriate balance for your circumstances. These preferences are likely to change over time as your situation changes—as you get married, have children, change careers, retire, etc.—so you may find yourself performing this exercise many times in your life.

# Deciding Among Alternatives

Many of the decisions you have had to make in college, just like many of the decisions you will face throughout the course of your life, require you to decide between competing alternatives—and usually you are only able to choose one major alternative at a time. As we have seen in several chapters in this book, choosing among alternatives has several components. First, you need to generate the possible alternatives that fit your general criteria. Second, you need to provide a weight to each of your criteria, prioritizing those that are the most important for you. Third, you need to evaluate how well each of the alternatives meet the needs of your criteria. Finally, you need to compare each option and make your decision.

Several chapters serve as good examples to return to for a refresher on how to determine what options to choose. They include chapter 2, where you make your decision about which colleges to apply to, and chapter 4, where you make your decision about which school to attend. Let's focus on chapter 2 for the first step in this process where you generate a list of all of the possible colleges you can apply to, based on a rough evaluation of what you're looking for (liberal arts college, geographic location, etc.). Moving on to chapter 4, once you've been accepted to or rejected from the schools you've applied to, your options are defined and you proceed to step two. In this step, you identify how important each specific criterion is to your decision. Is the location the most important? How about the majors offered at the schools? How will class size fit into your decision? After defining the relative importance of each criterion, you then move on to identifying how well each school you've been accepted to meets these criteria you've laid out. Finally, you make your decision based upon this complete evaluation of your options matched to your criteria.

Chapter 5, about decisions related to taking a gap year between high school and college, is also useful. It is important to consider multiple options in order to avoid limiting yourself. After all, if you don't consider an option, such as joining the Peace Corps, you won't be able to decide to select that option. Once you have all of your options, you need to map them into your goals or objectives, considering how well each of the options you've generated will help you achieve each of your objectives. Then you will be able to make a more informed decision about which alternatives best apply to your current situation.

Throughout the rest of your life, you're going to be facing decisions that will require you to choose between competing options. Many people don't take the time to approach these decisions in a way that will maximize their results. By focusing your efforts on 1) generating your possible options, 2) weighting your criteria, and 3) evaluating your options, you will ensure the best decision can be made. Some decisions that you will face with these competing characteristics will include job and career options, purchase options, and options for vacations, to name a few.

For example, just as you did with choosing which colleges to apply to and, ultimately, which college to attend, when you are considering a new job, you can apply a similar technique. If you break down each criterion into a set of categories (compensation, location, future potential, etc.) and weight each one, then provide some level of scoring for how well each of the options you're considering meets those criteria, you will have a better sense of how to evaluate each of your options. The same is true of many of the major purchase and action decisions in your life. This is truly one of the best tools in the decision toolbox to take with you after graduation.

## Shared Decisions

Throughout college—and your entire life up until this point—you have been required to make decisions in coordination with other people. Sometimes it's your professors. Sometimes it's your roommates. Most of the time it's your parents. When you were deciding which colleges to apply to (chapter 2), your parents had a lot to say. When you were deciding which college to enroll in (chapter 4), your parents had a lot to say. When you were deciding whether to take a year off from college (chapter 5), what to major in (chapter 10), what to do with your summers (chapter 11), whether to study abroad (chapter 12), and whether to live on or off campus (chapter 18), your parents had a lot to say.

Whether or not you decided to listen to them (you probably listened some of the time and probably did not at other times), they were involved in your decision-making process for a lot of good reasons. Most importantly, they were involved because they care about you and want to see you succeed. You've been able to use them as a valuable sounding board, asking them for advice when you weren't certain what to do. When you make a decision, your parents have a stake in the outcome of that decision, whether you know it or not.

Likewise with your roommates and your professors. Over the course of your college years, you've likely had to make many decisions where your roommates and your professors also had a stake in the outcome.

Your decisions will often have consequences for other people, too, whether their stake in your decision is small or large. This will continue to be true throughout your life. Some decisions will be yours alone to make, but you will seek out the advice of those who care about you and want you to do well. Other decisions will have to be joint decisions made with one or more other people, with each of you having equal say in what gets decided. And still other decisions will be made primarily by someone else, with you having a stake in the outcome but little ability to influence the decision other than in an advisory role.

These decisions are going to be common in all aspects of your life, including in your relationships and in your job or career. When you move in with your girlfriend or boyfriend, you will have to make joint decisions about where to live, what schedule to keep, when to go shopping, how to manage your finances, what to have for dinner, and even what television shows to watch. When you look into your future, you will have to make decisions about whether and when to get married, whether and when to have children, how many children to have, how to rear them, what schools they should attend, where to go for vacation, and a multitude of other decisions. In your job you're also going to have to make decisions with other people, especially related to specific projects, how to proceed in a given situation, and possibly whether to hire or fire people.

You also learned about how different people make decisions differently. Chapter 19 discussed the way personality types affect the way people make decisions. This is a valuable lesson that you can take with you and use throughout life. Try to appreciate and understand that the way you approach a decision may be very different from the way another person approaches it.

Since you will face so many decisions throughout your life that will either be shared or joint decisions, it's good that you have experience with these. Maybe you didn't always agree with your parents about which major to choose or where to study abroad. Maybe you didn't always agree with your professors about what paper topic to write about. Maybe you didn't always agree with your roommates about what schedule to set or when to have friends over. But disagreement, agreement, compromise, and making decisions that have an impact on someone else are lifelong skills that you will continue to hone. Having a strong foundation for how to do this from your college experiences will help you with these decisions throughout your life.

# Playing the System

Many decisions that you have made regarding college were made according to someone else's rules. Chapter 3 discussed the decision process that colleges use to select which applicants they're going to accept for admission and which ones they're going to reject. When you applied for college, you had absolutely no control over their decision process. Likewise, chapter 22 discussed the financial aid process and the decisions that you need to make with regard to paying for college—decisions that are made within a system created by your college and the federal government. While you can't change the process of either how colleges choose to admit students or the process for how colleges and the federal government award financial aid (including scholarships, grants, and loans), what you can do is try to understand these decisions so that you can use them to your advantage as much as possible.

Throughout your life, you will make many decisions within the structures and systems that others create. You will have little—if any—ability to change the processes that are laid out for you, but if you understand the system, you can "play the system." Structures are created by those who have the power to create them—governments (national, state, and local), as well as colleges, corporations, organizations, and, really, anyone who has anything that you want from them.

The government sets tax policies that you are required to follow, but if you understand how the system is structured, you will be sure to take the specific deductions that will enable you to pay the least amount in taxes that you can (legally, of course). Your company may have restrictions on matching funds for a 401(k) plan, but if you understand how the company's system works, you can make decisions about withholding from your paycheck that will ensure that you get the most matching funds possible. A baseball team may create a structure for how and when fans can buy tickets to its games, but if you know the system well, you can make your decisions about how to strategically play the system to get tickets to the games you want to attend. A person selling a house you want to buy may set a particular price for the house, but if you understand the process, you may be able to get more from them in terms of concessions than they originally expected to offer you.

Here is an example. Justin was competing for a job he really wanted. He realized that the company's decision was similar to the black box decision process he learned about in chapter 3, so he tried to understand how the company would make the hiring decision by asking questions during the interview. How was the decision going to be made? Who would be making the final decision? What were the most important characteristics the company was looking for? What characteristics were less important? How did they think he fit the job requirements? How did he compare to other candidates? Justin then used the answers to these questions to better position himself to get the job.

Justin got the job. Interestingly, the manager who hired him told him that he not only fit the requirements best, but they were also impressed by his initiative and skill in trying to figure out how the decision would be made. They realized it was a skill that would be useful in the job and one the other candidates had failed to demonstrate.

The list of decisions you will have to make while playing by someone else's rules is endless. But one of the lessons that you can learn from your college experience is that you can play the system only if you understand the rules of that system. Your decisions are not made in a vacuum. They are made within the structure of your life and your specific situation in life, along with those rules and restrictions that have been created by those in a position of power. By understanding the rules of the game, you're bound to be able to play it better.

## To Sum Up

Now that you're preparing to leave college and have made all of your major college-life decisions, it would be wasteful to forsake all that you have learned about good decision making. While this book focused exclusively on those specific decisions that you need to make related to college, it's important for you to look back and see that many of these techniques and lessons are ones that will travel well into the rest of your life. You can and should take them with you. From ensuring you make decisions intentionally and using an appropriate decision-making structure to understanding the unintended consequences of your decisions and how to make decisions that will impact other people, these lessons are just as important and applicable after college as they were in college. As you pack to leave college following graduation, remember to pack up your decision-making skills. It would be a shame to leave them behind.

# About the DecideBetter.com Web Site and Community

The popular and rapidly growing DecideBetter.com Web site is an exciting additional tool and resource for anyone who wants to make better decisions. It features a sample of the decision-making lessons found in the first edition of *Decide Better! for a Better Life*. These are some of the other invaluable resources available at DecideBetter.com:

- "Ask Michael," a section that allows users to ask a decision question of the decision-making expert and get advice
- Quizzes and decision polls that ask DecideBetter.com visitors to test their decision-making skills and compare them to others
- Customized collection of tailored decision worksheets (especially for college students and applicants) that can be downloaded for making and expediting specific decisions

❶ Other ongoing valuable resources designed to help individuals improve their decision-making skills

❶ Announcements of upcoming author interviews, conferences, and media appearances

Visitors to DecideBetter.com may access and download free resources and worksheets, and they can also register to receive regular e-mail newsletters. These updates include featured lessons, selections from the Ask Michael section of the Web site, and information about new features and resources on the site.

# http://www.DecideBetter.com

# About the Author

## Christopher K. McGrath

As a lifetime student, Chris has been involved in numerous key decision-making scenarios throughout his academic career that enable him to provide a unique perspective on how to make better decisions in college. Chris has learned to improve his decision skills through good decisions—lifelong lessons that have not only helped him to succeed in college but to successfully transition into adult life.

Throughout his time in college, Chris was extremely active in dozens of activities and carried on a very active social life, while concurrently earning an impressive GPA. This experience provided him with a unique understanding of how to balance academics with social life as well as extracurricular activities. In addition to serving in the student government, writing for the college newspaper, running academic-related activities, planning events, bringing speakers to campus, and being involved in a number of administrative committees, Chris also found time to study abroad in London, England, and in Grenoble, France. He also interned at the U.S. Environmental Protection Agency and the Royal Institute of International Affairs and served as a research assistant for a professor.

Chris is a graduate of the class of 1999 from Skidmore College with a Bachelor of Arts in Government, and he earned his master's degree in International Affairs from the Elliott School of International Affairs at the George Washington University in 2002. He spent several years working on political campaigns, including two presidential campaigns, and also worked on several international elections projects around the world. He is currently pursuing his doctorate in Political Science at George Washington University. He lives in Washington, D.C., with his wife Becca and dogs Samson and Delilah.

# About the Author

## Michael E. McGrath

Michael E. McGrath is the creator of Decide Better! and the author of the book *Decide Better! for a Better Life*. He is an experienced management consultant, successful business executive and respected visionary, entrepreneurial leader, author, and family man who has studied and applied decision making for more than 25 years.

Michael has established a reputation as a strong, yet personable and witty, decision maker and credits much of the success in his life to making better decisions. He created Decide Better! to further develop successful decision techniques and to promote these techniques through books and other insightful media to help others make better decisions.

With the initial book of the Decide Better! series, *Decide Better! for a Better Life*, Michael has been in demand for radio and television interviews on how to make decisions. Decide Better! has launched a renewed focus on helping people make better decisions.

Michael has always had a special interest in college education and helping mentor students, and he has experienced it from all perspectives. In addition to being a student, he taught at the college and graduate school levels. He has been through the anxiety and triumph of putting three children through college, with one more to go, and has been advising many others on college. He has also served on the board of trustees of a college for ten years, five of which were served as vice-chairman. Now with *Decide Better! for College*, he combines his college perspectives with his experience in decisions.

Michael currently serves on the board of directors of four corporations and four nonprofit organizations. He has a Bachelor of Science in computer science from Boston College and a Master of Business Administration from Harvard Business School. He lives with his wife Diane and his daughter Molly.